Coercive Persuasion

Coercive Persuasion

A Socio-psychological Analysis of the
"Brainwashing" of American Civilian
Prisoners by the Chinese Communists

EDGAR H. SCHEIN *with*

INGE SCHNEIER *and* **CURTIS H. BARKER**

Center for International Studies

Massachusetts Institute of Technology

W. W. NORTON & COMPANY, INC.

New York

Library of Congress Catalog Card No. 61-7483

41 680
July '61

PRINTED IN THE UNITED STATES OF AMERICA
FOR THE PUBLISHERS BY THE VAIL-BALLOU PRESS, INC.

1 2 3 4 5 6 7 8 9

CONTENTS

Preface and Methodology   7

Introduction   15

PART   I   *The Context of Coercive Persuasion*

    1   The Persuasion Theme in the Development of the Chinese Communist Party   25

    2   Thought Reform After the Take-over   43

    3   The Passion for Unanimity   62

PART   II   *Coercive Persuasion: Its Structure, Effects, and Determinants*

    4   A Socio-psychological Model for the Analysis of Coercive Persuasion   117

    5   The Special Role of Guilt in Coercive Persuasion   140

    6   The Effects of Coercive Persuasion   157

    7   The Determinants of Belief and Attitude Change   167

PART   III   *Theories of Coercive Persuasion*

    8   Theories I: Stress, Learning, and Psychoanalytic Theories   199

    9   Theories II: Socio-psychological Theories   221

PART   IV   *Implications for a Theory of Influence*

    10   The Ritualization of Belief   259

    11   Coercive Persuasion in Non-Communist Settings: Some Parallels   269

CONCLUSIONS   283

Appendixes   286

Bibliography   305

Index   314

PREFACE AND METHODOLOGY

THE STUDY to be reported below was an outgrowth of research which began in 1953. At the time I was serving as an Army research psychologist at the Walter Reed Army Institute of Research, Washington, D.C. With the settling of the terms of the armistice in Korea came the problem of how to handle the prisoners of war who were to be exchanged; specifically, how to determine what experiences they had undergone and how to assess the effects of such experiences on the men. As is well known by now, the decision was made to give an extensive battery of interviews and psychological tests to all the repatriates, and, to accomplish this, a large group of intelligence officers, psychiatrists, and psychologists were gathered together to work in Tokyo, Inchon, and on board ship carrying the repatriates home (Segal, 1954; Lifton, 1954).

Underlying this decision was the concern which we had that the Chinese had been able to sway many of our soldiers to their way of thinking, as evidenced by reports of extensive collaboration, by propaganda broadcasts made by some of the prisoners, and by letters and other documentary evidence of collaboration. The publication of Edward Hunter's book, *Brainwashing in Red China* (1951), provided further evidence of the Chinese Communists' intentions to wage a total ideological war and provided information concerning some of the techniques used on the Chinese mainland to secure the allegiance of politically neutral or hostile Chinese to the Communist cause. We were all concerned to find out whether the Chinese had "brainwashed" our troops, and if so, what this meant and by what means it had been accomplished. The possibility that the repatriates would need psychiatric care upon their return was seriously faced and provisions were therefore made to have a psychiatrist interview each repatriate prior to his arrival in the States.

I was one of a number of psychologists who were sent to the Far East to participate in this program, specifically, to support the psychiatrists by being available to give tests where such were called for. As it turned out, the exigencies of the local situation did not allow much time for psychological testing. Consequently, a number of us turned our attention to the research program which had also been built into the processing of the men, and, as part of this research program, I began to devote time to a socio-psychological analysis of the situation which had existed in the Chinese prison camps (Schein, 1956). The opportunity to conduct these interviews met my needs very well because of long-standing interests which I had in group psychology and the social psychology of influence and attitude change.

One of the major conclusions which came out of these interviews was that the much-feared Communist program of "brainwashing" was really more of an intensive indoctrination program in combination with very sophisticated techniques of undermining the social structure of the prisoner group, thereby eliciting collaboration which in most cases was *not* based on ideological change of any sort. In other words, the indoctrination was not very effective but the social control exercised by the Chinese Communists was (Schein, 1956). Clearly the Chinese Communists had a novel approach to dealing with a large captive group, but the low rate of ideological influence in this group left unanswered the question of whether the Chinese had discovered or were using some new techniques of changing the political beliefs of captives. There appeared to be ample evidence of the success of their indoctrination techniques with segments of their own population, but not until some time after the repatriation had been completed was there any further available evidence concerning the effectiveness of these techniques with Westerners who were known to have been initially hostile to the Communist regime.

A group of American and European students, doctors, businessmen, and missionaries began to be repatriated into Hong Kong in 1953, and among these were a goodly number, including some Americans who had been studying in Peking, who were arrested after the outbreak of the Korean War and imprisoned for periods of three to five years. Within this group were some individuals who stated to the press when first interviewed in Hong Kong that they had been spies for the United States, that they had been justly arrested, that they had deserved the punishment which they had received, and that, in fact, they had been treated very leniently by the Chinese Communist government. These statements seemed fantastic inasmuch as there was absolutely no evidence that any of the repatriates had committed any of the crimes to which they had confessed, and because of evidence from other repatriates and defectors (as well as from the subjects' own later admissions) that their imprisonment had been anything but lenient, and had, in fact, been quite brutal by Western standards. It seemed then, that these cases represented more truly instances of what Hunter had called "brainwashing"; that is, cases of genuine ideological conversion seemingly accomplished by coercive means.

The present study was then undertaken in an attempt to find out what had happened to this small group of Americans, what these events meant to the prisoners, what attitude changes had actually taken place and why, what long-run effects could be observed in them following their return home, and, finally, the meaning of all these events for the social psychology of influence and attitude change.

The study was sponsored by the Center for International Studies at the Massachusetts Institute of Technology and was carried out in collaboration with Inge Schneier and Curtis H. Barker from 1957 to 1959.

Our original plan was based on the assumption that if we were to understand "brainwashing," or coercive persuasion as we came to call the process, we should have to understand a great deal more about the context in which it operated (i.e. the cultural, social, and political situation in China and the history of the Communist takeover) and about the histories of the people who were arrested and coercively persuaded. It was apparent that what had happened to these Americans was part of an extensive program which the Chinese Communists themselves call "thought reform" or "ideological remolding." *

Since we were not China experts, it seemed that the way to gather this kind of background contextual information was to set up a project which would provide for the editing of a volume, the contributors to be China experts who would write articles on the various phases of the thought reform program and its effects. Our intention

---

* The first good reports of thought reform were published in 1956 and 1957 by Robert Lifton, who also worked at the Walter Reed Institute of Research and who based his conclusions on interviews conducted in Hong Kong with defected Chinese and expelled Westerners (Lifton, 1956b).

was not only to treat thought reform in the context of Chinese developments and Chinese Communist history, but also to relate it to other kinds of contexts such as Soviet types of indoctrination and totalitarianism in general, as well as to other kinds of mass persuasion attempts in history such as the Papal Inquisition. The analysis was also to include chapters on theory by representatives of the fields of psychology, psychiatry, sociology, political science, and anthropology, who would give a theoretical analysis of the process based on their particular disciplinary point of view.

The first step in carrying out our plan involved a series of interviews with experts in the field.* The purpose of the interviews with these experts in Chinese affairs, Russian affairs, history, psychology, sociology, and anthropology was to try to answer the following questions:

1. Was the project feasible, and if so, what suggestions did they have for organizing it?

2. Could they suggest reading material?

3. Could they suggest names of people who might be contributors to the project, who would have the kind of knowledge that would

---

* Among the persons interviewed were:

Allport, Gordon	Harvard University
Bauer, Raymond	"
DuBois, Cora	"
Kluckhohn, Clyde	"
Schwartz, Benjamin	"
Korol, Alexander	MIT
Letwin, William	"
Milliken, Max	"
Morison, Elting	"
Pool, Ithiel	"
Pye, Lucian	"
Borton, Hugh	Columbia University
Dallin, Alexander	"
Roberts, Henry	"
Robinson, Geroid	"
Berle, Adolf	New York
Borsiczky, Sandor	New York
Fisher, George	Brandeis University
Kecskemeti, Paul	RAND Corporation
Krader, Lawrence	American University
Monroe, James	Society for the Investigation of Human Ecology, New York
Moseley, Philip	Council on Foreign Relations, New York

allow them to write a chapter for us without having to do extensive original research?

In general, the persons interviewed expressed the opinion that the project was very worth while and important, but somewhat too ambitious and too broad. Most important, however, was the finding that the number of candidates who were suggested for chapters was quite inadequate in terms of how we visualized our end product. It was evident that the kinds of questions we were asking were important, but could not be answered without extensive original research. We were seeking (1) ways of bridging the gaps between areas of knowledge and (2) broad sets of relationships between different events that occur in totalitarian societies. But such questions in particular were ones which we found most political scientists or historians unwilling to get involved with. Hence, the major conclusion of our interviewing was that it would be quite unlikely that we should be able to find contributors for the bulk of the areas which we had chosen to investigate.

Since it was not possible to get contributors who would answer the questions we had originally posed, we decided that it might be best to reorient our work outline toward questions that perhaps we ourselves could answer, not by investigating primary sources (most of which would, of course, be in Chinese), but by pulling together material from various secondary sources and analyses. In terms of the literature which we felt might be available to us, we asked ourselves what kind of a research outline we could reasonably set up for ourselves, i.e. what kinds of questions we might be able to answer. Through a series of discussions we arrived at the following outline:

1. A discussion of the political-social-cultural context in which coercive persuasion operates, stated as a set of hypotheses. This discussion would include analyses of any historical, social, and cultural factors which we could identify in totalitarian society in general and in the Chinese situation in particular which bore on the development of the thought reform program and its operation in the 1950's.

2. An analysis of the institutional devices for carrying out the process of coercive persuasion, i.e., penal institutions, revolutionary universities, organized group discussions, and so on.

3. A consideration of the individuals or groups which serve as the agents of the institutions discussed above, i.e., the sorts of people who are the change agents in the day-to-day business of producing ideological change.

4. A consideration of the victims or target individuals and groups, i.e., who became involved in the program and why. The consideration here of why Westerners, why prisoners of war, and why Americans became involved is obviously a crucial one.

5. A consideration of the interpersonal process between the agent and the target. What goes on, for example, in the political prison which leads to a change process in the target individual?

6. A consideration of what might be called the intrapsychic process within the target individual. What kinds of changes were produced and by what kinds of psychological mechanisms are these changes to be understood?

7. A consideration of various kinds of psychological, psychiatric, sociological, and other theories which pertain to the change process or the influence process, with an attempt to evaluate what kinds of theoretical models are best suited to explaining what happened to the target individuals.

8. A consideration of parallel phenomena either at other periods in history or in our own contemporary society, in which we should attempt to spell out what sources of influence in our own society resemble the coercive persuasion that one witnesses in China. By making the comparison, we hoped it would be possible to illuminate both the process as it occurs in China and the process as it occurs in our own society.

We realized that we could not cover each of the above points with equal intensity or sophistication, particularly on the contextual side. We hoped, rather, to draw together what information other people had gathered and to summarize and integrate rather than produce original research. Our original contribution is primarily in the analysis of the interpersonal process that occurred in coercive persuasion between the change agent and the target individual, and the internal effects of this process on the target individual.

Having determined an outline for organizing our study, the question next arose of how best to gather the information relevant to the various topics. We chose to look at four kinds of data, or, rather, we chose four different approaches to the gathering of data in these areas.

1. Reading existing analyses of Communist China, the Soviet Union, and totalitarian society in general.

2. Reading autobiographical accounts of victims of coercive persuasion, both victims of Soviet imprisonment, forced labor, and indoctrination, and victims of Chinese Communist thought reform.

3. Discussions with various China experts as particular questions arose and as we needed clues to new sources or answers to specific questions.

4. Interviews with Americans who actually experienced thought reform and who allegedly were successfully "brainwashed." Such interviews were of interest not only from the point of view of getting information about the methods of thought reform, but also from the point of view of gathering follow-up data some three to five years after the experience. In choosing the subjects for interviewing we were not attempting to obtain a representative sample of civilian repatriates. Rather we were seeking people who had experienced the full force of thought reform in a prison setting and either had been influenced or had resisted influence successfully. Our final sample therefore consists of only fifteen people, but the accounts of these individuals have been supplemented by material from published reports, government documents, first-hand observations by others not imprisoned, and consultations with others who are studying modern Chinese affairs.

The report which follows is the result of amalgamating the data gathered through these four approaches. As will be seen, the report does not follow our original outline at many points and there is far more emphasis on some of the points in the outline than on others. It is our hope that many of the assertions we make throughout the report will be treated primarily as hypotheses contributing to the understanding of events which have been little understood thus far, and that the reader will approach our study with a spirit of inquiry rather than with a hope of finding final answers. It is also our hope that we have been able to convey the complexity of the coercive persuasion phenomenon and to avoid the kind of oversimplification which has characterized some of the early efforts to understand it.

A few words are in order concerning our own division of labor. All three of us worked on all phases of the project. We divided our reading responsibilities and concentrated on different questions but basically hammered our conclusions out jointly. We each did some of the interviewing and each worked up portions of the material. It is therefore difficult to give credit for any particular set of ideas to any one of us. They were always a joint product. The only exceptions are the historical outline in Chapter 1 (developed by Curt Barker), the categories which underlie Chapter 5 on types of guilt (developed by Inge Schneier), and the theoretical model of coercive persuasion which underlies Chapters 4, 8, 9, and 10 (which is my own). Specific contributions by Curt Barker can also be found in Appendixes 2 and 3 (group methods and the agent). The final draft is my own version of our joint conclusions.

The encouragement and support of many of our colleagues helped us to sharpen our ideas, and their critical evaluation of our conclusions helped us to avoid premature or unwarranted generalizations. We would like to extend special thanks to James Monroe of the Society for the Investigation of Human Ecology for his consistent support of this project and for his generous offering of his own knowledge of psychological warfare to us.

The support which we received from the Center for International Studies was immeasurable. Particularly helpful were the efforts of Miss Alice Riedinger, the Center librarian, and Don Blackmer, Arthur Singer, and Richard W. Hatch whose encouragement and support were unflagging. The tireless efforts of a number of secretaries, particularly Miss Jane Isherwod, also deserve special mention.

Finally, I must give special thanks to my wife, who not only provided the moral support necessary to complete the study, but whose editing of the entire manuscript improved its quality immeasurably.

Our thanks also to our subjects, whose interest in our study and willingness to give freely of their time and thoughts made the interviews productive and rewarding experiences.

EDGAR H. SCHEIN
Cambridge, Massachusetts

INTRODUCTION

The purpose of this study is to analyze the experiences of a small number of American civilians who were imprisoned by the Chinese Communists between 1950 and 1956. These cases are of interest to the psychologist because almost all of these individuals are alleged to have made confessions of a politically damaging nature and a small percentage of them appeared upon repatriation to have been converted to Communism. Though there was no evidence at all of their having worked for the United States Government, and though it became known through others and from their own later accounts that their imprisonment had been illegal and quite brutal by Western standards, they made statements like the following upon their repatriation:

"In China today a person who is not guilty of a crime could never be arrested or convicted. . . . Before I was arrested in my heart I knew that I was guilty of being a spy, but I wouldn't have admitted it . . . our conditions were so good! The People's Government took care of us so well! . . . We had no pressure put on us."

"When I was arrested I was absolutely guilty of the crime of espionage . . . I knew in the first place that I was guilty. . . . In order to gain self-respect one has to confess. . . . We are grateful for such light sentences. One has to be penitent to be released."

Because the beliefs, attitudes, and values of these persons had apparently been drastically altered by coercive means, the label "brainwashing" came to be applied to the experiences they had undergone, and it was widely assumed that the Communists had developed a new and powerful weapon to use against the mind of man.

The dramatic confessions of Communist Party members in the Soviet purge trials of the 1930's, the confessions extracted by the Soviet and satellite secret police from Cardinal Mindszenty, William Oatis, and Robert Vogeler had given ample forewarning of Communist willingness and ability to obtain confessions, but not until the publication of Edward Hunter's book *Brainwashing in Red China* (1951) did it become widely apparent that the Chinese Communists were waging a far more extensive battle for the mind of man, which included confession extraction as only a small, though key, part of a more elaborate process of re-education. And not only was such political-ideological re-education limited to political prisoners, but it was widely applied to all segments of Chinese society. The attempts to indoctrinate United Nations prisoners of war in Korea and the successful extraction of germ warfare confessions from some of them was but one segment of this total program of ideological re-education.

The term "brainwashing," introduced into the English language by Hunter, derives from the Chinese phrase *Hsi Nao,* which is used to refer to the idea of washing away the vestiges of the old system (literally "cleansing the mind") in the process of being re-educated to assume one's place in the new Communist society. The concept is alleged to have been used in reference to re-education by Mao Tse-tung in his early speeches on Chinese Communism, but is not commonly in use within China today. The more common way to refer to the program of re-education is the phrase *Szu Hsing Kai Tsao,* which translates into "thought reform" or "ideological remolding" (Lifton, 1956$_b$).

The term "brainwashing" quickly became associated with all Communist efforts to extract confessions and indoctrinate captive audiences, as well as with their internal educational and propaganda efforts. Analyses of the psychological processes underlying such a widespread program of mental coercion have sought general principles like Pavlovian conditioning which could account for the seemingly involuntary compliance that the behavior of prisoners suggested. In the attempt to find the common core of methodology in brainwashing, the actual events and the experiences of prisoners were often lost, however. This led to some quite erroneous conceptions of what the Chinese approach to re-education actually is, and what sort of psychological theory is appropriate to the explanation of its outcomes.

On the other hand, those studies which have attempted to analyze a limited set of events like the Soviet purge trials (Leites and Bernaut, 1954), the Soviet approach to education and propaganda

(Inkeles, 1950), the Chinese "revolutionary university" (Lifton, 1957), or the Korean prisoner of war (POW) episode (Schein, 1956) have typically revealed that situational factors or unique aspects of the total experience are crucial for an understanding of the outcome. And as carefully conceptualized studies of different aspects of Communist control operations have been published, the image of the master plot based on Pavlov has begun to fade. Important differences have been turned up between the practices of the Soviet secret police and the Chinese Communist secret police (in spite of common origins and some overlap in methods). Where the Soviets have put emphasis on confession extraction to justify public trials (prior to eliminating the victim), the Chinese have from the beginning emphasized the role of confession as a step in rehabilitation and reform, and have relied more heavily on persuasion than coercion. Where the Soviets have traditionally isolated the prisoner and undermined his resistance by depriving him of any social contact, the crux of the Chinese approach has been to immerse the prisoner in a small group of others who are more advanced in their reform than he and who operate as the key agents of influence. Where the Soviet methods have supported an image of "scientific" interrogation and confession extraction, the Chinese have stimulated the image of a zealous, enthusiastic, almost evangelical mass movement sweeping converts into its ranks by virtue of the intrinsic merit of its message. In neither the Chinese nor the Soviet case has any evidence been turned up of any connection with Pavlovian psychology or any systematic use of his findings.

It is in the spirit of adding detailed analysis of a limited phenomenon that we have built the present study around the experiences of the rather small number of Americans who were imprisoned on the Chinese mainland and were subjected to unusual and intensive pressures designed to change their beliefs, attitudes, and values. We shall not attempt to encompass any of the many other Communist efforts to indoctrinate, nor shall we be seeking theoretical explanations which will account for the confessions and conversions of captives in the Soviet Union or the satellites. We shall not even extend our analysis to the experiences of the American POW's during the Korean War; partly because such analyses have already been made (e.g., Lifton, 1954; Segal, 1954; Santucci and Winokur, 1955; U.S. Department of Defense, 1955; Strassman, Thaler, and Schein, 1956; Biderman, 1956, 1957; Schein, Hill, Williams, and Lubin, 1957; Segal, 1957; Singer and Schein, 1958); and partly because a detailed explanation of why some men collaborated, why some twenty-one of them refused repatriation, and why some allegedly came home brainwashed would require a study at least as long as the present one. Of course if one conceives of brainwashing as a process of producing genuine, extensive, and *lasting* belief, attitude, and value change in a person resisting such change, then only the small number of American civilians imprisoned on the Chinese mainland are true cases of brainwashing.

Since its introduction into the English language, the term brainwashing has acquired a whole range of usages. Most commonly, when the word is used in a semi-technical sense, it refers to Communist efforts to break an individual prisoner by a prolonged and scientific program of mental destruction, and then to empty him of his old beliefs and attitudes and pour in new Communist beliefs and attitudes. This image of brainwashing as an esoteric technique of systematically destroying the mind of an individual has been strongly supported by the frequent claims of psychologists, psychiatrists, and neurophysiologists that their researches on conditioning, sensory deprivation, implantation of electrodes into the brain, and psychopharmacology have direct relevance to the understanding of brainwashing (Lilly, 1956, 1957; Miller, 1957; Huxley, 1958).

The experiences of the prisoners do not fit such a model, however; hence we have abandoned the term brainwashing and prefer to use the term coercive persuasion. Coercive persuasion is a more accurate descriptive concept because basically what happened to the prisoners was that they were subjected to unusually intense and prolonged persuasion in a situation from which they could not escape; that is, they were coerced into allowing themselves to be persuaded.

We are not implying by the choice of this term that the experience for the victim was not painful. What we are trying strongly to underline at the outset is that the phenomenon with which we are dealing here is a completely understandable one, and that it occurred in people who were not broken or psychotic during or after their imprisonment. By inserting the concept of persuasion we are further asserting that a genuine clash of beliefs and points of view was involved in many phases of the process; it was not merely a case of a Machiavellian Communist inserting into a docile prisoner ideas or beliefs which would make good propaganda for the Communist.

From the outset the purpose of this study has been to analyze these cases of attitude change from a socio-psychological point of view. We are not concerned with providing a detailed description of the experiences of the prisoners, nor are we concerned with the political implications of the whole thought reform movement. This is not a study of China or its methods of education. Rather, it is a study of a particular approach to the problem of influencing beliefs, attitudes, and values and our main purpose is to contribute to the social psychology of influence and attitude change. This is not to say that we shall ignore the fact that the events of coercive persuasion took place in Communist China and that they have obvious political relevance. Nor is it irrelevant to consider some of the implications of these events for a totalitarian society. What we are trying to delineate is our central focus or orientation, which is basically psychological.

A preliminary survey of literature and a set of interviews with experts on China and on Communism led to the conclusion that the process of coercive persuasion and its outcomes in the American prisoners could not be understood without a careful consideration of the context in which it occurred. The coercive persuasion of the prisoners took place as part of the general thought reform program which was sweeping China, and this program had qualities which derived partly from the history of the Chinese Communist movement and partly from the fact that it was a particular manifestation of the passion for unanimity which has characterized a number of totalitarian systems. Consequently we have devoted Part I of this study to a consideration of these historical and political-social factors. Our purpose in presenting this contextual material is not to provide a definitive piece of history or political analysis; rather, it is to trace the theme of coercive persuasion back to some of its roots in totalitarianism in general and Chinese Communism in particular. As part of this analysis we shall also present what appear to have been some of the major aspects of the thought reform movement of the 1950's, its explicit and implicit aims, and the manner in which it led to the arrest and coercive persuasion of our American cases.

In Part II we shall suggest a conceptual scheme for organizing sequentially the many facets of the coercive persuasion experience; discuss the special role which guilt played in accounting for some of the changes observed in the prisoners; describe the kinds of belief, attitude, and value change which occurred in the prisoners; and state some hypotheses about personal predispositions and certain categories of experience which, if they were present, tended to increase the likelihood that the prisoner would undergo extensive belief, attitude, and value change.

Part III concerns itself primarily with the relevance of various psychological, physiological, psychiatric, and sociological theories to the understanding of the events and outcomes of coercive persuasion. We shall examine theories and conceptual schemes which have been suggested to account for its effects, and attempt through a critical analysis of these suggested theories to move toward a synthesis and integration of them. The kind of theoretical model which begins to emerge in rough outline from this attempt is not only intended to encompass the coercive persuasion experience of our cases in Communist China but is also generalizable to other kinds of social influence situations, some of which occur in our own society.

In Part IV we examine some of the implications of the points developed in Part III for the analysis of influence situations which exist within our own society and for a general theory of influence.

A word is in order about our methodology. We do not pretend that our conclusions are based on an exhaustive analysis of all Americans who were imprisoned by the Communists; indeed, we do not even have a representative sample of them. Rather, we are building a theoretical analysis around a very small number of cases of individuals who demonstrated extensive and lasting belief, attitude, and value change. We obtained as much material as was available on these cases, including reports of interviews with them prior to, during, and after their imprisonment; observations of them at repatriation and at various times thereafter; follow-up interviews with them some three to five years after their repatriation which we conducted ourselves; autobiographical accounts which were in some cases published, in other cases available only for our own use.

The reader will note that we have not, however, included very much case material in our analysis. The basic reason for this is that the persons concerned are so few in number as to make it almost impossible to disguise their identity sufficiently to protect their anonymity. Our subjects were more than willing to explore extensively their experiences and their feelings about them, but much of this material was obviously private. There is, however, an additional reason for the minimal amount of first-hand material—we found in analyzing the experiences of our cases that adequate documentation of our points would require virtually complete biographical accounts. Since it was not our intention to be descriptive, but rather to be analytical, we decided that detailed descriptive material could better be obtained by the reader if he consulted one of a number of excellent autobiographical accounts (Bull, 1955; Bonnichon, 1955; Rigney, 1956; Ford, 1957; Rickett and Rickett, 1957; Becker, 1958) or more descriptive accounts like those of Lifton (1956b) or Barnett (1953, 1956).

Wherever possible we checked our hypotheses with those of others, like Robert Lifton and Doak Barnett, who were thoroughly familiar with the events of thought reform and who had conducted careful studies of samples of American and European repatriates from Communist China. We cannot ignore, however, the real danger that a *post hoc* analysis of events as complex as those surrounding the coercive persuasion of a few Westerners contains within it. Though we often state our points as conclusions, the reader should always remind himself that basically they are hypotheses to be checked against further data wherever and whenever such may become available. And ultimately the test of our theoretical model will have to come not from further analysis of cases but from empirical investigations of comparable phenomena within our own society where we have the opportunity to repeat observations and check conclusions constantly against new data.

PART ONE *The Context of Coercive Persuasion*

THE PHENOMENON of coercive persuasion occurred * in the context of the thought reform movement which the Chinese Communist Party (CCP) launched to deal with their problems of social control and reconstruction. This movement permeated all segments of Chinese society after the take-over, including the prisons and the prisoner of war camps. It involved a number of Americans who were arrested on suspicion of espionage or on other charges designed to discredit the West, to assert Asian superiority at home and abroad, or to serve as a bargaining point in international negotiations.

It is very doubtful that any Westerners were imprisoned and subjected to thought reform techniques for the primary purpose of being reformed. Rather, their treatment subsequent to arrest was typical of current Chinese Communist penal methods for "enemies of the people," whether Chinese or Western.

It is the attempt to *reform* "enemies of the people" which distinguishes the CCP from other Communist Parties. The Bolsheviks may have been masters at eliciting confessions, but such confessions were designed to destroy their authors and remove them from society, while the emphasis in the CCP was to "cure the disease and save the man" for a productive role in the society. To understand better the institutions and processes which this emphasis has pro-

* We use the past tense here and in other parts of the chapter because we do not know whether the combination of events we have labeled "coercive persuasion" is now occurring or will in the future occur again. We do not have any evidence that current penal practices are in fact different; rather, we are asserting that we simply do not know whether they are or not.

duced, it is necessary to look at those aspects in the history of the CCP which throw light on the development of the thought reform approach. Following this we shall briefly describe the operation of the thought reform movement in the early 1950s and then set forth the manner in which Americans became exposed to it.

1

The Persuasion Theme
in the Development of the
Chinese Communist Party

A KNOWLEDGE of a number of historical factors is essential to an understanding of the thought reform program as it operated in the 1950's, particularly to the understanding of the treatment of the Westerners in political prisons. Some of these historical factors pertain specifically to the development of the Communist movement within China, which was in many ways different from classical Marxist theory of revolution and from the Communist experience in the Soviet Union; some pertain to cultural themes which lent themselves very well to the themes that the Communists introduced; and some pertain to the organizational know-how which the Chinese Communists acquired from their Soviet counterparts, particularly in secret police work and prison management.

MAO'S PEASANT BASE

As a political party the CCP had considerable difficulty in its early attempts to make a place for itself in Chinese politics (Schwartz, 1951). Not the least of these difficulties was the lack of a proper base of popular support—that is, the absence of a po-

litically conscious, powerful urban proletariat. In 1925, instead of
seeking the support of the urban proletariat, Mao, who was then
still a fairly low-level party secretary, was organizing a peasant base
of support in the province of Hunan. This activity was not sanctioned by the party elite or by Moscow and resulted in Mao's political ostracism from the CCP for a number of years (he was
charged with "adventurism").

Although the possibility of relying on the peasants in a revolutionary movement had been considered by Lenin, it is a major
premise of Marxist ideology that proper class consciousness can
only come from proper class origins, and these origins can be found
only in the *urban proletariat*. Peasant origin is considered to lead
to the antithesis of the desired Communist attitude because the
peasant would tend to be ultra-conservative in his preoccupation
with property, and classical ideological appeals would therefore
have little effect on him. In organizing the peasants, therefore, Mao
had to rely on specific ideological themes (i.e. the disaffection in the
peasant groups with their landlords and the government) and had
to build from these particular themes an adequate working ideology.

One can imagine Mao, always reputed to have been a highly
practical man, appealing to the peasants primarily in terms of their
grievances against the "corrupt landlords supported by a corrupt
government," and winning only the support of malcontents in the
younger generation of farm children. That such discontentment
within the family existed prior to the rise of Communism in China
has been well documented (e.g., Fried, 1959). It only remained for
the Communists to find the sources of discontent, like the absolute
authority of the father and elders, the complete subjugation of
women, the lack of freedom to choose a marital partner, and so on.

Mao had faith that the movement could be built by this means on
a peasant base of support, and implicit in this faith was an assumption which underlies the entire thought reform movement—namely,
that class origins do not *irrevocably* fix political attitudes, but, rather,
that political attitudes can be learned and unlearned. It has been
observed that it was already a Chinese tradition to assume a
tabula rasa at birth and that through reason and rote learning one
could engrave on it what one would. Hence Mao was working in

keeping with Chinese tradition and the then current trends when he undertook to educate the peasantry to fulfill the traditional role of the proletariat (Wright, 1959).

Of course it was not only the force of Chinese tradition, but Mao's own background and experience which must have underlain this faith in education to class consciousness. Mao and other leaders were aware that they themselves did not have appropriate proletarian class origins and that they had, in fact, learned the ideology and developed the appropriate attitude (class consciousness) intellectually.

But beyond this faith there was the necessity of creating support for the party. And Mao, the realist, could see that in a society whose base was overwhelmingly agrarian, and whose major grievances were those of the peasants, it was most practical to seek and organize peasant support. Since the Chinese Communists were not in a position to win the peasant support with actual programs to alleviate their plight (although they attempted in the mid-twenties various land reforms such as reduction in their rent and even some confiscation of the landlords' land [Wright, 1959]), they had to woo them with the tools of persuasion and agitation. Thus, their position led them to "a total inversion of certain Marxist presuppositions. Instead of deducing ideological tendencies from class affiliations, they decided to deduce class affiliations from ideological tendencies" (Brandt, Schwartz, and Fairbank, 1952). They had the faith that they could teach such new ideological tendencies to any "correct thinking" individual. It should be noted that this assumption differs markedly from the early Soviet assumption that elements of society which were, from the viewpoint of class origin, unfit for a contribution to Communist society were useful at best as slave labor (though a more common course was simply to eliminate them).

THE EXIGENCIES OF GUERRILLA WARFARE

The blockade strategy of the Kuomintang (KMT) in the early 1930's and of the Japanese in the 1940's forced the Red Army to become primarily a guerrilla operation using hit-and-run tactics rather than a well-based and well-supplied series of military garrisons. The very nature of these operations required extensive de-centralization of administrative authority, a wide scattering of forces, and dependence for basic supplies of food on the local peasantry. Only if the local peasantry was willing to support the Communists actively by supplying food could the movement survive, a condition which required reliance on persuasion (to insure *active* support) and extensive local decision-making power both on short-run operational policy and on ideological matters.

. . . the Communist areas of China have, with few exceptions, been the scene of practically continuous guerilla warfare. Successful guerilla warfare demands the active support of the great majority of the population. The normal situation has been that the population of any area have been in a position to ensure the defeat of the local Communist forces, not by actively opposing them, but simply by ceasing to give them whole-hearted support. This has made actual popular support a material fact of supreme importance which could not be explained away or distorted to fit into a system of Marx-Leninist dogma. If the masses in any area disliked Communist policy enough to stop giving active support to the local Communist army, that army would be defeated. The Communists might believe that the masses did not understand what was good for them, that they were the victims of superstition, feudal traditions or reactionary propaganda, but this was all irrelevant to the practical problem. However mistaken the masses might be, the Communists faced the choice between winning their support and being defeated by the Kuomintang or Japanese. [Lindsay, 1950, pp. 24–25]

Whatever the merits or demerits of the orthodox Marxist-Leninist ideology, it had to be used operationally on a day-to-day basis as a tool of persuasion. Furthermore, because guerrilla contact with the local people of an area was likely to be on a diffuse person-to-person basis, it was necessary that all members of the guerrilla movement have the ideological tools with which to carry out such persuasion. Clearly, it was not enough for a few leaders to be the custodians of the ideology when it was the rank and file who were in the day-to-day business of persuasion, nor was it sufficient to limit ideological training to the teaching of orthodox theory. The rank and file had to learn it as a working ideology. Lindsay describes very well the results of such experience:

The effect of this sort of experience could be seen very clearly in individuals as well as in the party as a whole. Cadres whose career in the party had been passed entirely in headquarters organizations, in the most stable base areas or in underground work in enemy areas, were very often similar to the typical cadres of other Communist parties. There was seldom any doubt about their genuine desire to serve the people or about their unselfish devotion to the party and the cause they believed in. But often their minds were completely closed to any experiences or ideas that could not be fitted into a dogmatic system determined by Marx-Leninist theories and the Party Line. The one sacrifice they were not prepared to make in the service of the people was to jeopardize their quasi-religious faith in Communist doctrines by the exercise of critical scientific reasoning and observation of the material world. Cadres whose careers in the party had been mainly in the front-line areas and especially in the guerilla areas were a noticeable contrast to this. They believed the same Communist doctrines but, in most cases, believed in them as scientific theories and not as religious dogmas. Their minds were usually much more open to new experiences and new ideas and they would make room for observed facts by adjustments in their system of Communist beliefs in the way that a scientific theory is adjusted to new observations. This contrast can be explained by a process of natural selection. The work of a Communist official or mass-movement organizer in the guerilla areas was extremely dangerous (Central Hopei lost one-third of its hsien magistrates in one year), and he could only survive if the local population was prepared to make considerable sacrifices and take very great risks in order to protect him. He had to win the confidence and loyalty of a large number of individual peasant families. Someone who refused to consider the real individual Chinese peasant as he actually was, who refused to take account of differences with the ideal Chinese peasant as he should have been according to Communist theory, was unlikely to survive. Work in the guerilla areas was, therefore, a very effective education in modifying Communist theory to fit the facts, with a high probability of sudden death for those who failed to benefit from this education.

All this has made the Chinese Communist Party unique in the high proportion of its leaders and cadres who are prepared to use practical common sense and who are prepared to make a scientific and objective estimate of the facts of a situation and, if necessary, to modify their Communist doctrines to take account of these facts. It is this unique objectivity and consistent materialism that have made the Chinese Communist Party develop Communist principles in ways which differ very considerably from developments in the West. [Lindsay, 1950, pp. 24–25]

EXPERIENCES IN "LIBERATED AREAS"

This factor is closely related to the previous one in that the CCP found itself in a position of having to administer areas which came under its control fairly early in its history, and saw the necessity for a program of "cultural" education emphasizing basic literacy training for the masses of illiterate peasants. This program provided an ideal opportunity for political tutelage, insofar as it made evident the Communists' "genuine concern" for the ultimate welfare of the peasant; at the same time, it could be used as a vehicle for political propaganda, e.g., first teaching those few characters which were essentially political slogans and generally teaching only those characters which would make it possible for the peasants to read CCP literature and propaganda. The general function of political tutelage, teaching the peasants the rudiments of the Communist ideology, was, of course, to insure that if the areas were democratized the vote would still be strongly for the CCP.

It was, however, inevitable because of the decentralized administration that different ideological as well as practical solutions to problems would be developed in different areas, and some of these were in clear conflict with central party policy. Just as proper class consciousness could be learned, so it could be unlearned or learned wrong. And without tight centralized control the leadership operating from Yenan could do little to prevent personal ambition, inadequate training, excessive fanaticism, and other situational factors from threatening the security of the CCP. It was no doubt factors like these which led eventually (in the 1940's) to the *Cheng feng* (Party Reform) movement for "the correction of unorthodox tendencies," which will be discussed in greater detail below.

RECRUITING MANPOWER IN THE CIVIL WAR

The CCP relied on two basic sources of manpower—young people from the rural areas and villages through which the Red Armies moved, and defectors from KMT forces or prisoners captured during military engagements. We have not been able to determine how many former KMT troops and officials actually became integrated into the Red Armies or the exact reasons for the alleged large-scale KMT defections, but in almost every account one reads, it is stated that such personnel were a key source not only of manpower but also of weapons for the Red Armies. The problem of making reliable soldiers and Communist Party workers out of uneducated youths, defectors, or prisoners was no doubt a considerable one. The feature which stands out in the CCP approach to this problem, is the great emphasis on political indoctrination for all troops as a primary technique of insuring loyalty and high performance.

". . . every Red Army man is fighting for the same purpose, so the command is followed as one man and discipline is perfect . . . the Red Army is not only militarily but politically well disciplined and conscious." [Chu Teh, quoted in Wales, 1939, pp. 259–60]

In a more general vein, Ch'en Yun wrote in *How to be a Communist Party Member:*

"Revolution is a stupendous and trying undertaking and the conditions of the Chinese revolution and the revolutionary movement are particularly complex and kaleidoscopic; the reason why the CP is able to control, under changing and complex circumstances, the great revolutionary movement and guide it towards victory is because it possesses a revolutionary ideology. Accordingly, a CP member must understand this revolutionary ideology; then he can find a way out of highly complex situations; he can work out his course in the ever-changing (revolutionary) movement, and can carry out his revolutionary assignments successfully. Unless he does so, he will lose his way and direction in the midst of his complicated and ever-changing revolutionary environment. He will be unable to work independently and will fail to carry out correctly the assignments and resolutions of the Party. Thus, every CP member must learn through work whenever and wherever possible, elevate his political and cultural level, increase his revolutionary knowledge, and deepen his political vision." [Quoted in Brandt, Schwartz, & Fairbank, 1952, pp. 334–35]

The political education of the troops occurred in a context in which the shared experiences of hardship, stress, and success during, for example, the Long March from 1934 to 1936 must have already created strong emotional bonds and loyalty based on commitment to the cause. But such solidarity was apparently not left at a purely emotional level; instead it was continually rationalized and placed into a political context through extensive education and propaganda.

The approach which was used with captured or defected enemy soldiers who might have been expected to represent an ideologically hostile group was to rely once again on re-education, that is, to treat the prisoner or defector as one who was misguided and could be shown the true path (Wang Tsun-ming, 1954). His bourgeois or even anti-Communist background was not held against him unless he showed himself unco-operative in his re-education.*

. . . enemy prisoners would be treated with unexpected leniency and encouraged to express all of their grievances against their officers and landlords—"vomit bitter waters," as it was called; the Communist "instructors" would help the prisoners ascribe the causes of their misfortune to the former regime—"dig up the roots"; and the prisoners would be encouraged to become part of the forces of the revolution—the "one heart movement." Communist soldiers stressed morality and dedication through personal example. [Lifton, 1956b, p. 193]

The important point is that this approach was the result of trial-and-error and its use was the result of the many successes the CCP had when applying it to initially neutral or hostile recruits.

* The reader will recognize in this approach the "lenient policy" which took the American POW so much by surprise in the Korean conflict of a decade and a half later (Schein, 1956). A good description of this policy is given in Appendix 1.

COALITION GOVERNMENT AND "UNITED FRONT" STRATEGY

Another factor in the history of the CCP was the commitment on the part of the leaders of the party to a "united front" with other parties, particularly with the KMT, and their tolerance for or actual encouragement of coalition government. Having committed himself to coalition government, Mao could not very well rely on outright coercion to insure that his party would remain in control.

Administrative and bureaucratic authority tended to be weak in most of the rural Chinese areas; hence a reliance on *military* force as a way of maintaining control of an area and establishing administration had a long tradition (Pye, 1956). Many of the villages had local militias which were of considerable strength. Mao chose to try to persuade such village militias to work with him, to become part of his military force, rather than to waste his own manpower by trying to subjugate them and risk losing the support of the people in the process. Everything would go more smoothly from his point of view if he were able by persuasion to win over whatever pockets of armed resistance he might meet.

Coalition government also meant the sharing of power with other parties in parliamentary activities, which gave the CCP a façade of legality but also forced Mao to rely more on public opinion than he probably wished. Of course, the political tutelage given to the people, in combination with extensive use of activists and Party workers in the liberated areas, usually insured that they would "voluntarily and spontaneously" vote for the CCP candidates.

THE *CHENG FENG* MOVEMENT

The *Cheng feng* movement of the early 1940's was an attempt by the CCP leadership to "purify ideologically" its administrative and military organization. Because it was similar in many respects to the post-takeover thought reform movement and foreshadowed many of the techniques of coercive persuasion, we shall look at the *Cheng feng* movement in some detail.

The movement for the "Correction of [unorthodox] tendencies" was probably launched with the aim of rallying and reconsolidating the forces of Chinese Communism in order to overcome the blurring and unsettling effects of the united front strategy. It may also have been launched with a view to preparing the Communist movement for the contingency of a possible disintegration of the united front at some time in the future. Essentially it involved a reclarification of basic Chinese Communist positions on all matters of doctrine and organization. It re-emphasized certain perennial core elements of the Communist tradition, and also clarified the New Democracy line in various spheres of activity. By thus clarifying Party positions on all issues, the CCP leadership could more easily separate the sheep from the goats—i.e., separate "right and left opportunists" from faithful followers of the Party line.

The movement concerned itself with three types of tendencies: (1) in learning, (2) in the Party, and (3) in art and literature. But at the heart of the whole movement there lay the question of proper Party organization and Party discipline. For so long as the basic Leninist principles of Party organization are not accepted, incorrect tendencies in other spheres of Communist activity are an ever-present possibility. Thus Mao Tse-tung constantly insists on "objectivity" in applying Marxist-Leninist doctrine to concrete Chinese realities. But the norm of what is objective and what not, must be fixed by the Party leadership, just as in many churches the correct interpretation of the Scriptures is always fixed by ecclesiastic authority. The proper understanding of the Leninist concept of the Party lies at the very heart of the whole *Cheng-feng* movement. [Brandt, Schwartz, & Fairbank, 1952, pp. 353–54]

Going into more detail Brandt, Schwartz, and Fairbank give the following reasons for the *Cheng feng* movement:

(1) *The problem of unorthodox thought.* Ever since the outbreak of the Sino-Japanese war on July 7, 1937, the CCP had suffered from an increasing shortage of trained (especially ideologically trained) personnel. This was a result both of expanding personnel in the enlarged guerilla areas and of losses through war-time casualties. A few hundred trained cadres turned out at Yenan each year were quickly swallowed up in the vastness of the country. The sudden influx of new Party members had created tension between the old and new comrades and made for an increase in careerism and unorthodoxy. Evidently some Party members, especially among the new recruits, had interpreted the spectacular shifts

of the united front period to mean that the concepts of Western liberalism could be imported into the CCP itself. On the other hand, other more doctrinaire Party members were disturbed by the shift from the ideology of the Soviet period and by what seemed to them to be discrepancies between the Marxist texts and the actual practices of the CCP, particularly with regard to the relations between proletariat and peasantry and between Communism and the growing nationalism of the period. Liu Shao-ch'i had expressed the uneasiness of the Party leadership in his speech *On the Intra-Party Struggle . . .* when he said, "Recently a great number of intellectual elements and new Party members have entered the Party, bringing with them to the Party strong bourgeois, liberal ideas. Ideologically, politically, and organizationally they have not been tempered by the iron discipline of the proletariat . . ."

(2) *The problem of the sinification of Marxism.* The accumulated effect of war-time nationalism was also clearly manifest in the *Cheng-feng* movement. Mao Tse-tung . . . says, "If we have only read this theory [of Marx, Engels, Lenin, and Stalin] but have not used it as a basis to study the historical reality and the revolutionary reality and have not created our own specific theory in accordance with China's practical needs, then it would be irresponsible to call ourselves Marxist theorists." A similar remark was made by Mao in his speech, *Reform Our Learining,* in May 1941, that "Youths of seventeen or eighteen are taught [in the cadres' school at Yenan] to digest *Das Kapital* and the *Anti-Duhring.* As a result, an abnormal psychology is created among the students, who lose interest in Chinese problems and neglect the directives of the Party. They only worship the words passed on to them by the teachers, holding them to be dogma that will remain forever valid." In short, it had become evident that Marxist theory could not be effective in China unless applied very practically to Chinese conditions.

(3) *Problems of intra-Party morale.* The *Cheng-feng* movement also served to carry out intra-Party reforms and tighten Party discipline. The *Decision on the CC's resolutions and Comrade Mao Tse-tung's report concerning the correction of three unorthodox tendencies,* adopted by the Propaganda Bureau of the CC on April 3, 1942, calls the movement a "spiritual revolution" and states that "All the organizations and schools should thoroughly study and vigorously discuss the above [*Cheng-feng*] documents . . . everyone should think hard and penetratingly about his own work and thought and life. The same applies to the examination of

other people. . . . The responsible heads of various departments (both Party and administration) should, after studying and discussing these documents, think about the work of the department and its personnel. Also they should exchange views with others, map out plans to check departmental work, proceed to do so according to plan, and then draw conclusions as to how the work could be improved. . . . Thus the *Cheng-feng* movement was developed as a catalytic procedure to invigorate Party and organizational activities. . . . [Brandt, Schwartz, & Fairbank, 1952, pp. 373–75]

The attitude toward this reform which we have pointed to previously is best summarized by Mao himself in a speech on "Correcting Unorthodox Tendencies in Learning, the Party, and Literature and Art":

"Lastly, in opposing subjectivism, sectarianism, and Party formalism, two principles must be observed. The first is, 'Punish the past to warn the future,' and the second, 'Save men by curing their ills.' Past errors must be exposed with no thought of personal feelings of face. We must use a scientific attitude to analyse and criticize what has been undesirable in the past so that more care will be taken in later work, and so this work will be better performed. This is the meaning of 'Punish the past to warn the future.' But our object in exposing errors and criticizing shortcomings is like that of a doctor in curing a disease. The entire purpose is to save the person, not to cure him to death. If a man has appendicitis, the doctor performs an operation and the man is saved. If a person who commits an error, no matter how great, does not bring his disease to an incurable state by concealing it and persisting in his error, and if in addition he is genuinely and honestly willing to be cured, willing to make corrections, we will welcome him so that his disease may be cured, and he can become a good comrade." [Quoted in Brandt, Schwartz, & Fairbank, 1952, p. 392]

And again, in his *Opposing Party Formalism*, Mao points out:

"The task of destroying and sweeping away these conditions is not an easy one. It must be properly done, which means that a reasonable explanation must be given. If the reasoning is good, if it is to the point, it can be effective. The first method in reasoning is to give the patients a powerful stimulus, yell at them, 'you're sick!', so the patients will have a fright and break out in an over-all sweat; then, they can be carefully treated." [Quoted in Brandt, Schwartz, & Fairbank, 1952, pp. 395–96]

It should be noted that the preoccupation with ideological purification reflects the assumption that political attitudes can be learned *and unlearned*. Even the very favorably placed person in the party hierarchy may become disaffected. The potential enemy is always present, even within the innermost party circles; hence continual purification, ideological purging, and mutual surveillance are necessary and justified.

. . . Heresies are thus likely to emerge in any quarter. The only ultimate criterion of Party loyalty is the disciplined acceptance of the Party line at any given moment, no matter how that line may shift. It can be seen that the tasks of intra-Party struggle are unending. [Brandt, Schwartz, & Fairbank, 1952, p. 355]

The struggle is, of course, as unending in Chinese as in Soviet Communism. There is, however, a fundamental difference in the approach which the Chinese have taken to dealing with the problem.

. . . We should note and ponder the fact that within the ranks of *Chinese Communism* in the New Democracy period—*as opposed to Russian Communism in the same years*—there is almost no record of the destruction of certain comrades by the Party or by other comrades, through the means of official purges leading to execution or by mysterious assassinations or disappearances. *Moral suasion or reindoctrination appear to have taken precedence over violence as the means of settling intra-Party disputes.* In this and many other respects the experience of Europe or of Russia may be an inadequate guide to the future of China's ancient society. Traditional traits and ways may persevere among the Chinese people with extraordinary tenacity. Today the esteem given the scholar is still such a trait; and this no doubt accounts in part for the CCP effort to win over and work with the intellectuals, even though Mao Tse-tung

has evidenced little but contempt for the traditionally bookish scholars
of the past. [Brandt, Schwartz, & Fairbank, 1952, p. 476; italics added]

The kinds of techniques used in this purification effort again
reflected leniency * and involved: (1) encouragement of grievances
against non-Communist groups or ideas combined with the presentation of highly acceptable positive goals (to reconstruct China, fight
Japan, and later fight American aggression in Korea, or, in the
case of dealing with American POW's, to fight for world peace);
(2) heavy reliance on group discussion, creating an atmosphere in
which each student had to commit himself and subject himself
to detailed scrutiny and analysis; (3) the use of criticism and self-
criticism to stimulate self-examination and to permit group members
to compete with each other in self-exposure and mutual exposure
with the aim of denigrating and thus destroying all emotional ties
with the past; (4) systematic rewarding by group members and
authorities of self-exposure, confession, and self-criticism, thus
setting the tone that any man was redeemable provided he was
willing to allow his "reactionary tendencies" to be exorcised; (5)
learning Communist doctrine and its practical meaning in a group
setting in which each member had publicly to think through and
apply to his own case whatever the theoretical point was.

To conclude:

In the years from 1936 to 1946, while these Chinese Communists were
busy expanding and recruiting new members from the general Chinese
population, they gradually developed a highly organized and vigorous
indoctrination program. It was aimed at all potential recruits who happened to fall into their ranks. Uneducated peasants, city workers, and
captured KMT troops, as well as interested students from the universities,
were subjects for this indoctrination.

In order to create in this heterogeneous group a feeling of comradeship

* ". . . Loyal comrades in the Party who have committed errors should not
be utterly denounced from the start; instead they should be persuaded, educated, and tempered with a friendly, sympathetic attitude, and only when
absolutely necessary should they be publicly attacked and expelled." [Liu
Shao-ch'i, "On the Training of a Communist Party Member," in Brandt,
Schwartz & Fairbank, 1952, p. 343.]

and identification with the peasant Communists, it was necessary to make them "cut their ties to the past." Therefore, the training program included a deliberate assault upon all of the traditional "bourgeois," "reactionary," "upper-class" attitudes, beliefs, and practices the recruits brought with them.

Trainees were forced to abandon their refinements of speech, manner, and behavior, their reverence for family ties and worldly goods, and to adopt the crude and earthy attitudes and behavior of the new "people's army." This questioning and discussion of behavior and value systems was accompanied by the inculcation of a fanatical enthusiasm for the Communist movement, built around the ideal of the rejuvenation of China and its re-establishment of a dynamic, modern society (an ideal which had been shared by the majority of Chinese intellectuals and reformers since the days of Sun Yat Sen). The combination of Communist practices, such as public confession and self-criticism, with traditional Chinese methods of learning by rote and repetition resulted in a highly effective method of persuasion. [Hinkle & Wolff, 1956, pp. 35–36]

CULTURAL THEMES IN CHINA AND SOVIET CONNECTIONS

The Chinese Communists' approach to thought reform has many elements which are, in a sense, their own invention, or at least were born out of their own experience. They have not, however, failed to take advantage of cultural traditions and specific institutions which worked in their favor. Both China and the Soviet Union had a long tradition of autocracy which created a readiness in the population to accept still another authority, albeit one which purported to rely more on ideology than raw power. Many of the institutions which might have been expected to be most hostile to the intrusion of Communism (e.g., the tightly knit family) had been weakening since the turn of the century from the impact of Western ideas, war, and general social upheaval. There was a strong predisposition to accept Western approaches, of which democracy, socialism, and communism were seen as some of the more interesting which might be tried in China.

At the same time, the strong nationalism of the Chinese, which the Communists certainly fanned, and the hostility toward the West, which was an outgrowth of a long history of exploitation by the West, led most Chinese to be somewhat ambivalent toward Western ideas. They wanted to become westernized, but at the same time they wanted to reject Western ideas and do things their own way. It may have been such ambivalence which stimulated concern with converting Westerners such as in the POW camp or the political prison. Perhaps the Chinese felt that they needed to prove to the Westerner that the Oriental was in fact superior and that they could do this best by forcing him to accept a new ideology, though the irony of it was that this "new" ideology was itself Western.

As far as more specific cultural themes are concerned, a number of them are relevant. For example, the traditional emphases on learning by rote and on learning by systematic self-examination have been exploited in the methods of thought reform; the belief that man can be re-educated has been previously mentioned as an important underlying assumption; the practicality of Chinese culture and the tendency of the Chinese to treat things expediently would suggest an easy acceptance of a movement like thought reform but a withholding of deep involvement in it; the contemplative emphasis which stems from Buddhism and Taoism would facilitate tendencies toward self-analysis but would obviously make difficult the active involvement sought by the Communists; Chinese sensitivity to interpersonal relations, the ability correctly to diagnose what is happening emotionally in another person, would, of course, become one of the most potent weapons in the service of thought reform if sufficient involvement was obtained to get individuals to use it "destructively" (in the sense of destroying bourgeois remnants) in their mutual criticism and other group discussion activities.

Lifton (1956b) also points out that those aspects of thought reform which run strongly counter to traditional values (denouncing close members of the family, willingness to be publicly humiliated by making public confessions, renouncing ancestor worship and other religions, etc.) still proved to work in favor of the acceptance of thought reform because of their appeal to the rebellious and the young.

Specific techniques such as the use of group discussion for indoctrination and the extensive use of self-criticism were certainly well known and highly developed long before the advent of the Chinese Communist movement. Many of them go back to early Marxist experiences and were learned in the process of developing stable and reliable cells. Many of them were products of Lenin's organizational genius.* There is no evidence that they were extrapolations from scientific principles of psychology, psychiatry, or sociology.

The extraction of public confession and public self-analysis may be techniques taken over from the Soviets; certainly there is more precedent for this kind of institution in Russian culture and religion than in the Chinese. For example, Berle (1957), in discussing the legal origins of Communist techniques of interrogation and indoctrination observes:

> . . . in the Slavic Balkans and in South Russia the Greek-Orthodox Catholic practice of confession differed somewhat from our more familiar Roman Catholic practice. The penitent made his confession to the "pope" or priest, in a sort of running conversation. The priest felt quite justified in questioning him to discover whether he had told all the truth, and frequently sent him home admonishing him to search his conscience and memory, and to return to make fuller accounting. When the priest was satisfied that he had a fair or adequate disclosure, he imposed penance and gave absolution. [Berle, 1957, pp. 646–47]

The important point here is that the priest, operating as an audience and judge, could, in effect, interrogate the subject and exhort him to continue self-analysis just as fellow group members do in thought reform. The use of public confession as a political device was, of course, extensively exploited in the Soviet Union during the purge trials.

Many of the specific techniques of confession extraction and indoctrination in a political prison derive from the long experience of the Soviet secret police, which in turn had antecedents in

---

* This statement is not intended to imply that the Marxists invented these techniques. Rather, they used methods which have been used in religious, fraternal, and other orders throughout history. It is possible, however, that the Communists are the first to use group methods specifically in the service of *political* indoctrination.

Czarist secret police experience (Hinkle & Wolff, 1956). The Chinese did introduce some major variants in their treatment of the prisoner, specifically the use of group pressure as a central technique both of confession extraction and indoctrination. It is important to remember, however, that the basic plan of prisoner handling was typical of Communist police procedures everywhere.

2

Thought Reform
After the Take-over

THE POST-YENAN period (1945–49) was a period of moving back into the cities, of further civil war, and of the gradual take-over of the mainland. For our study, the events of this take-over have their main significance in terms of the image which the Communists created in the minds of those Westerners who were later to become prisoners. For some of these Westerners the predominant image was one of a highly moral, puritanical, well-disciplined, ideologically zealous Red Army "liberating" cities and villages from the oppression of a government supported by "Western imperialism," thus making possible for the first time in Chinese history a united China based on ostensibly genuine concern for the people.

Such an image appeared to predominate either among those who had witnessed only the early phases of the Communist take-over or those who had spent most of their time in cities like Peiping where a special effort was made by the Communists to conduct their operations in an exemplary fashion and where unfavorable information coming from other parts of China could be suppressed by the control of the mass media. If stories of brutality and terror filtered through to the intellectuals in Peiping, it was second-hand knowledge which could easily be discounted by anyone exposed only to the exemplary conduct of the troops within the city; and even if those in Peiping became intellectually aware of the fact that Communist take-overs have typically been brutal affairs, they could hardly have felt the impact in the same sense in which it must have been felt by the missionaries in the villages where most of this brutality manifested itself in the Land Reform program.

These missionaries and other civilians who found themselves in the path of the Red Army also reacted initially with surprise and with admiration for the behavior of Communist troops. Typically, the missionaries were reassured that the regime was not hostile to religion *per se,* and that they had nothing to fear if they did not actually interfere with or harm the new People's Government. However, as many accounts have documented (Bauer, 1954; Becker, 1958; Report of Three Canadian Jesuits, 1955; Dejaegher & Kuhn, 1952; Tennien, 1952), after a honeymoon period of reassurance and co-operation, there inevitably followed increasing pressure on the missionary to give up all of his local influence, property, and status, eventually leading either to voluntary abandonment of the mission or to confiscation, imprisonment, and often thought reform.

The image of the Communists which these groups had at the time of their imprisonment was therefore quite different from that of the intellectual or the unexposed resident of the big cities. They had usually seen the brutal totalitarian side of the Communists; and, by seeing the Communist operation over a period of time, had had an opportunity to see that behind the exemplary Red Army lay the party with its willingness to use any means to achieve given ends.

How did the CCP organize Chinese society once its own power position was secured, i.e., how did it approach the broad problem of social control and how does thought reform fit into it? Basically the CCP approach to the control problem was to use a complex mixture of coercion and persuasion.

On the one hand, there is ample evidence that Mao and his lieutenants were and still are completely willing to use any amount of force necessary to achieve their goals. The brutality of Land Reform and the extensive *physical* liquidation * of the landowner

* In Chinese Communist usage the term "liquidation" has meant the psychological wiping out of certain class attitudes. Thus, following adequate re-

class is but one example of their following the traditional totalitarian pattern. At the same time, they have instituted extensive measures of coercive control by reviving the old *pao chia* system of mutual surveillance (in which every citizen is made responsible for some other group of citizens to report any counter-revolutionary activity *), by encouraging children to spy on and, if necessary, denounce their parents, and by the liberal use of secret police terror, forced labor, and political imprisonment (Wei, 1955; Chen, 1955).

Secret police organizations exist in Communist China under both the Ministry of Public Security of the government and the Bureau of Social Affairs of the party's Central Committee, but not a great deal is known of their operations. They do not appear to be as omnipresent as their counterparts in the Soviet Union. One important public manifestation of police state controls, however, is a system of so-called Public Security Committees, established on a nationwide basis in 1952. These committees, composed of three to eleven members each, are to be organized in every village, factory, institution, and organization in the country "to organize and lead the masses to help the government and public security organs to denounce, supervise, and control counter-revolutionary elements" and "to protect the state and public order." In short, it is an organized, nationwide system of police informers. Anonymous denunciations have also been legalized and systematized by such devices as "people's opinion boxes" run by the local representatives of the Committee of People's Control. These and similar measures have contributed to a general atmosphere of mutual suspicion which effectively inhibits the expression of any opinions in conflict with the official line. [Barnett, 1953, p. 48]

On the other hand, the Communists have made extensive use of persuasion and reform, as outlined in our previous historical section. The use of these techniques in all echelons of Chinese society has been one of the most dramatic departures from ex-

---

education and reform of landowners, they might say that the landowner class had been "liquidated."

*Mutual surveillance is a powerful weapon of control. If a given person A failed to report person B, and some other person C reported person B, then A would be guilty of failing to report and would therefore be just as suspect as B himself.

pected totalitarian rule. But their extensive use also creates a paradox in that they are so heavily supported by the coercive police apparatus. As Barnett puts it:

> The efficiency of instruments of coercion which the police state apparatus in China possesses should not obscure the fact that the Chinese Communists rely to a great extent upon persuasion in dealing with the Chinese population. A tremendous amount of energy is devoted to propagandizing, educating, indoctrinating, and in effect trying to convert the Chinese people. The fiction is consistently maintained that virtually everything that people are forced to do is done "voluntarily," and the spectacle of people "enthusiastically" doing things which are obviously in conflict with their own personal interests is one of the most remarkable phenomena observable in China. Actually the line between coercion and persuasion is so blurred as to have little meaning in China today. The populus is persuaded to take "voluntary" action, but the Communists' persuasiveness rests to a considerable degree on the instruments of coercion they possess, the periodic campaigns of controlled terror they have conducted, and the under-current of fear which permeates Chinese society under Communist rule. Nonetheless the Chinese Communists' efforts at mass persuasion are impressive. [Barnett, 1956, p. 125]

The approach through persuasion rests on several kinds of institutions or programs. One of its basic supports is the complete control of the mass media. The mass media are in effect made an extension of the party propaganda apparatus (which, by the way, the Red Chinese explicitly admit and of which they are apparently very proud). All information from the West is censored and all unorthodox ideas are excluded from the carefully co-ordinated complex of media (e.g., the newspapers, the movies, the radio, loudspeakers in public places, dramatic productions, cartoons, comics, magazines, books, pamphlets, painting, poster art, dances and songs, operas, and village storytellers). All the media are used to present to all of the people a single party point of view propagating the current official line (Barnett, 1956).

Supplementing this audio-visual propaganda network is an oral-agitation network designed to reach the high number of illiterates.

Oral propagandists, operating at a village level, "deliver propaganda to the door"; they are even advised, without a trace of humor, to get ordinary people to "replace family gossip with talk on current events." The organized propaganda apparatus is so extensive that the Chinese Communists claim that during special campaigns they can mobilize fifteen per cent of the total population actively to propagandize the remaining eighty-five per cent. [Barnett, 1956, p. 126]

Such campaigns seem to play a major role in communicating the party line, mobilizing the population for certain particular programs, and serving as a further vehicle of indoctrination. For example, during the summer of 1950 the Land Reform movement began involving large numbers of the rural population in "people's tribunals" to help get rid of "oppressive" landlords. The Korean War late in the summer of 1950 served as the basis for the "Resist America, Aid Korea" drive in which citizens were expected to contribute heavily both material resources and manpower (Chen, 1955). In early 1951 a "Hate America" campaign was organized involving extensive propaganda posters, cartoon books, and movies. In 1952 the famous "3-Anti" (anti-corruption, anti-waste, and anti-bureaucratism in government and party) and the "5-Anti" (against bribery, tax evasion, fraud, stealing state property, and theft of state economic secrets) drives were launched. Also during 1952 the "ideological remolding" or "thought reform" movement for intellectuals was officially launched as well as further judicial reform and agrarian reform movements. In 1953 there was the "5-Too-Many" drive in recognition of the fact that there had been so many campaigns and drives that people did not have enough time to do constructive work.

In 1954 the party's decision to doom the "rich peasant economy" and strengthen the agricultural producers' co-operatives led to the "high tide of socialization in the Chinese countryside," resulting in the establishment in early 1956 of the co-operatives and the "voluntary" transformation of private industry and commerce by the device of "joint" state-private operation. In 1957 there was the spectacular drive to "Let Flowers of Many Kinds Bloom and Diverse Schools of Thought Contend." Mao highlighted this new line on ideological remolding and stressed an alleged ideological freedom in his speech on "The Correct Handling of Contradictions Among the People" in February, 1957. Very quickly this drive was followed by a new ideological rectification movement (1957–58) which was directed against the "bourgeois rightists" who had shown their true colors during the "Flower" period. This was followed by a series of Socialist "solidarity" and "re-construction" drives which culminated in the 1958 drive directing that the collectives be consolidated into communes. The widespread participation of the people in these communes, "the best form of organization" and the "basic social units in Communist society," has been the object of this latest drive.

For our purposes the drives that are of greatest importance are, of course, the ideological remolding movements of 1952, 1957, and 1958. These drives were implemented through widespread group indoctrination which extended from the most remote rural areas to the most urbanized centers. The essential technique was again the group discussion:

One of the unique features of Chinese Communist rule is group indoctrination on a very large scale. Contrary to some opinion, the techniques labelled "brainwashing" by Westerners are not restricted in their use to inmates of Communist jails or labor camps. Although prisoners of the regime are subjected to indoctrination in its most intensive forms, similar techniques, which show great psychological insight into means of manipulating and controlling men's minds, are used in small study groups to which millions of ordinary citizens belong. These study groups, averaging ten or twelve members, meet regularly in places of work or residence, often for an hour a day, to read, listen to talks, and discuss materials provided by the official propaganda agencies of the regime. Each group is headed by a leader who makes regular reports to higher authorities. Discussion within the group is often prolonged and intense. Members can, and in fact are expected to raise doubts about the official "correct" view on any subject; but when this happens all other members are expected to argue in favor of the official line. The final objective is mutual agreement and unanimous support of the official line. Every member of such a group must take an active part; one cannot be passive or silent.

The result is described by some Chinese as a situation in which there is "neither freedom of speech nor freedom of silence." [Barnett, 1956, p. 127] *

Because of the regime's extensive oral-agitation network it was possible to bring such group discussion techniques into even the more remote rural areas of China, but, of course, they were effective only to the extent that the cadres who made up this network were themselves properly trained for and committed to their job.

We noted in our historical section the importance of creating cadres who could work more or less independently and without close party supervision. The necessity for cadres to work alone existed even after the take-over because of China's great size and population. Facilities were therefore needed for training cadres and imbuing them with a sufficient sense of commitment and dedication to make them reliable party workers who would resist the personal aggrandizement which their power position often made possible. This job of training has been undertaken by a number of educational centers modeled after the training centers of the Yenan period, which in turn were designed by graduates of Moscow training schools for Chinese Communists (Gourlay, 1952). Such educational centers, usually labeled "Revolutionary Colleges" or "Universities," taught courses lasting from a few months to several years (Walker, 1955); the essence of their training was a very intensive program of persuasion aimed at the severance of the student's emotional ties with his past and the adoption of a new identity (Lifton, 1957; Liu Shaw-tong, 1953; Yen, 1954). These Revolutionary Universities were also places where intellectuals and others whom the regime wished to "reform" were sent if their crimes were not so serious as to warrant imprisonment. Since similar programs of ideological reform were instituted within the regular universities, virtually no one in the society could escape exposure to them (Guillain, 1957).

For students who proved to be recalcitrant or who needed a more "fundamental" kind of re-education, and for professionals, intellec-

* A more detailed description of the use of groups in thought reform is given in Appendix 2.

tuals, and party members whose occupations might make their class consciousness too parochial (and thus not proletarian), there was "reform through labor." Prisons sometimes sent their political prisoners through "reform through productive labor" programs. Revolutionary Universities also carried "productive labor" as part of their regular program, and more recently everyone has had to spend a day or so per week working in the fields or factories. The regime justified "reform through labor" in terms of the assumption that there is no better way to acquire and maintain the proper proletarian outlook and correct class consciousness than by actual manual labor. Judging by the reaction of many Chinese to the prospect of such reform, this program was often little more than a somewhat dressed-up version of Soviet slave labor. It was perceived by the Chinese as punishment similar to Soviet slave labor, in spite of its manifest reform image and its accompaniment of fanfare and jubilation.

For those individuals (whether Chinese or foreign) who were accused of or suspected of counter-revolutionary activity, i.e., whose actions were dangerous above and beyond their incorrect attitudes, there were many kinds of prisons. However, it is noteworthy that the Chinese political prisons, too, operated on the assumption that the inmates should and could be reformed. Thus they were unlike their Soviet counterpart where the major goal was confession extraction prior to liquidation, or penal servitude in forced labor camps. The whole Chinese penal reform scheme emphasized that prisoners were to be treated leniently in order to be rehabilitated; leniency, of course, meant that good treatment would come only to those who co-operated with the government in changing their attitudes (Lifton, 1956b, 1957).

The implementation of a program of confession extraction, indoctrination, and reform was far from perfect in many prisons, and one should not make the mistake of assuming that the prison's *only* role was to reform. Rather, the reform and indoctrination emphasis often entered prison management in the same way that the other programs entered it. The Communist leaders would emphasize the importance of reform, and soon thereafter everyone in the society was expected to intensify his participation in it. The drives would extend into the prison's routine and intensify its reform aspects. As one reads the accounts, one must conclude that sometimes the reform emphasis entered the prison structure primarily in response to external pressures, and that the sophistication with which it was then administered as a program varied sharply with the quality and training of the prison personnel and with their geographic distance from the political center (Peiping). It varied also with what seemed most effective in each prisoner's case.

Although prison procedures were apparently in accordance with an over-all plan formulated by the central ministry and handed down to all sub-committees (Lifton, 1956b), the elaboration of the plan was left to the individual bureaucrats. The manuals used by all prisons were general in nature (of the kind that Liu Shao-chi provided in *How to Be a Good Communist*, 1951), not psychologically technical or specific. Thus the actual reform techniques used in a prison varied with the sophistication, facilities, and motivation of each prison official. If the guards, administrators, and interrogators had assimilated some of the dynamic qualities of the reform movement, understood its premises, and believed in its validity, they could implement it effectively. But in some prisons the authorities did not really understand it, did not have adequate ideological training to implement it effectively, and did not have the support of their own superiors (e.g., the pressure to get a quick confession may have been sufficient to make some prison authorities fall back on "illegal" coercive methods). In some cases the prison personnel had no more than a three-months' indoctrination course (similar to that given to prisoners) before they became interrogators (Tennien, 1952).

The geographic distance from Peiping had an impact on the effective application of reform techniques, in that communication problems made guidance and surveillance from the center difficult. There appeared to be also a "selection of the fittest" for the major centers. Peiping, by virtue of the fact that it is the coveted center of Chinese life today, was much in demand. Thus only the best, the "Stakhanovite," who would experiment with the most refined techniques of persuasion to achieve the ends required of him, could manage to stay at his job. The high motivation of the authorities and superior physical facilities thus made the Peiping prisons the most effective centers of reform.

In summary, from an *ad hoc* technique, designed to meet pragmatically the problems of the emergent revolutionary movement, persuasion became an institution in name and function: "thought reform." While thought reform thrived primarily on the assumption that people could be re-educated if they were given a chance and that their desire for re-education could be "brought out" in them, and while it was, in intention, basically a program of education and persuasion, it should not be overlooked that it was strongly supported by a monolithic coercive apparatus in which the person who became the target of thought reform really had no choice but to reform himself if he wished to keep peace with the regime. This mixing of coercion and persuasion was most dramatically exemplified in the treatment of apolitical civilians (many of them Westerners) in political prisons.

THE AVOWED AIMS OF THOUGHT REFORM

Creation of a "New Man"

The ultimate avowed aim of thought reform is, of course, the "new man" who will be ideally fitted for the Communist society of the future.* The "new man" has the following characteristics. He should be completely concerned about "others," "The People," and the ideology. He should not look at things subjectively, from a self-centered or selfish point of view, but "objectively," recognizing that the greatest good for himself is that which is the greatest good for the group as a whole. He should be an *active* enthusiastic supporter of the cause (apathy and indifference are tantamount to opposition). He should be enthusiastic about physical labor and manual labor as the essential means to the glorious "ends" of the revolution rather than being concerned with intellectual and aesthetic activities, which are often pursued selfishly as ends in themselves; intellectual and aesthetic activities should be pursued only

---

* Most revolutionary movements have generated pressures for this kind of reform shortly after their successful seizure of power, and in many of them it has become the justification for the worst kind of terror.

for the purpose of effectively communicating the Communist conception of society and rallying others' support of it. He should be enthusiastic about the simple, unembellished life rather than being concerned with material possessions and the luxuries of life; he should adopt the simple values and standards of the working people and peasants, including their language, manners, and morals. In short, the "new man" should be truly *collectivized.**

The image of the "new man" was continually held up by the authorities and by the propaganda organs as the ideal to strive for, and any tendency of a citizen or a prisoner to behave in a manner not consistent with this idealized image could and did lead to his being severely criticized.

Teaching Communist Point of View on Specific Issues

The creation of a "new man" is the long-range goal, but the more immediate task was to reveal the "incorrect" attitudes of the prisoner or citizen and to encourage him to change these by adopting the Communist point of view, "the people's standpoint," toward certain issues which had to be dealt with on a day-to-day basis. For the American POW this might have meant the adoption of "correct attitudes" about the question of who started the Korean war, who were the aggressors in the world picture, who stood for peace, whose policies should be supported, and so on. For the peasant the issue might have been the adoption of "correct attitudes" toward having his land collectivized, paying high taxes to the government, having some of his hard-won crop shipped to the Soviet Union even though his family was starving, and so on. For some citizens whose social origin had allegedly predisposed them to "reactionary" tendencies, the adoption of "correct attitudes" might have meant that they should denounce members of their family or loved ones, that they should divorce husbands or wives who were political liabilities to their own career, that they should give up personally profitable businesses to the government, and so on. For the political prisoner the adoption of a "correct attitude" might

* This term was suggested to us by Malcolm Bersohn.

have meant that he should recognize how various of his past activities actually or potentially hurt "the people's" cause, that he should confess to crimes by this standard, and should help to locate other actual or potential criminals by denouncing them. In other words, the adoption of a "correct attitude" often meant accepting highly desirable ethical principles which would make the person feel morally uplifted, and at the same time accepting tremendous personal sacrifices for the sake of a government which promised a future utopia.

THE IMPLICIT AIMS OF THOUGHT REFORM

Creation of Obedient Citizens and Cadres

If we extrapolate only slightly from the avowed aim of teaching people to adopt the "correct attitude," we come to what is probably a major implicit aim of thought reform, namely the creation of a well-motivated worker for the regime, one who will be completely obedient to the party, yet be able to apply the party line independently and creatively in new and unanticipated situations. Whether he is an ordinary citizen, low-level cadre, or party member, he must be willing to accept and justify the party line, be able to derive from it the relevant consequences for his own behavior, and be able to subordinate himself so completely to the system as to be willing to sacrifice himself physically or socially for its sake. That is, if and when a program fails he must be willing to accept responsibility for its failure by confessing that it was his implementation, not the basic theory, which was at fault; at the same time he must be creative in applying party policies and avoid the sin of "formalism" (being too theoretical and unable to apply theory to local situation) or "bureaucratism" (being too slavishly obedient to the party line and hence failing to take into account the exigencies of the local situation). Also he must be willing to employ any means prescribed by the party in the achievement of prescribed ends, no matter how immoral they might seem or how distasteful they might be to him, and he must be willing and able to justify them enthusiastically in terms of the higher morality which is defined by the utopian goals of the Communist ideology.

Conversion of an Entrenched Bureaucracy into an Arm of the Communist State

Because the regime had so few trained administrators it had to work through the existing bureaucracy which had traditionally been independent of specific political ideologies. The political conversion of members of this bureaucracy to bring them into reliable service for the Communists, and their initiation into Communist society were thus important implicit goals of thought reform. Obviously, the more entrenched they were, the more severe this initiation had to be to stand any chance of success. A similar attitude had to be taken by the regime toward the intelligentsia and any other groups whose services were required by the Communists, yet whose initial attitudes might be anti-Communist or neutral.

Creation of Ideological Unanimity

The high degree of obsession with unanimity which totalitarian regimes seem to develop is well illustrated in the case of Communist China. Tremendous effort was expended to bring the ideological message to every member of the society, and tremendous effort was expended to insure that all citizens overtly express their ideological unanimity whenever possible. Thought reform provided the mechanism and the energy for converting anyone and everyone, whether he was initially friend or foe, native or foreigner.

In the next chapter we shall discuss in detail some hypotheses concerning the reasons for such preoccupation with unanimity in a totalitarian state. For present purposes we need only to emphasize that the thought reform program touched every person with whom the Communists came in contact. The involvement of our Western subjects could in no way be construed to be the result of a specific policy of reform aimed at them in particular. Rather, they unwittingly became involved in something which was sweeping all of Chinese society.

VISIBLE EFFECTS OF THOUGHT REFORM

We do not have data which would permit a detailed evaluation of the effects of thought reform on the Chinese citizen, but there is sufficient consistency in the reports of Westerners and Chinese defectors to warrant certain tentative conclusions. The first of these conclusions is that behavioral conformity and verbal unanimity seem to have been achieved on a wide scale. Almost everyone who has had contact with Communist China in recent years has been struck by the degree to which all the citizens look alike, speak alike, and act alike (e.g., Guillain, 1957). In fact, many observers feel somewhat terrified by this massive conformity because it implies a tremendous power potential and has a strong appeal for anyone seeking to lose himself in a powerful cause.

It has also been observed that the disciplined efforts of masses of the population have led to a number of tangible accomplishments, ranging from increasing productivity in some sectors of the economy to the stamping out of certain vices. The fact that there are apparently no more beggars on the streets of Peiping recurs in the accounts of our subjects with dreary regularity, suggesting that this sort of accomplishment has almost become a symbol of the success of the new regime. Clearly there is in a number of these accomplishments a strong basis for great pride and great hope for the future.

The ascetic moralistic tone of the message of thought reform lends itself well to acceptance by a serious young generation bent upon bringing the "New China" into the front ranks of world powers. There is no doubt that among many of the young and rebellious the "correct attitude" has been accepted and internalized, leading to zealous and sincere proselytization of others. Our POW's and our civilian subjects encountered many completely converted cadres and Red soldiers in the prison camps and prisons, and it was often their sincerity which caused our subjects to be swayed by them.

On the other hand, evidence that thought reform has not gone deep in many segments of society was provided by the flood of criticism that followed Mao's "Let 100 Flowers Bloom" speech, and from the frequent reports by our subjects that the prisons were filled with unreconstructed critics of the regime, as were many of the cities and rural areas. The presence both of outspoken supporters and outspoken critics was important because the group with which our subjects came into contact created much of their initial attitude toward thought reform.

By way of summarizing:

There is no doubt that the Chinese Communist regime, despite its totalitarian character, does have a solid basis of support which is by no means small. There are millions of people in China who work for the regime and its myriad organizations and who have a vested interest in it. Although their financial rewards are small, they acquire power, status, and prestige in return for their support. In China, also, there are clearly many people who, although undoubtedly objecting to some Communist policies, apparently accept the proposition that China requires violent social surgery to change and develop the country and that totalitarian methods are therefore justified. There are certainly other Chinese whose intense nationalism has led them to accept totalitarianism and justify its necessity because they want to see China acquire national power and international prestige. In addition, the Chinese Communist regime appears to be attracting positive support from a sizeable proportion of the youth of the country; it is convincing many of them that the Communists' policies are inevitable and right, historically unavoidable, and desirable. . . . active supporters of the regime constitute only a relatively small minority of the total population and . . . a large majority of Chinese dislike Communist rule and have been alienated by Communist policies during the past seven years. The Communists' performance has been far different from the slogans and promises before 1949. Their ruthlessness, totalitarian control, and use of violence have disillusioned millions who were once hopeful about what a change of regime might bring. The Communists have undermined the position and attacked the interests of groups making up a great majority of the population. They have undoubtedly alienated most of the peasantry by collectivism, the majority of businessmen by socialization, and many intellectuals by campaigns of "thought reform." In the past seven years the Communists have clearly come to rely increasingly on repression and control and decreasingly on voluntary support. It is a reasonable guess, therefore, that the majority of Chinese, if they were now offered a choice of regimes . . . would reject the Communists, and that if there were some practical political alternatives which they believed achievable . . . they would probably choose to be ruled by another group of leaders. [Barnett, 1956, pp. 127–29]

REASONS FOR THE IMPRISONMENT OF WESTERNERS

One of the major reasons for the arrest and imprisonment of Westerners was the belief on the part of the regime that there were spies and enemies among this group (particularly among the ones who stayed in China after the outbreak of Korean hostilities). The intensive attempts to force them to confess were probably straightforward attempts to break "spy rings" by learning the names of others involved. It must be noted that from the CCP point of view it was considered preferable to arrest many innocent ones rather than to let one guilty one escape; clearly the safest procedure was to arrest all Westerners against whom any degree of evidence was available. It must also be noted, however, that by no means all the Westerners were arrested; rather, the regime seemed to build up its case against particular individuals before proceeding with the arrest.

A second reason for imprisoning Westerners was to provide an adequate basis for propaganda. As some of the CCP programs failed, and as certain Western ideas had to be discredited to facilitate CCP consolidation of power, it became convenient to arrest Westerners and pin the blame on them directly if possible, or at the minimum discredit them. To this end it was obviously desirable to obtain confessions which could be publicized as evidence of the regime's claims. For example, one suspects that many of the priests and medical missionaries were arrested to discredit the work which the missions and their hospitals had done, and thereby to discredit the notion that the West had ever done anything good for China. During the Korean conflict, when most of the arrests occurred, it was obviously not possible to fan suitable hatred for the enemy if, in the midst of China, American missions were doing basically good work for the Chinese people. Some of the more fantastic propaganda, like charges of infanticide against nuns running primary schools, probably served the functions of fanning hatred in support of the war effort.

A third and closely related reason was that the Chinese undoubtedly wanted the properties and facilities of the missions and their hospitals. Since they maintained an avowed policy of freedom of religion and promised not to persecute priests, they could not very well make such expropriations without first discrediting the work of the missions. Hence, charges of sabotage or counter-revolutionary activities had to be developed to justify arrest and expropriation. The lengths to which the Communists went to justify the premise that the priests and doctors had exploited the Chinese people is reflected in some astonishing incidents. For example, one story tells of the charge that some ten years or more ago some-one from a mission had stolen an egg from a farmer. This egg's theoretical productive capacity over the ten-year interval proved to be roughly equivalent to the value of the mission; hence to repay the "people" for the theft of the egg, the missionary was now expected to give up the mission. It was probably not difficult in any of the mission areas to find someone with sufficient personal grievances against the Western priests, doctors, nurses, and teachers to denounce and accuse them. In a way the surprising thing is that the CCP had as much trouble as it did. In most places the local populace supported the missions very strongly and only after real threat to the people in the area was it possible to get them to participate in the discrediting of the missionaries.

A fourth reason for imprisoning Westerners was undoubtedly the need to collect hostages to be used in bargaining with the West for political advantages. Some of the more unpredictable adventures of our subjects are probably related to this purely political factor. For example, some of the cases wound up with unusual rapidity after international argeements had been reached on the release of Americans held in China. Whether these individuals had confessed or changed their attitudes became irrelevant once the decision was made to release them on political grounds. Nevertheless, while in prison they were subjected to the standard prison regimen including thought reform.

A fifth reason was perhaps one which the Chinese themselves would not explicitly recognize but which no doubt played a part in their manner of handling the Western prisoners, namely the opportunity to revenge themselves on the exploiting West and at the same time prove their own superiority by humiliating the prisoner and in the end converting him. The pride which Chinese guards showed in exhibiting POW's to native populations, for example, suggests strongly that there were deep emotional factors involved, at least for those Chinese who had the opportunity to have direct contact with the Western prisoners. The rapidity with which reformed prisoners were expelled from China after their cases had been settled also makes one wonder whether this was in part motivated by a desire to show off the power of the Chinese Communist methods of re-education. Another factor which makes one think that desire to prove Asian superiority entered strongly into the picture was the tremendous sincerity and zealousness of many of the authorities who dealt with Westerners, their pride in Chinese accomplishments, their sensitivity to any kind of criticism, their desperate attempts to emulate the more "civilized" ways of the West (for example, not using torture on prisoners), and their desire to have it be clearly understood on the outside that they felt that Communism was doing something constructive for the prisoners.

As can be seen, there were many overlapping reasons for the arrest of Westerners and their subsequent exposure to the thought reform program. As we have previously pointed out, there is little evidence to suggest that thought reform was specifically designed to convert Westerners; there was no Machiavellian program of brainwashing designed for the treatment of certain groups of captives. Rather, they became involved with thought reform by virtue of being held in prisons in which it was a normal part of the prison regimen. Thus it was only a fortuitous set of circumstances which made the combination of imprisonment, traditional emphases on confession extraction, and an atmosphere of reform the powerful blend of forces which we have labeled "coercive persuasion."

CONCLUSIONS

1. Thought reform as an approach to a prisoner was but a manifestation of a wide program of social and psychological control which permeated all segments of Chinese society in the 1950's.

2. Thought reform as an approach to the problem of social con-

trol had a fairly long history in the development of the CCP and had its roots in both Soviet Communism and Chinese culture.

3. The avowed and implicit aims of thought reform are, respectively, to create a new man, to change attitudes, to produce an obedient and energetic party worker, to initiate into Communist society individuals who are not yet committed ideologically, and to produce ideological unanimity.

4. The effects of thought reform on the Chinese population were seen by some of our subjects as being very deep, by others as being very superficial. Probably by objective evaluation one would find certain segments of society more deeply influenced than others. The perceptions and the kinds of contacts which our subjects had, of course, influenced their later reactions to their own imprisonment and the effects of the reform program on them.

5. Westerners were arrested in order to expose spies and other enemies, in order to discredit Western ideas and programs, in order to expropriate Western properties, in order to have hostages for international bargaining, and in order to assert Asian superiority.

6. One should not confuse the reasons for arrest with the reasons for being subjected to thought reform. The reasons for being "thought-reformed" are probably fortuitous, in the sense that it was not planned to have prisons engage in reform of Westerners; rather, this was part of the regular prison routine in which Westerners happened to get involved.

7. While the emphasis on thought reform is very widespread throughout China, it would be a mistake to assume that the same programs and techniques are employed everywhere. There are significant variations in the practices found in different situations and at different times.

3

*The Passion for Unanimity**

CHINESE COMMUNIST thought reform is a dramatic instance of the totalitarian passion for unanimity, both in the intensity with which it has been pursued and in the wide range of participation which it has demanded. Is this purely a Chinese phenomenon, or are there forces in any totalitarian society, particularly in a revolutionary period, which can account for the elaborate unanimity rituals like parades, elections with predetermined outcomes, "spontaneous" mass demonstrations, and society-wide campaigns; the extensive proselytizing among the "heretics" or the "infidels"; the purges, programs of re-education, and other repressive measures aimed at deviants; the deep infringement on the part of the government into areas of life ordinarily considered to be private; and the extensive efforts by the leaders to legitimize whatever coercion of overt behavior is present?

We propose to examine this general question by considering what functions ideological unanimity serves for the system as a whole, for the leaders, and for the followers. Most of our examples will deal with Communist society but will highlight those aspects which it shares with other totalitarian societies. Our basic purpose is to show that unanimity pressures can be deduced from many different forces acting in a totalitarian society and that achieved unanimity serves many different functions. In particular we wish to demonstrate the fallacy of assuming that any single level of analysis—the political,

* We are indebted to Ruth Ohlin (1954) for this concept and for a number of the ideas in this chapter.

sociological, or psychological—is any more valid than any other level in providing an adequate explanation. Therefore our approach will be to discuss each of the forces which act at these various levels one at a time and as if it were the only one acting. The interaction between the forces, their relative strength, and their degree of interdependence are, of course, important determinants of the final outcome. We have set as our goal, however, only the identification and discussion of the separate forces, considering them to be some of the basic variables of any final theory of the passion for unanimity:

The forces we shall consider can be categorized in the following manner:

Forces deriving from the movement's ideology.

Forces deriving from the goals of the leaders of the movement or state.

1. The necessity of projecting an image of unanimity for external consumption.
2. The necessity of projecting an image of unanimity for internal consumption.
3. Keeping control over any ideas which could become the basis of resistance.
4. Creating or eliciting motivation for social and economic change (rapid industrialization or other pressing goals which the movement or state may wish to attain).

Forces deriving from the definition of the movement or state as being in a state of "combat."

Forces deriving from psychological factors in the leaders of the movement or state.

1. Basic personality traits of the leaders.
2. The psychological consequences of success.
3. The effects of coercing unanimity.

Forces driving from psychological factors in the followers or citizens of the state.

1. Dependency, alienation from self, need to merge self with larger movement.
2. Effects of crisis or disillusionment.
3. National character factors.
4. Missionary zeal.

A system organized explicitly around an ideology probably shows the effects of the ideology in all areas of its functioning, yet it is usually quite difficult to specify precisely the nature of these effects. In the case of Communist society the difficulty lies partly in our inability to determine precisely the role of classical Marxist ideology in the psychological organization of the leaders; partly in our inability to determine precisely in what manner the ideology enters into the education of the young and integrates itself with existing cultural themes; and partly in the nature of the Communist ideology itself insofar as it is a dynamic philosophical system with a large number of components, many of which are loosely tied together, many of which are susceptible of redefinition as suits the needs of the leaders, and many of which are ethical generalities and platitudes which do not clearly distinguish it from many other ideologies. In the section on ideology we shall present those aspects of classical Marxism-Leninism which bear directly on the question of unanimity, recognizing that the existence of this ideology does not necessarily imply its use by the leaders in actually seeking unanimity; in subsequent sections we shall discuss some of the specific effects of the ideology on the psychology of the leaders and followers in the society.

COMMUNIST IDEOLOGY

Communist ideology, as a philosophical system, contains a number of features pertaining to unanimity. First, because it is a deterministic, all-encompassing set of beliefs based on psuedo-scientific laws, it cannot, as a religion cannot, admit the possibility of any other truth. Any idea or piece of behavior not in line with Communist principles is *ipso facto* blasphemy, sacrilege, or heresy depending on the nature of the deviance. As Talmon puts it:

The totalitarian democratic school . . . is based upon the assumption of a sole and exclusive truth in politics. It may be called political Messianism in the sense that it postulates a preordained, harmonious and perfect scheme of things, to which men are irresistibly driven and at which they are bound to arrive. [Talmon, 1952, p. 2]

Second, though the ideology is supposedly based on a scientific analysis of history, it contains in its assumptions the refutation of any competing theory. It is thus completely untestable, while maintaining the appearance of rational truth. For example, the plea on the part of a prisoner to subject an assertion by the interrogator to "scientific" test is immediately refutable on the grounds that the scientific method as conceived of by the Western prisoner is a capitalist invention and therefore, *ipso facto*, not valid. On the other hand, it is asserted that the validity of the Communist point of view can be perceived only by adopting the correct cognitive frame of reference, which means, in effect, the *a priori* acceptance of its basic premises.

Third, the basic goals, i.e., the Communist vision of utopia, are highly acceptable generalities concerning the brotherhood of man, complete harmony of outlook, and a world of freedom and plenty for all. The reiteration of such broad ethical generalities as the justification for the operation of the Communist state not only increases the possibilities of easily obtaining unanimity on a very general level but also sharply decreases the likelihood of successful ideological deviance or resistance. The ideology is too general and broadly acceptable to be vulnerable.* However, the acceptability of a broad ethic by no means guarantees that it will be easy to obtain unanimity concerning the means used to achieve the utopia. From the point of view of the leaders of the movement, outspoken unanimity on basic utopian goals is probably important to serve as a set of rationalizations or justifications for a concrete program which, it is anticipated, may lead to strong resistance on the part of the followers or citizens. Whatever resistance arises can be neutralized by affirming the proposed means as the *only* way to achieve the ends that everyone has agreed to already, or can be eliminated by being branded as standing in the way of the achievement of the ultimate goals.

It has been pointed out by Talmon that all utopian ideologies,

---

* Erikson (1958) has pointed out that the ideological utterances of successful leaders of mass movements are often distinguished more by their invulnerability to attack than by their intrinsic appeal. Part of the success of the ideological program lies in the neutralization of potential opposition.

even those eighteenth-century philosophies which underlie the development of the Western democratic state (e.g., Rousseau's idea of "the general will" as a rational way of integrating separate individual wills), contain the assumptions that make a totalitarian system possible.

It is of great importance to realize that what is today considered as an essential concomitant of democracy, namely, diversity of views and interests, was far from being regarded as essential by the eighteenth century fathers of democracy. Their original postulates were unity and unanimity. The affirmation of the principle of diversity came later, when the totalitarian implications of the principle of homogeneity had been demonstrated by Jacobin leadership. [Talmon, 1952, p. 44]

The very idea of a self-contained system from which all evil and unhappiness have been exorcised is totalitarian. The assumption that such a scheme of things is feasible and indeed inevitable is an invitation to a regime to proclaim that it embodies this perfection, to exact from its citizens recognition and submission and to brand opposition as vice or perversion.

The greatest danger is in the fact that far from denying freedom and rights to man, far from demanding sacrifice and surrender, this system solemnly reaffirms liberty, man's self interest and rights. It claims to have no other aims than their realization. Such a system is likely to become the more totalitarian, precisely because it grants everything in advance, because it accepts all liberal premises *a priori*. For it claims to be able by definition to satisfy them by a positive enactment as it were, not by leaving them alone and watching over them from the distance. When a regime is by definition regarded as realizing rights and freedoms, the citizen becomes deprived of any right to complain that he is being deprived of his rights and liberties. The earliest practical demonstration of this was given by Jacobinism. [Talmon, 1952, p. 35]

The impact of this circumstance on the citizen is described well by Ferreus.

. . . the adoption of the artificial communist creed must produce guilt complexes, as does, within a communist-controlled nation or within the party, the negation of the "accepted" code. Many of these guilt complexes are essentially social and political in nature—"I have sinned against my class," "I am a saboteur and exploiter"—and they expose the person to the dangers of nonconformism. Whenever the communists succeed in convincing people that they are a sort of incarnation of humanity's social conscience and that they are history's anointed arbiters of any action undertaken by non-communists, a person will tend to be apologetic about any doubts he may be harboring concerning communism. Opposition to or deviation from communism is tantamount to a negation of mankind's loftiest ideals and of mankind's inevitable future. [Ferreus, 1957, p. 102]

Fourth, in its basic assumptions (and supported by its own semantic rules) the ideology tends to dichotomize the world, reflecting an almost complete lack of tolerance for ambiguity. Thus statements are either absolutely true or totally false; people are either friends or enemies; the world can only be capitalistic or communistic; future developments are either inevitable or impossible; given actions are either prescribed or forbidden; there is in any given situation just one "correct line" of policy, all others tend to lead to ruin; and so on. The philosophical assumption behind this aspect of the ideology is that objective truth is attainable:

When . . . a Party member is given instruction in Marxist ideology, the first thing that is impressed upon him is that there exist, and can exist, only two possible philosophical positions, idealism and materialism. . . . He is told that there are many forms of idealism, but that all assert that mind is primary, and that matter, if it has any reality at all, is secondary. Idealism contends that we can have no *final* knowledge of the world of phenomena, because such knowledge is conditioned by our senses. A knowledge of "things in themselves" is thus impossible. To men born in green or red spectacles the snow will appear green or red, and they have no means of discovering that it is, in fact, neither. On the other hand, materialism insists that reality is not mind but matter; that the existence of matter precedes that of mind; that the material world, so far from existing only in our minds, possesses an objective existence apart from our perception of it; and that we can therefore obtain a knowledge of the world which, though incomplete, like a jigsaw puzzle from which certain parts are missing, contains an indestructible core of absolute truth which is continually growing as our knowledge increases. [Hunt, 1957, p. 36]

Undoubtedly this kind of position creates forces toward unanimity in that any degree of deviation or lack of support can be defined as *total* rejection should the regime choose to apply the definition. Only by complete outspoken acceptance can the citizen guarantee for himself some measure of safety (though, as we shall see later, even this may not be an iron-clad guarantee).

Fifth, the ideology states that it derives its main dynamism from the thought and needs of the proletariat. In fact, it claims to be an expression of the will of the proletariat. It is therefore implied that any member who fits the definition of proletarian ought to think in a Communist manner and support the movement. If he does not, he has been contaminated or infected by incorrect ideas and must be taught the truth. Because it would damage the image of the ideology to have its *a priori* faithful actually be heretics, it is clearly justifiable to expend considerable effort to prevent them from becoming or continuing to be unfaithful.* For this same reason, perhaps, great emphasis was given by Lenin and others to the Communist Party as the leader and embodiment of the will of the masses (the proletariat). If the masses do not express their own will, the leadership must "make them conscious of it" and express it for them.

For the Chinese Communist Party this ideological problem was exacerbated by the fact that the masses supporting the revolution were primarily drawn from the peasantry instead of the urban proletariat. This circumstance forced Mao to reconsider the correctness of the basic Marxist premise that only the urban proletariat could provide a proper mass base for the revolution. His successful peasant movement validated the concept that people with improper class origins could be re-educated and, in so doing, he laid the foundation for thought reform.

---

* Other groups in the society are judged by the ideology to be *a priori* *un*enlightened and in varying degrees to be incapable of re-education (e.g., capitalists, landowners, small shopkeepers, intellectuals, soldiers, etc.). With respect to these groups the government has the alternatives of liquidating them, stripping them of power and status and tolerating them, imprisoning them, or re-educating them.

Sixth, the ideology stresses the unity of theory and action. Among other things this concept implies that intellectual knowledge alone is useless and that apathy or lack of support is as evil and intolerable as outright opposition. Hence there results continuous pressure for outspoken, active support.

Marx teaches that . . . sensations, which were held to give us faithful images of the external world, did not provide *immediate* knowledge but only stimuli to knowledge which completed itself in action; for if sensations were purely passive, it was impossible to explain why they should result in conscious activity; and if men were unable to react on their environment and change it, revolutions could no longer be regarded as a form of human activity and were simply incidents in a mechanical process. Hence, he insisted that we only preceive a thing as a part of the process of acting upon it, just as a cat when it sees a mouse immediately pounces on it. . . . Marxists have always insisted that theory and action are one. A theory of which the truth is not confirmed by action is sterile, while action which is divorced from theory is purposeless. The two stand in much the same relation to one another as do faith and works in Christian theology. [Hunt, 1957, pp. 34–35]

In the same vein, Mao said in 1942:

"How can half-intellectuals be transformed into intellectuals with a title corresponding to reality? There is only one way: to see that those with only book knowledge become practical workers engaged in practical tasks, and see that those doing theoretical work turn to practical research. In this way we can reach our goal." [Quoted in Brandt, Schwartz, & Fairbank, 1952, p. 381]

The need for activity as proof of loyalty follows:

Totalitarian terror has not only this negative function to perform (elimination of misfits or deviants). Operating within the context of enforced unanimity, it becomes a stimulant to more enthusiastic expressions of support for the regime. It classified men's behavior according to degrees of loyalty, and mere absence of opposition to the regime becomes insufficient as proof of devotion to it. Positive action is demanded, and men compete in loyalty. It is no accident that secret police files in the USSR stress, first of all, whether a given individual is passive or active. Needless to add, one can be active in a totalitarian society only on behalf of the regime. [Friedrich & Brzezinski, 1956, pp. 135–36]

In China, the pressure for active support has reached even greater intensity:

The regime desires unanimous approval even in the prison camps. We must not imagine that the pariahs can fulminate against the system within their cell walls or under the sun of the Gobi desert. The pressure on them is so great, as we have learned from those who have managed to return from the Chinese prisons to the free world, that the prisoners are zealous to bow to the warders, accusing themselves of all manner of crimes and thanking the People's Republic which has reformed their way of thinking. Unanimity must nowhere be in default, and even Hell itself must echo with approval and praise. [Guillain, 1957, pp. 288–89]

The society, led by the party, must actively work to achieve the utopia, not merely wait for its arrival, and must be willing to use any means to achieve the utopian goals. The dictatorship of the proletariat, excessive terror and coercion, and the combat atmosphere to be described below are all consistent with and justified by this ideological premise.

A seventh and final point which should be made about the Communist ideology is that it is an all-inclusive philosophy of life.

It recognizes ultimately only one plane of existence, the political. It widens the thought and action as having social significance, and therefore as falling within the orbit of political action. Its political ideas are not a set of pragmatic precepts or a body of devices applicable to a special branch of human endeavour. They are an integral part of an all embracing and coherent philosophy. Politics is defined as the art of applying this philosophy to the organization of society, and the final purpose of politics is only achieved when this philosophy reigns supreme over all fields of life. [Talmon, 1952, p. 2]

All aspects of life become related to the political, hence all areas of life become the target of political scrutiny, and the demands for unanimity, though they may originate in a purely political sphere, often spill over into the most minute details of daily living. This same all-inclusiveness also operates as one of the powerful appeals of the ideology. In a revolutionary period when traditional values are strongly undermined, or at a time when such values no longer serve to mediate between an individual and the problems he faces in the world, a new ideology which can serve to orient him to all aspects of his external world has more appeal than one which orients him to only a portion of it.

COMMENT. Having mentioned some general points about the Communist ideology, we should now consider the question of the level at which unanimity is actually demanded in a totalitarian society. We have already made the distinction between behavioral conformity and ideological unanimity, but must further refine the latter concept because the ideology consists of a number of components, not all of which are equally important at all times. These components range from very fundamental premises, philosophical assumptions, and basic goals (the vision of the utopia) to very operational principles which apply to specific situations and may change from day to day. The distinction made by Smith, Bruner, and White (1956) in reference to political attitudes between a person's *basic orientation,* or attitude toward something, and his *policy stand,* or concrete proposals for action in regard to it, can be useful here in considering the components of ideology.

As we have implied before and shall see again, unanimity on basic orientation is often easier to achieve than unanimity on policy stand. From the basic philosophies of most ideologies it is possible to derive several alternative policy stands, each designed to achieve the ultimate goals at which one is aiming. In principle this flexibility also exists in the Communist ideology, but in practice it must often be denied because of the party's position as the only valid formulator of policy stands. If one allowed the possibility of alternatives, then the position of the party as the sole legitimate power would be brought into question. To avoid this possibility the system arrives at a paradoxical conclusion: that unanimity must be shown not only on basic premises but also on any given policy stand (the regime must at all times be publicly upheld as correct); yet that the populace must be prepared to change its mind overnight and become unanimous about new policy stands whenever the party line changes, at the same time pretending that this change has not occurred or that there is no inconsistency at all between the previous and the current position.

In other words, in Communist society certain basic premises and goals must be genuinely accepted by all members of society (including the premise that the party and its leaders are the legitimate leaders of the society), while other principles concerning the day-to-day means of operation must appear to be accepted by all members of the society, regardless of how often they change. It can be seen that for the individual citizen or party member this set of circumstances leads to a difficult psychological situation. He must be committed sincerely to an ideology, but he must not think through the consequences of this ideology for himself; instead he must be prepared ritually to affirm what his leaders dictate and must be able to rationalize his leaders' conclusions in terms of the ideology.* The citizen must be prepared to do extensive rationalizing of his leaders' policy in any public situation where he is under the scrutiny of others who have some degree of control over his fate. This kind of pressure to think through and discuss the ideology in various kinds of peer-group situations is, of course, one of the main features of the Chinese Communist approach to producing unanimity.

The components of the ideology also differ in the degree to which their content is relevant for given segments of the population. Certain basic premises must be accepted throughout the society by the masses, the rank and file, the cadres, and the top elite alike. Beyond this, the content of the ideology, and the degree of acceptance re-

---

* It is probably for this reason that the intellectual communist, the man who believes in all portions of the ideology and thinks it through for himself, is often considered to be the real enemy of the system. His "formalism," to use the phrase Mao used in condemning certain factions in the Chinese Communist movement (Brandt, Schwartz, & Fairbank, 1952), makes him unreliable as an obedient citizen and makes him ineffective if he has to adapt the ideology to a situation for which no formal solution has as yet been worked out or promulgated, a situation which arose often in the Chinese case.

quired, are tailored to the concerns and needs of each target group and the goals which the leaders have in mind for this group. To the peasants the party brings theories, promises, and programs for land reform; to the workers it brings the theory of the proletariat as the true base of the revolution and promises of labor owning the means of production; to the cadres and party members the leaders bring promises of power and glory for aiding the advancement of the revolution; to the political prisoner or prisoner of war they bring the opportunity of redemption, re-education, and identification with a glorious cause; and so on. Within each group unanimity must be expressed concerning the specific content and program proposed; across groups there must be unanimity about the wisdom of the leadership which has brought these programs into existence, and about the amount of energy, devotion, and loyalty which should be exhibited in their implementation.

From the point of view of the leadership this process not only consists of properly extrapolating from the basic premises of the ideology to a concrete situation but also, more importantly, involves careful diagnosis of the actual demands of a given situation and careful choice of a program (including such details as the language in which to make the ideological appeal).*

In summary, it is evident that the Communist ideology has in it many themes which suggest the need for unanimity, but that it is a complex enough philosophical system to preclude the prediction that from its characteristics alone one could specify how the society in which it operates will handle the unanimity problem. The role which ideology plays in the society at a given time, the stage in

---

* Mao, for example, said the following in a speech on "Opposing Party Formalism": "As soon as a man talks with another man he is engaged in propaganda work. If he is not mute, he always will have a few words to say. Therefore, our comrades must all study languages. In studying various languages [they must] pay special attention to the language of the workers, peasants, and soldiers and the masses. If we do not study the language of the masses, we cannot lead the masses." (Brandt, Schwartz, & Fairbank, 1952, p. 400). In another context he says: "The people's language is very rich in expression; it is lively and vigorous and presents life as it is. Many of us have not mastered it, and as a consequence, in writing articles and giving speeches, we do not use lively, vigorous, really effective language; we only have a few varicose veins." (Brandt, Schwartz, & Fairbank, 1952, p. 399)

which a revolution finds itself, and the psychological commitment which the leaders actually feel to it (as contrasted with public commitment which may serve purely political or social functions) all enter into a consideration of how an actual program of creating unanimity may come about and its specific character.

THE GOALS OF THE LEADERS

Maintenance of Power by Presenting a Correct External Image

It is a tenable assumption that the leaders of Soviet and Chinese societies, regardless of their degree of commitment to the ideology, have as their primary goal the securing of their own position and the securing of the power position of their nation. Insofar as the leaders see themselves as being in a struggle for survival with other nations in the world, one may expect that they will utilize whatever means are available to give the appearance of being powerful. Therefore the leaders are committed to creating and projecting a certain image of themselves and their society—an image of solidarity, unanimity, and legitimacy.* They must show that the society accepts them and their program unanimously and with enthusiasm, and that their citizens will fight to defend the new system. If they can successfully project such an image, two very important functions are served: the solid front which is offered as a proof of strength actually reduces the likelihood of threat from other nations; unanimous popular acceptance as proof of the legitimacy of the regime is a powerful weapon in international bargaining and in proselytizing among neutral national groups.

COMMENT. A regime's need to prove its legitimacy and exhibit its

* The following news release is a good example:
"London, April 26, 1958 (Reuters)—Following is from the text of President Tito's speech today to the Yugoslav Communist party congress at Ljubljana, as issued by the official Yugoslav news agency Tanyug:
"The seventh congress of the League of Communists of Yugoslavia today finishes its fruitful work.
"We can indeed be pleased and proud of the extraordinary ideological political unity and unanimity which has found full expression during the work of the congress. Whoever has been present at or otherwise followed the work of this congress can no longer have any doubts as to the force which moves and guides the entire process of development of our Socialist society.'"

power in the form of unanimity is probably greatest when the society and its leaders are in reality most insecure and least powerful. If the Chinese Communists were in fact at their weakest during the civil war and in the immediate post-takeover days, one would expect to see the greatest pressures toward unanimity at those times. The Chinese Communist leadership relied more from the very beginning on ideological re-education for anyone who came into contact with the movement and did intensify their efforts during the civil war in the *Cheng feng* movement and after the take-over in the thought reform movement.

The importance of unanimity as a means of presenting an image of power to the external world can be seen daily in the impact which Chinese Communist society has on the foreign visitor. Time and again what impresses him is the solidarity and uniformity and the huge numbers of people involved in any public demonstrations.

Maintenance of Power by Presenting Correct Internal Image

The regime's power position is also supported by an image of unanimity and solidarity projected within Communist society. Such an image serves at least three functions: it isolates the actual or potential dissenter psychologically and thus prevents the organization of dissent or resistance; it diverts attention from actual disagreement among members of the ruling groups; and it provides the psychological basis for increased dedication and loyalty to the regime by reassuring the followers that they are indeed part of a powerful and rightful social movement.* Many kinds of rituals such as parades, demonstrations, campaigns, and elections seem to have as one of their primary functions the production and dissemination of such an image.

The importance of the first of the above functions can be seen by an examination of the consequences of lifting totalitarian pressure, as in Hungary in 1956, or in the "Let One-Hundred Flowers Bloom" speech of Mao Tse-tung. As soon as a few disaffected individuals begin to speak their mind, others discover that they have not been

* The reassurance which such unanimity provides to the leaders themselves will be discussed below.

alone in harboring grievances against the regime, leading to a rapid build-up of resistance. In the Hungarian rebellion, once a small group had impulsively initiated resistance action, other disaffected Hungarians risked going into the streets to fight, only to discover that all their neighbors whom they had mistrusted for years were also joining in the fight. The sudden recognition of solidarity and the destruction of the image of a nation solidly standing behind Communism opened the floodgates of rebellion. Of greatest significance is the fact that the image of unanimity, though invalid, had kept hundreds of potential dissenters from ever broaching their dissension to any but their closest friends or family members. Most had believed that their neighbors were Communists and informers.

The regime can prevent the growth of rebellion only by enforcing complete conformity in public utterances, thus insuring that no one will know to whom to turn to seek social support for an anti-regime opinion. Continuing mutual surveillance such as was described in the discussion of social controls in Communist China (Chapter 2) is also necessary in order to undermine private interpersonal relationships and, in fact, to destroy the concept of a legitimate private world. As close friends and members of the family are seduced into becoming agents of the totalitarian system (e.g., children informing on parents), it becomes increasingly difficult for the citizen to interact with others in anything but a "public" frame of reference. Nothing remains safe from government scrutiny.

. . . perhaps more important than what totalitarianism does to mass communication is what it does to private communication. Mass communication receives a new content, but remains mass, whereas private communication is transformed and ceases to be private. No matter what the context, on the street talking to a stranger or in the intimacy of one's home, one must say only the right thing. And one must say it as publicly as possible. Private communication becomes suspect, for to speak privately implies the desire to speak without being overheard by others. And the wish not to be overheard suggests that one is saying forbidden things—for if they were not forbidden, blasphemous things, would you not be proud to say them aloud for all to hear? In the end, even silence becomes suspect, for it may mean an unwillingness to reiterate the catechism which the mystique requires all to intone, and hence mark one out as an alien, a non-believer, and a potential source of contamination. Thus, private communication becomes public communication, and along with mass communication is subverted to fulfilling the imperatives of the mystique. Communication is communalized. [Inkeles, 1954, p. 102]

As this process takes hold, one may expect that individuals increasingly lose their ability to identify what others really believe, because it becomes increasingly difficult to check the accuracy of their perception. To the extent that the government succeeds in creating an image of the world as a place in which what a person says publicly is taken to be equivalent to what he believes privately, it undermines the individual's confidence in the belief that he and others have a private world or makes him forget how to go about looking for it.*

It is an interesting fact that such social isolation can be produced merely by coercing public utterances. It does not matter how disaffected the citizen is privately. As long as he does not speak his mind to others, his disaffection is, in effect, irrelevant to the security of the system.† The point is well summarized by Friedrich and Brzezinski:

* Inkeles also points out that it is a distinctive feature of totalitarian society to subordinate the individual by first subordinating those social institutions through which he obtains his status and identity as an individual. For example:

"Clearly, if the subordination of the individual cannot be complete without the subordination of his associations, then it follows further that *absolute* subordination of the individual requires absolute subordination of all the human associations which form the web of society. But it is not on these grounds alone that the totalitarian exempts no organization from being measured against his Procrustean rule. The mystique implies a plan of the good society. It provides a single metric for all forms of human organization. The totalitarian rejects outright the principle which inheres in the formula 'render unto Caesar the things which are Caesar's.' He accepts no distinction between the sacred and the profane, the public and the private, in social life. The demands of the mystique determine what decision shall be taken in regard to any particular institution, but all institutions are equally subject to review." (Inkeles, 1954, p. 94)

† Of course, one may expect that such disaffection would have other negative consequences for the regime such as likelihood of low productivity, defection, etc.

. . . The atmosphere of fear it creates easily exaggerates the strength of the regime and helps it achieve and maintain its façade of unanimity. Scattered opponents of the regime, if still undetected, become isolated and feel themselves cast out of society. This sense of loneliness, which is the fate of all, but more specially of an opponent of the totalitarian regime, tends to paralyze resistance and makes it much less appealing. It generates a universal longing to "escape" into the anonymity of the collective whole. *Unanimity, even if coerced, is a source of strength for the regime.* [Friedrich & Brzezinski, 1956, p. 137]

The second function of an internal image of unanimity is to obscure actual diversity.

. . . Behind the totalitarian façade, the struggle of the elite formations of Soviet society for power and influence continues to find expression. The Party apparatus, the police, the army, and the administrative bureaucracy vie with one another for preferment, and the local and departmental interests of different sections of the bureaucracy exercise their counterinfluence on the Party. The public affirmations of unanimity on which all totalitarian regimes insist serve to obscure the diversity of interests which they can neither eliminate nor dare openly acknowledge. [Fainsod, 1953, p. 328]

If the regime's legitimacy rests solely on its claim of being the official interpreter of an absolute ideology, it could hardly gain in power by allowing to become public the disagreement among leaders concerning the interpretation of doctrine. As Orwell so well foresaw in his *Nineteen Eighty-Four* (1949), even outright falsification of history, manipulation of statistics and public records, and the faking of elections is justified in the pursuit of an image of unanimity when diversity threatens to become evident.

The third function, that of providing the image of a powerful and righteous social movement, will be discussed in greater detail when we consider the psychology of the follower. Suffice it to say at this point that, if the follower is a person who wishes to lose his sense of self by identifying with a powerful social movement, he will be aided in his quest if the members of the movement are unanimous and outspoken about their unanimity. This result follows both for cognitive and emotional reasons. On the cognitive side, it has been well demonstrated that ease of identification with another person or group is a function of the clarity of that person or group as a model. On the emotional side, the perceived power of the movement, which is again a function of its unanimity, will determine its attractiveness to all those whose desire is to identify with a powerful cause upon which they may become dependent (Hoffer, 1951; Meerloo, 1956).

The compulsive concern with active participation in the thought reform movement obviously aids in the maintenance of the image. The "student" who does not commit himself actively mars the image just as much as if he uttered heresies, for silence can only mean lack of acceptance or unspoken heresy. The student must think out loud and thereby show the manner in which he recognizes the error of his past; he must publicly confess his sins to show to all others who may yet be wavering how the regime is permitting him to become a penitent and redeemable person. Thus he provides a model of how to become part of the movement at the same time as affirming his solidarity with it, a device frequently used by religious mass movements.

Maintenance of Power by Controlling Ideas

It is a stated assumption of the Communist leaders that correct political behavior is based on correct political ideas. Such an assumption is embodied in Communist ideology (unity of theory and action) and is clearly reflected in Communist law in the concept of guilt for holding ideas which if logically carried out would lead to crimes against the party (Leites & Bernaut, 1954; Berle, 1957). Such an assumption is also reflected in the boundless optimism verbalized by the leaders, especially the Chinese, concerning the malleability of men, and in their energetic program to create "a new man."

Harsh repressive measures against incorrect ideas are justified because, if one can root out such ideas and create a "new man," one can then dispense with coercive controls.

The Chinese Communists have always stressed the importance of ideological homogeneity as a means of control. Believing that action springs from thought, they consider the control of thought even more fundamental than the control of overt behavior. All errors in action, they maintain, are traceable to errors in thinking, or, in other words, to ideological deviations. Consequently, the history of the Communist movement is in part a story of unceasing ideological struggle against tendencies of deviation from the correct orthodoxy sanctioned by the Party leaders. [Chen & Chiu, 1955, p. 177]

Furthermore, permitting incorrect ideas to exist, whether they are in the political area or not, is likely to contaminate loyal citizens and lead inevitably to rival centers of power which must grow from such ideas (Inkeles, 1954).

To achieve ideological homogeneity, the regime controls completely the flow of incoming information, while saturating the mass media of communication with those ideas considered to be correct, and reinforces the correct ideas by thought reform wherever it is considered necessary. This technique was clearly seen in the POW camps where all publications, news broadcasts, movies, mail, and contact with outsiders was carefully filtered for its ideological purity. Western literature and personal mail were permitted only if they supported the Communist ideology or could serve some other important function, e.g., mail was permitted to go through which contained bad news in order to demoralize the prisoner and to undermine the support which he might be getting from identification with reference groups (Schein, 1956). In the political prison the more extreme measure of cutting the prisoner off from all information was sometimes used (Lifton, 1956a, b; Hinkle & Wolff, 1956).

COMMENT. Much of what the Chinese Communists do in reforming a prisoner or citizen is inconsistent with much of what they say theoretically about such efforts, in that the outright coercion of behavior is given at least as much emphasis as the initial control of incoming ideas or persuasion. As we saw in the previous chapter, tremendous overt and covert pressure is brought to bear on everyone to conform publicly, to participate actively, and to work hard, while a façade is maintained that such conformity and dedication is entirely voluntary or the product of successful ideological persuasion. It would appear, then, that the regime not only holds the assumption that correct behavior results from correct beliefs, but also holds the assumption that correct beliefs result from correct behavior. Actually this assumption is also stated explicitly and is strongly supported by ideological underpinnings. The whole concept of reform through labor (learning the attitude of the proletariat by experiencing directly what the proletarian does), the notion of identifying potential progressives or reactionaries by means of a study of their class origins and what they have done in their lifetime, the rejection of the sophisticated intellectual Communist who has never engaged in political action, all support this assumption.

These apparently inconsistent assumptions can be seen to be consistent if we consider what kinds of ideas or beliefs the good Communist is expected to learn. As we have previously noted, acceptance of the basic utopian premises is one level of idea or belief that everyone is expected to share and which can presumably be inculcated by information control, propaganda, and persuasion alone. But to have correct political beliefs also involves the absolute acceptance of and belief in the party as the official interpreter and implementer of the ideology. This latter class of ideas and attitudes can be taught *only* by coercion,* but, once thoroughly learned, does indeed lead ritually to "correct political behavior," i.e., obedience to party directives and policies.

In neither case are we dealing with a class of ideas, beliefs, or attitudes which serve the person as a way of defining his own role in relation to his environment, which express his own needs and personality, which grow and change as his experience changes, or which guide a whole range of overt behavior because of their inner logic. In Communist society, particularly under the impact of the "passion for unanimity," beliefs and attitudes function only as a way of appraising reality and relating to others, particularly to others in positions of authority. To the extent that they cease to express anything about the personality of their holder they become at once coercible and determinative of overt behavior, i.e., they become ritualized.† The person who operates in terms of ritualized ideas

---

* Except insofar as the person's needs for complete dependency are sufficiently dominant to make him a willing accomplice.

† See Chapter 10 for a more detailed discussion of ritualization of belief.

and beliefs guides his behavior by such ideas or beliefs but is completely dependent on external authority to define for him what his ideas and beliefs should be in any given situation. Thus for the budding Communist his practical training consists of learning how to obey and rationalize party directives in concrete situations or how best to attune himself to what these might be if he is in a situation in which he is cut off from direct party authority.

Eliciting Motivation for Rapid Social and Economic Change

In the period immediately after the take-over, one of the primary goals of a regime is to build up the new society economically, industrially, and socially. In order to accomplish this goal according to the rapid time scale which the regime usually sets for itself, a high degree of motivation and dedication is needed on the part of the citizens. The regime does not have time nor is in a position to earn this kind of loyalty and motivation because it neither has available, nor is willing to produce, the material goods which would serve as real incentives for hard work and loyalty. It must fall back, therefore, on ideological goals and symbolic incentives. However, persuading people of utopian conceptions when their standard of living is only slowly improving is not likely to be successful. Furthermore, with the consolidation of power by the new regime come aspects of life which may be highly unattractive to the citizen: lack of freedom of physical movement, lack of privacy, heavy taxation, longer working hours, and the like. The result may be that the ideology stands in danger of being actually disconfirmed for the man in the street in the immediate post-takeover period.

Under these conditions the regime has two alternatives: to cut back its own programs or time schedules (as in Lenin's New Economic Policy); to tighten discipline and coerce the acceptance of the ideological goals, and the regime's means to achieve them, as a dogma rather than as empirically derived knowledge. The validity of the means and ends is simply stated as a fact not to be questioned, and the unpleasant conditions of the post-takeover period are explained and justified as being an essential stage in the achievement of the ultimate goals (the Dictatorship of the Proletariat), and/or the result of sabotage and counter-revolutionary activity. The all-encompassing and absolutistic nature of Communist ideology makes its conversion from a system of pseudo-scientific knowledge into a dogma a relatively easy matter.

As we have seen at other times in history (e.g., the Papal Inquisition of the Middle Ages, the French Revolution), when faith or knowledge becomes converted into dogma, the passion for unanimity grows apace, for dogma is far more vulnerable than faith or knowledge to the diversity of opinion which rational examination of means and ends entails. When the dogma is a justification for the tremendous self-sacrifice demanded of the citizen in the industrial reconstruction, one may anticipate great pressure against any ideological deviance which could even suggest the possibility of errors in ideological premises or their implementation by the party. Thus we see in totalitarian society the whole coercive apparatus of the state brought to bear on any individual who questions the regime's policy or even advocates that it be subjected to rational discussion.

COMMENT. As the regime is able to build up its industrial base and concentrate on consumer goods, the need for this artificial motivation declines. One may hypothesize that the greatest pressure for unanimity will therefore be present when the maximum rate of industrial and social change is called for and when the fewest alternative motivations such as nationalism or fear of attack are readily available.

Converting ideology into dogma can build some measure of collective motivation, but collective ideological goals do not meet the citizens' personal needs for status, and if such needs are not fulfilled the collective motivation cannot be maintained. To fulfill the needs for status, individual incentives must be provided in the form of reward for and recognition of individual contributions to the collective effort, as have in fact been provided in the Soviet Union and in China in the form of medals, publicity, luxury vacations, extra privileges, and so on.

While at work, the workers are constantly exhorted by their party organizations and by the trade unions to engage in "socialist competition" among themselves, and collectively with the workers of other factories, trusts or institutions. Special rewards are given to those who excel in overfulfilling their norms, the so-called "shock-workers"; since the thirties the successful shock-workers have been known as Stakhanovites, after Stakhanov, a shock-coalminer. The Stakhanovites receive special medals, and badges, as well as financial rewards. They are entitled to certain privileges, such as free railroad travel, while in some cases their children are entitled to free education. It was estimated that in 1948 some 87 per cent of the labor force in the USSR was engaged in "socialist competition." [Friedrich & Brzezinski, 1956, p. 283]

It should be noted that the acceptance on the part of the population of such incentives also tends to deflect attention from a rational examination of the underlying goals of the regime.

By accepting the regime's policies as dogma, the citizen solves a number of problems for himself. He is able to reduce the external pressures impinging on him; he is able to rationalize and justify to himself a course of action which he has reason to believe the regime would impose by force anyway; he can gain some measure of status; and he is able to maintain hope for a better future. It should not be assumed therefore that the citizen's clinging to the dogma is merely an expression of fear. Its acceptance may fulfill a number of psychological needs.

One important limitation of the above argument is that, by itself, it does not explain the tremendous encroachment of the government apparatus on the private lives of the citizens. It does not account for the conformity demands in widespread areas of behavior such as the arts and the manner of dress.

THE COMMUNIST MOVEMENT DEFINED AS A "COMBAT" ORGANIZATION

We have alluded in a number of places to the fact that the Communists perceive themselves to be in a struggle for survival with many enemies both inside their movement and in other countries, and to be organized therefore according to military combat standards rather than peacetime standards. The overt emphasis on these conditions is, of course, greatest during and immediately after the take-over, when the actual number of enemies inside and outside the movement may be expected to be greatest. For example, the 1945 Constitution of the CCP states in its preamble:

"The CCP is a unified, combat organization, built on the principle of democratic centralism, and held together by the discipline which all Party members must observe conscientiously and voluntarily. The strength of the CCP rests on its solidarity, unified will, and integral action. The Party cannot tolerate any internal action which deviates from its programme and Constitution or is detrimental to discipline; it cannot tolerate any demand for autonomy within the Party, factionalism, or two-faced deeds which pretend to obey the Party while opposing it in practice. The CCP must constantly purge from its ranks those who violate the programme, Constitution, and discipline of Party membership, and who are incorrigible in their mistakes." [Brandt, Schwartz, & Fairbank, 1952, p. 424]

Pye, in commenting on "People's Liberation Movements" in Asia, notes that their reliance on armed struggle is to a degree a reflection of the general importance which armed power has traditionally had in Asian politics. It also reflects the situational demands of a prolonged revolutionary struggle, consisting of the gradual "liberation" of rural areas prior to gaining control of the urban centers.

. . . Conceiving of themselves as existing in an environment dominated by violence and as struggling against enemies who seek to maintain their control by military means, the People's Liberation parties have readily turned to the task of creating their own military forces. [Pye, 1956, p. 27]

"Confronted with such enemies, it is inevitable for the Chinese revolution to take on a 'protracted' and 'ruthless' nature. . . . Confronted with such enemies, the method and principal form of the Chinese revolution must necessarily be militant and not peaceful. . . . It is absolutely correct for Stalin to say, 'One characteristic peculiar to the Chinese revolution is opposition against the armed counter-revolutionaries by the armed revolutionaries.' Hence any tendency to make light of armed strug-

gle, of revolutionary war, of guerrilla warfare, and of the work of the
armed forces, is altogether wrong." [Mao Tse-tung, quoted in Pye, 1956,
p. 29]

Several general consequences follow from the system's definition
of the situation as one of combat which can be found in most post-
revolutionary regimes or in non-revolutionary situations where regimes feel themselves to be threatened (e.g., the Papal Inquisition).*
1. In a state of combat there is the need for highly centralized
authority to achieve efficiency in implementing the goals of the regime and maintain adequate co-ordination among decentralized
forces.† Highly centralized authority makes possible a greater degree of arbitrariness of decision and thus lays the groundwork for
inquisitions and persecutions of deviants.
2. Organizations or regimes which conceive of themselves as being
under threat or in combat tend to replace authority by legal process
with authority by administrative decision. The source of this trend
is probably to be found in the desire of the leaders to maintain as
much power in their own hands as possible, but it is also justified
as a means of reaching disciplinary decisions rapidly and efficiently,
and preserving a solid front by avoiding the full airing of issues
which accompanies the usual legal process.

Essentially, the Communist legal system in this respect approximates
the situation in other legal systems in States where *Church and State are
combined,* and where the law and procedures are assimilated to and
governed by ecclesiastical and religious practice. The difference lies in
the fact that the Communist system, being materialist, discards any external or transcendental criteria: doctrine is made by the Communist
Party of which the State is an expression; there can be, therefore, no
principle, let alone law, superior to it. Police, administrative officials and
Courts are obliged to adapt the "law" (meaning thereby decrees and
regulations, and so forth) to this doctrine, and to handle the accused

---

* In this section in particular, we are shifting our level of analysis. Our purpose is to show that some of the characteristics of totalitarian movements can be
explained without explicit considerations of their ideology.
† High centralization may in fact be the product of the power drive of the
leaders, but it is likely to be rationalized and justified in terms of its efficiency.

accordingly. Leaving out the transcendental element, the Communist legal system is probably merely a new version of the practice prevailing in trial of crimes against the State under the Byzantine Empire (in which the Emperor was also dominant in the Church) and of the actual though less rationalized practice in many political cases under the Czarist Empire. [Berle, 1957, p. 649]

There appear to be several corollary effects, particularly as the system operates in Communist China: the automatic assumption of guilt if any member of the administrative apparatus makes an accusation; the inadmissibility of any defense by the accused because such defense constitutes a questioning of the authority and is therefore a revolt against established power; the unavailability of any legal text to which the accused can turn to discover the nature of his crime (which has a striking counterpart in the Papal Inquisition of the twelfth and thirteenth centuries in the outlawing of the Bible for popular consumption [Lea, 1887]; the person in authority defines the law simply by his position); the definition of crime purely in terms of expediency and the demands of the moment, which in turn leads to rather vague categories like "counter-revolutionary activity," "sabotage," "reactionary tendencies," and so on (Berle, 1957); repressive measures which maximize the odds for the government by inferring from a minimum of evidence the actual or probable criminal intent of anyone who is in any way a threat to it.*

Given these circumstances, the actual or potential deviant has little chance in the system. If he is accused by anyone, he can quickly be arrested, tried, and convicted by virtually any administrative authority. It is the recognition on the part of the prisoner that the demands for confession and thought reform are backed by completely arbitrary authority which more than anything else creates a hopeless situation for him. Just as the witch or heretic of the Middle Ages could only defend himself or herself by accepting the frame of reference of the inquisitors (which meant accepting at least the

* These factors have been noted by a number of students of legal practices in post-revolutionary states. A particularly concise analysis of the Chinese Communist legal system is given by Bonnichon (undated), a jurist who was himself imprisoned. A more detailed discussion can be found in Wei, 1955.

validity of the premise that devils and witches do exist), the prisoner of the Communists can survive only by accepting the ideological frame of reference of his captors and the validity of their premise about "struggle," "combat," "ceaseless vigilance against counter-revolutionary activity," and so on.* He soon learns that if his judge or interrogator says he is guilty, he is in fact guilty. Bonnichon describes the situation this way:

"Therefore, two ways lie open to you: either you confess and implore the clemency of the government, in which case the government will be lenient, or you resist and subject yourself to the severest of punishments." This speech has been repeated to every accused, both in the field of political crimes and that of ordinary crimes; in each case, it has been repeated many times; it was clear that judges and interpreters alike knew these words by heart. It is understandable, therefore, that to plead innocence is to offend the government; and moreover, you are told so: "So you dare accuse the government of frivolity or injustice!" That is another offence which makes your case worse. Thus, not only is the accused presumed guilty, but he is forbidden to prove the contrary: to try, is to revolt.† Not only does the judge have nothing to prove, but he is even dispensed from the necessity of pronouncing a precise accusation: You are guilty; we know it; accuse yourself. When I ask: "Guilty of what?", I am told that it is not for the accused to put questions; there is only one thing he can do: confess and ask the government's pardon.

Thus it is the knowledge on the part of the prisoner that he has absolutely no recourse which forces him ultimately to give in to the

* The generality of this phenomenon was recently demonstrated in the post-takeover phase of the Cuban revolution in which Fidel Castro set aside the legally arrived-at acquittal of a number of pilots who had fought for Batista, and by administrative act condemned them to life imprisonment on the basis of his personal conviction that they had murdered innocent women and children in their strafing.

† This presumption is irrefutable to such a degree that the "political instructor" of the prison, assistant to the judge in the "reform of our thoughts," told me one day: "The very fact that you do not see what crimes you have committed makes your case even worse, because it proves your obduracy." [Bonnichon, undated, p. 8]

system. At the same time, the administrative official knows that his own position depends entirely upon the adequate fulfillment of his superior's orders and this motivates him strongly to produce total conformity in the prisoner at virtually any price (short of losing him by death or psychosis). The combat atmosphere, strongly supported by ideological premises, makes him particularly sensitive to any evidence of crime and deviance, no matter how tenuous or circumstantial; the confessions he finally elicits, of course, confirm his suspicions.

3. Conditions of threat or combat tend to produce a *shift in the frame of reference used to evaluate behavior.* Behavior which under peacetime conditions might be ignored or might result only in mild censure can and does become, under combat conditions, a serious offense punishable by imprisonment or even death. Such severe penalties are applied both for behavior which constitutes failure to achieve a stated goal (such as failing to stay awake on guard duty or to clean one's rifle) and for behavior which increases danger by breaking security (such as telling of a troop ship departure to an unreliable person).

The Chinese Communist definition of such offenses as espionage and sabotage is an excellent example of this kind of shift in frame of reference. As one reads the kinds of charges which have been brought against Western prisoners, one is initially struck by their utter incongruity—a student accused of espionage, a priest or nun accused of sabotage or infanticide, and so on. However, many prisoners in time come to be able to understand the frame of reference from which the conclusion follows that crimes have been committed. This frame of reference, usually called "the people's standpoint," is characterized primarily by the degree to which it attaches serious criminal intent or effect to any action which in any conceivable way could hurt the Communist regime. The justification for this extreme kind of interpretation is the notion of perpetual combat with enemies within and without. For example, a letter to an American friend by a priest who had just traveled through some rural areas, in which he described the landscape and the kind of farming he observed, was espionage according to the judge because, it was pointed out, from the Chinese "people's point of view" combat was not restricted solely to military engagement but included also political and ideological struggle. Hence "intelligence" is not limited to matters of military significance but includes also matters of economic, political, and social significance. If information about a farm in China could conceivably be used as the basis for a psychological warfare campaign against the peasant, for example, it is automatically "intelligence" and its transmitter is deliberately or unwittingly engaging in espionage. The fact that between 1950 and 1953 the United States and Communist China were technically at war with each other supported this logic. It is not at all unlikely that in a situation of comparable threat any nation would adopt a course of maximum security and treat many seemingly innocent actions with suspicion, especially if those actions were committed by members of an enemy nation.

We have belabored this point to establish clearly the distinction between a set of Communist attitudes which derives from their ideology and a set which derives primarily from their preoccupation with struggle, threat, and survival. The point is crucial because many victims of Communist Chinese imprisonment found it much easier to understand and accept the fact that their own behavior was harmful because it represented a threat in a situation which was defined as one of combat than it was for them to accept the ideological premises and rationale that led to such a definition of the situation in the first place. For example, Robert Ford, a British citizen working as a radio operator for the Tibetan government when captured by the Communists, recognized shortly after his arrest that from the Communist point of view he was certainly guilty of espionage (in terms of the circumstantial evidence against him), and that he might as well confess it rather than deny something he could appreciate intellectually. Only much later in his thought reform did the issue of the acceptance of Communist values arise (Ford, 1957).

To generalize the argument: it seems clear that if the Communist regime or any other regime can convince its population that they are under constant threat from enemies inside and outside the system, it is introducing a potent force toward unanimity and conformity because even slight deviance becomes highly suspicious and is severely dealt with. Every person can then be told that his own lack of conformity can be a severe threat to the system as a whole, and that such behavior is therefore not only against his own long-run interests but also gives justification to the harsh repressive measures used by the regime.

4. Conditions of struggle and combat, particularly in the period prior to take-over, require the recruitment and maintenance of effective fighting forces. If such forces are drawn from politically uneducated masses, and if, as was the case in the take-over of China, these forces have to wage scattered guerrilla warfare as well as to administer "liberated areas," the importance of ideology as a motivating force and guideline for action becomes exceedingly great. Hence, the Communists have placed great emphasis on political education and indoctrination within the armed forces, with the effect of making them more disciplined and providing for their politically untutored audience in the liberated areas an appealing model of the "good life" under Communism.

The ideology operates not only as a unifying force and a guideline to action in ambiguous situations, but also as a *language*, a set of semantic guides, which makes possible rapid and efficient communication of the wishes of the central authorities.* For example, if every soldier and cadre understands clearly what is meant by a term like "bureaucratism" (i.e., the slavish obedience to orders without consideration to the local political situation), then a campaign can be launched by the regime against this type of behavior simply by stating that bureaucratism is bad and must be avoided. Everyone knows precisely what is expected of him, what he is to criticize in others, and how to change his behavior in the future. Semantic clarity can be achieved only if unanimity of knowledge and interpretation is strenuously enforced. One function of intensive indoctrination, then, is to insure the widespread sharing of definitions of key terms of the ideology. If this goal can be accomplished, the communication process can to a degree be streamlined and wider active participation can be insured.

---

* William Griffith, in private conversation, has pointed out the importance of Western studies of Communist ideology as a basis for understanding even what their internal communications mean.

PSYCHOLOGICAL FACTORS IN THE LEADERS
OF THE MOVEMENT OR STATE

In considering the psychological factors in the leaders we must distinguish between the three sets of such factors: basic psychological traits or personality predispositions; the psychological consequences of success—attitudes and psychological mechanisms which result from the leader's *role* as one who has successfully engineered a revolution; and, feelings and attitudes which result from the leader's launching of a purge or a program for coercing unanimity.

Basically, the problem is to keep separate those psychological characteristics which motivate the individual to become a revolutionary leader from those characteristics which may be assumed to be the result of his experiences, as these are mediated by the position in which he finds himself at different stages of the revolution.

Basic Psychological Traits

Among the basic traits which have been attributed to successful leaders of revolutionary movements are fanaticism, intolerance for ambiguity, extremism, megalomania, idealism, authoritarianism, excessive self-righteousness, vanity, paranoia, asceticism, excessive sense of dedication or commitment, ruthlessness, cruelty, rebelliousness, psychopathy, opportunism, frustrated ambition, nonconformism, and cynicism. This bewildering diversity of traits, combined with a lack of good biographical data, argues strongly for holding in abeyance any hasty conclusion about a revolutionary type.

Instead, Brinton argues that revolutionary leaders represent the same kind of cross section of society as any other types of leaders (Brinton, 1952). In analyzing the "character and disposition" of the revolutionary, Brinton finds among them (1) "the gentleman-revolutionist, the 'misguided superior,' the man born on top, but perversely unwilling to stay there" (p. 113); (2) from classes below the ruling one: "fools, scoundrels, idealists, professional agitators, diplomatists, lunatics, cowards, and heroes" (p. 115); (3) "failures in the old society, men who were unable to attain the objects of their ambition" (p. 115); (4) "men of very practical abilities, men of the kind that even cautious and hard-headed conservatives must recognize as worthy of respect" (p. 117); (5) "men of blood (the terrorists)" (p. 117); (6) "the crack-brained schemer, the fantastic doctrinaire, the man who has a crazy gadget which will bring Utopia" (p. 119); (7) "the disputatious, contrary-minded person who loves to stand out from the crowd of conformists" (pp. 119–20); and finally, (8) the type most nearly the "perfect revolutionist," namely "the idealist" (p. 121).

The concept of "the idealist" who is devoted enough to his ideals to pursue them relentlessly and who is realistic enough to find a way to mold a revolutionary movement around them is well expounded by Inkeles in his discussion of the "totalitarian mystique" (Inkeles, 1954). He points out that the assumption of cynical power-seeking is not sufficient to account for the often seemingly irrational tampering with social institutions characteristic of totalitarian movements. Rather, the leader is primarily characterized by his conviction that he has *directly* perceived some immanent law of social development and by his "mystical" dedication to it.

This element of the totalitarian character is not conceived of as replacing the power drive, but rather as distinguishing the totalitarian from other individuals who also seek power, even absolute power. [Inkeles, 1954, p. 88]

Furthermore,

. . . this approach is assumed to manifest itself regardless of the particular content of the totalitarian's formal ideology—although it may be that only certain kinds of formal ideology will appeal to him; [*Ibid.*]

and

. . . the totalitarian's knowledge of the law is seen by him both as dictating necessary action on his part, and as guaranteeing the "correctness" of that action. [*Ibid.*]

We are not prepared to judge the validity of any of the character trait analyses. We can note, however, that certain of the traits which have been mentioned above, or which can be inferred from those mentioned, are highly relevant to our basic question—what functions does unanimity serve? Looking at this question now from the perspective of the personality of the leader, we can identify three kinds of traits which are relevant: the predisposition to feel anxious and insecure (which can be inferred from the preoccupation with security operations such as dedication to pseudo-religions, power-seeking, etc.); lack of flexibility in thinking and perceiving (which is either mentioned directly or can be inferred from a number of other traits mentioned); and activity proneness.

The first of these predispositions leads the leader to seek constant reassurance, which for one who sets out to be a leader can only be the unanimity of his followers. He needs not only the reassurance that his followers will remain loyal, but also the reassurance that they accept his legitimacy, that they grant that his ideology and course of action are correct. Furthermore, if his insecurity is rooted in emotional conflicts of childhood rather than being based on a realistic evaluation of his current situation, one may expect pre-occupations with reassurance which are out of all proportion to the objective situation.

The tendency to be inflexible in perceiving and thinking should lead to genuine inability on the part of the leader to see the virtue of any point of view other than his own. Other positions are likely to be viewed, at the minimum, as understandable errors of the un-enlightened (in which case re-education is called for), or, at the maximum, as inherently evil and dangerous heresies to be excised as quickly as possible. The latter position is more likely to be taken if, with the inflexibility, there is present a strong commitment to an ideology which is all-inclusive. Inkeles labels this phenomenon a "fear of contamination from within":

. . . It is a characteristic of totalitarian leaders that they see every social movement as having within it the seeds of its own destruction, and that they are ridden by fear that within their own movement and social organization there is such a potentially destructive foreign body which must be wholly and violently expunged—it is not enough to build anti-bodies against it—lest it cripple its host society from within. For Hitler it was the Jews and all other forms of "race mixture," whether of blood, of physical contact, or of ideas, which he saw as opening up the possibility of the disintegration of his particular mystical structure. For the Soviet Bolshevik it is the taint of capitalist thought remnants, or of various forms of "deviation." And I suppose that for Franco it is any sign of "socialism" or "anti-clericalism." [Inkeles, 1954, pp. 97–98]

When heresies or "inner taints" are discovered there is no choice but to destroy the carrier as well as the germ, thus leading to the possibility of endless preoccupation with purges and thought reform.

Activity proneness in the service of an ideology derives its importance from the fact that it leads the individual into an irreversible series of commitments from which is forged an identity to which the individual inevitably becomes strongly attached psychologically. It is in such behavioral commitment that the main difference lies between the intellectual Communist who may go so far as to discuss his ideas and beliefs with congenial friends or willing listeners, and the active revolutionary who is prepared to back up these ideas and beliefs with actions which may result in exile, imprisonment, or death.

The ideology becomes a component of the person's identity partly through his behavioral commitments and partly through his interactions with others who may join him in forging the revolutionary movement. This process of embedding a set of beliefs both in personal commitment and in lasting social relationships can lead only to increasing psychological commitment to them, which, in turn, should lead to increased efforts to convince others of their validity. One may expect this process to reach its greatest intensity at the point of greatest commitment, in the final struggle to take over the society and in the period immediately afterward.

The Psychological Consequences of Success

The successful take-over of a society by a revolutionary clique is obviously a product of the interaction of many political, economic, social, and psychological factors. The complexity of this interaction insures the conclusion discussed in the previous section that no one personality type will likely end up in the position of the successful leader. It is tenable to assume, however, that the psychological *consequences* of being a successful leader will show considerable uniformity, regardless of the personality of the individual in whom they manifest themselves. We shall hypothesize four kinds of psychological consequences and try to show how they relate to the passion for unanimity.

1. Successful take-over strongly confirms the ideology for the leader himself, and confirms also the identification of the leader with the ideology in the minds of the followers and bystanders. The ideology thus becomes not only the most convenient but also the only tenable basis of legitimacy for the new regime.

2. Successful take-over reinforces the leader's sense of confidence in himself, his sense of rightness, and consequently his sense of power. Gaining more and more power is supported not only by whatever personal power needs may be present but also by the newly reinforced sense of destiny which legitimizes these needs.

3. Successful take-over must involve a certain amount of guilt concerning actions which have been taken in the take-over process, though one might expect that this guilt would be fairly deeply buried psychologically. The more guilt is present, however, the more the successful leader must seek reassurance and legitimation, on the one hand, and the more paranoid he may become, on the other hand. The growth of paranoid feelings may result either because of fear of revenge or because of the leader's projection onto others of his own hostility toward established authority.

4. Successful take-over thrusts the leader into a position of having to fulfill the utopian promises of the ideology on which he rose to power, and to test his own ability as a person in a position of final authority. It is much easier to criticize the existing order than to create something better oneself. Therefore, under the leader's façade of confidence must lie a layer of doubt and insecurity concerning his own ability to bring to fruition many of the things he has talked about so glibly. As actual programs fail, this insecurity may be expected to mount, because both the ideology and the leader's own ability are then in danger of being disconfirmed.

From any one of these factors one could predict that the leader would initiate programs to liquidate those who are useless and uneducatable, to re-educate those who are needed in the new society and who are considered re-educatable, and to purge members of the faithful as a way of purifying and reaffirming the faith as well as consolidating his own power position. The important point here is that one can predict the occurrence of preoccupation with unanimity in the post-takeover period without postulating any specific basic personality characteristics in the leader. Different personality types may be equally prone to preoccupations with legitimacy and may equally share the need for reassurance because of the circumstances in which they find themselves.

The type of expression of unanimity demanded by the leader may, of course, be partially determined by the situation in the post-takeover period. The leader during this period not only requires reassurance that he will receive support; he also must be elevated to the great heights of a savior and be given a positive image and high status to insure ready acceptance of his position among other nations and to reward psychologically the masses who identify with him. To this end one may find great importance given to the more overt ritual expressions of unanimity—the demonstrations, elections, parades, and so on. However forced such demonstrations may be, they probably operate to give the leader a sense of power and control which enables him to go ahead with the process of rebuilding society, and which makes it possible for him to maintain face in his dealings with representatives of other nations.

Overtly expressed unanimity also serves the important function of absolving the leader of responsibility for irreversible courses of action. If the leader can feel that actions which lead to feelings of guilt or which threaten to have unpredicted consequences are in fact demanded of him by the ideology and the people (i.e., that he is only the agent of destiny), he can relieve himself of much psychological discomfort. The "People's Courts" in the take-over of China may serve as a good example. A landlord is to be liquidated. The party member launches into a harangue concerning the landlord's crimes against the people and demands to know what the people's judgment is. Agitators in the crowd shout for liquidation of the criminal. The malcontents pick up the theme and some of the timid go along from fear. Soon the whole crowd is swept by a frenzy of mob feeling and expressed hate, leading to the unanimous decision to execute the victim. Such demonstrations no doubt serve many functions. The one we wish to point to here is that the party member, though he knows he staged the whole thing, is nevertheless reassured and absolved by the final unanimous people's decision. Self-fulfilling prophecies are no less reassuring than other kinds, and in some sense perhaps more so.

An additional aspect to this need for legitimation which is often mentioned in analyses of the totalitarian system is the leader's need to be judged favorably by history (Friedrich and Brzezinski, 1956). Not only does he feel a need to be reassured in the present but his commitment to being an agent of destiny requires that ultimately he be proved correct no matter what the actual outcome of his decisions may be. To this end, then, are devoted the more fantastic rituals like the falsification of history so well described by Orwell in his *Nineteen Eighty-Four*. One may expect this process to take hold in totalitarian society to the extent that the leader or leaders can imbue the members of the party and the citizenry with the same sense of destiny which they themselves have.

The points discussed thus far refer primarily to the problem of dealing with power needs, legitimacy, and absolution from guilt. It remains to discuss the fourth factor mentioned in our list of consequences, the threat of personal or ideological disconfirmation. It is quite likely, the complexities of social systems being what they are, that the leader will make some predictions or put into operation some programs which will fail to materialize in the manner expected. Statistics can be falsified to preserve the public image of the leader's omniscience, but what of the effect on the leader himself? There is relatively good evidence that if an individual or group committed to a certain ideology makes concrete predictions about future events on the basis of the ideology, and such events fail to occur as predicted, the degree of commitment to the ideology will psychologically *increase*, and will manifest itself in sharply increasing proselytization (Festinger *et al.*, 1956). In other words, when a set of ideas to which one is committed is about to be proved false, the best way to preserve psychological balance is to reassure oneself that they are not false, and this can best be accomplished by convincing others of their validity. Thus, in the group which Festinger *et al.* studied first hand, a prediction was made, based on revelation from God, that the earth would be destroyed on a certain day at a certain time, but that the faithful would be picked up by a flying saucer and saved. When the original prediction and several revisions (based upon further revelations) failed to materialize, the group for the first time in its history actively began to seek publicity, to tell others of their religion, and to reaffirm it more than ever among themselves. The explanation of the earth's being saved was revealed also: the devotion of the group itself had led God to relent!

Because the leader of totalitarian society, particularly the first-generation leader, rises to his position by virtue of his commitment to an ideology around which a revolutionary movement was forged, it is highly unlikely that he would find it psychologically possible to become less committed even if the ideology proved to be quite useless in coping with concrete reality. It should be noted, by the way, that in a broad sense it is impossible to disconfirm an ideology like Marxism-Leninism. Apart from the unassailability of a humanitarian ethic and a utopian goal, the clear separation of means from ends and the concept that any means are justified to achieve the ends always make possible the explanation of short-run failure as the result of such things as incorrect choice of means, sabotage or counter-revolutionary activity, or poor administration at lower echelons. The same kind of semantic ambiguity which is introduced into a religion by successive revelations is present in Communist ideology because of its failure to define denotatively (except insofar as the definitions are provided by the leaders to suit the needs of the moment) what its basic terms mean. It is well and good to be against the "rich farmer" in a given campaign, but there remains the problem of defining precisely what constitutes a farmer and what constitutes rich.* Given such ambiguity, it is not difficult for the leader to convince either himself or others that his false predictions were actually not false, and that no one need lose faith.

---

* An excellent discussion of the problems this kind of ambiguity posed for a group of prisoners who were attempting to re-educate themselves in a Chinese Communist prison is presented in Bishop Quentin Huang's account of his experiences in prison (Huang, 1954).

Cynicism and an apparent lack of devotion to ideology are often cited as a characteristic of totalitarian leaders, however. Is the observation wrong, or should one assume that such feelings are the end result of repeated disconfirmation and/or the hard experience of dealing with the realities of power politics? We prefer a third explanation, suggested by Inkeles, that the totalitarian treats his ideology in a mystical pseudo-religious sense which permits cynicism, indeed encourages it, about existing worldly institutions. The argument is well stated in the following passage:

. . . I do not minimize the cynicism and the manipulativeness of totalitarians. Indeed I suspect the world has never seen cynicism and manipulation to surpass theirs. The questions are what makes them cynical and what are they cynical about? The mystique dictates their morality, indeed it stands above ordinary human morality and places its adherent outside the demands normally to be made of a man and leader. Hence the totalitarian may be cynical about and manipulate "law," "loyalty," "truth," "honesty," and so on. For as long as he manipulates these in the service of the mystique, his action is beyond question—it is law, honesty, loyalty, unto itself. [Inkeles, 1954, p. 92]

The callous disregard for the human suffering caused by the establishment of the totalitarian regime and the expensive human sacrifice which the leader is explicitly willing to make for the sake of the ideology can only be understood in terms of fanatic devotion to a higher morality and a mystical sense of omnipotence.*

An additional point, though one concerning which we have not

* Parenthetically, the degree to which leaders of the revolutionary movement come to be identified with the ideology of the movement was well demonstrated by Leites and Bernaut in *The Ritual of Liquidation* (1954), in which they showed convincingly how the public false confessions of prominent Communists could be understood best as a final act in the service of the party and the symbolic reidentification which this act then signified. Smith (1954), in comparing the Soviet purge trials of the 1930's with the English treason trials under Henry VIII, finds convincing parallel evidence that individuals accused of crimes they probably never committed nevertheless confessed when facing the scaffold as a final act of reaffirming their solidarity with the system. After all, to judge the government to which one has devoted one's whole life as wrong makes a mockery out of one's own past. It is easier to see oneself as wrong and to reaffirm the system.

located data, is that the role of the ideology in the total personality probably shifts as the career of the member of a movement, organization, or society progresses. It appears to be generally true that the person is overtly most committed and most fanatical when he first enters the movement or organization. In the early stage of his career he must prove his worth, and part of his initiation is the total emotional acceptance of the ideology. As the person enters higher positions of authority he finds himself increasingly in a managerial role, and the managerial attitude must be maintained alongside the ideological conviction. If the ideological commitment remains as emotionally consuming as it was in earlier years, it becomes impossible for the person to function effectively in a managerial capacity, and thus effectively blocks his rise to power. To be an effective leader he must develop perspective, that is, he must be able increasingly to see the ideology in relation to other considerations. This implies no diminution in commitment to the ideology, but it does imply an increasing concern with other aspects of life.

A useful parallel can be drawn here with religious orders. To become a high official of the order generally requires administrative ability and a high degree of worldliness, yet one does not get the feeling that the high official is therefore any less devout. Rather, with rising rank the person learns more and more how to fulfill his religious goals in a complex environment. Similarly, when a totalitarian leader rises to a position of high authority he takes on a managerial role without, however, being any less influenced by the ideology. If anything, his increasing administrative ability may teach him better how to accomplish ideological goals; where the fanatic might fail at the helm of a society, the managerially competent leader might succeed.

The conclusion for our purposes is that one may expect in any program of coercive persuasion a mixture of rational and irrational elements. The leader of the regime may see the rational functions outlined in earlier sections of this chapter, but also may be emotionally swayed by needs either which he has always had or which have resulted from his accession to power.

The Effects of Coercing Unanimity

Partly for the psychological reasons described above, partly to facilitate rapid reconstruction of society, partly to build an image of legitimacy, and partly to consolidate his power by isolating the potential dissenter, the leader initially commits himself to a program of coercing agreement or unanimous acceptance of the ideology. However, the more the regime coerces unanimity in the political area, the fewer criteria it has for determining whether there is genuine acceptance or not. The more fear there is created in the citizenry and in the bureaucracy, the more of a communication vacuum is created around the top leadership because of the fear of passing upward any information which could in any way be used against anyone below.

This failure to communicate effectively, both within the hierarchy and with the rest of the people and the world, we have called the phenomenon of the vacuum. There develops within the regimes a kind of empty space around the rulers, which becomes more and more difficult to penetrate. A slow disintegration affecting all human relations sets people against each other and causes mutual distrust so that ordinary people are alienated from one another, all the bonds of confidence in social relationships are corroded by the terror and propaganda, the spying, and the denouncing and betraying, until the social fabric threatens to fall apart. The confidence which ordinarily binds the manager of a plant to his subordinates, members of a university faculty to each other and to their students, lawyer to client, doctor to patient, and even parents to children, as well as brothers to sisters is disrupted. The core of this process of disintegration is, it seems, the breakdown of the possibility of communication—the spread, that is, of the vacuum. Isolation and anxiety are the universal result. And the only answer the totalitarian dictatorship has for coping with this disintegration of human relationships is more organized coercion, more propaganda, more terror. [Friedrich & Brzezinski, 1956, p. 166]

At the same time, the more uniform everyone's behavior becomes, the more difficult it becomes to distinguish the active enthusiastic supporter from the mere conformist. Thus the very mechanism initially designed to reassure the leadership actually leads to greater insecurity, which in turn leads to greater demands for reassurance and, therefore, to more widespread coercion. One result of this cycle is the broadening of the sphere of the citizen's activities which the regime begins to take an interest in. That is, behavior in initially non-political areas comes to be considered indicative of what the person might say or do in public on potilical issues. Such broadening of surveillance is justified, as we have previously indicated, by the demands of the totalitarian ideology for total active participation on the part of the citizen. It is easy to show, in terms of the premises of the ideology, that the "new man" in the society should have no private life, or any need of it, and that all activities are basically political anyway.

As the regime's demands and areas of surveillance increase, the citizen, to protect himself, begins to conform in more and more areas of his life, thus making those areas once again useless as criteria for loyalty and resulting in still further searching by the regime into his private life. The only way this cycle can be slowed down is by the citizen's total acceptance of the regime's paranoia, in effect giving up all claims to a private life separated from a public one, and a wholehearted co-operation with the regime in "hunting out its enemies." When mutual surveillance in the service of the regime completely replaces surveillance by the authorities the process is complete.*

As we have previously suggested, the main effect of this social process is that political-ideological beliefs do get confirmed for the leaders and are learned by the citizenry, but at the same time these

---

* Inkeles in his discussion of the totalitarian mystique argues that the deliberate destruction of certain social institutions (e.g., primary group relationships) as a way of destroying the very basis of individuality is inherent in the system. While this may be true, it implies a high degree of sociological sophistication on the part of the leaders. Our explanation suggests that whether he deliberately set out to do so initially or not, the totalitarian leader soon finds himself forced to attack institutions like the family and friendship ties anyway. It is quite possible that he then discovers empirically what the good and bad consequences are of destroying primary group relations and the "private" life, often leading to a deliberate reversal of policy (e.g., reaffirming the solidarity of the family).

beliefs increasingly assume the form of a ritual rather than remaining or becoming viable, growing, expressive cognitive responses. The form, the time of expression, and the content all become so rigidly prescribed that the belief ceases to serve any function other than reassuring the regime and making life safe for the citizen. That is, the citizen learns not to invest too much of himself in the political belief and learns not to take its content too seriously, although he does accept the importance of the principle that "one must have the correct political belief and must express it appropriately."

From the point of view of the regime, the fate of the coercion-insecurity–more coercion cycle will probably depend on the following considerations: whether the leader's insecurity is based on stable personality dispositions or on a realistic evaluation of the likelihood of disaffection in the citizenry (especially under the pressures of forced industrialization) and the actual degree of success of the social system in reconstruction, industrialization, war, providing consumer benefits, scientific or cultural accomplishment, etc. If the leader's insecurity is strongly rooted in his personality one may expect no diminution of coercion through his lifetime. If on the other hand it is based on a realistic assessment of the state of feeling of the citizenry, one may expect coercion to decline as success is achieved by the system; that is, as the basis of consent and legitimacy begins to shift from purely ideological grounds to rational grounds in terms of the successful performance of the leaders.

PSYCHOLOGICAL FACTORS IN THE FOLLOWERS

Thus far we have concentrated on the functions of unanimity for the system as a whole and for the leaders of the system. It remains to discuss what may be a most significant additional dimension of the problem—the functions which unanimity serves for the followers, functions which may be of sufficient importance to lead the masses not to resist the regime's demands for unanimity and at given times even to demand it.

A number of authors writing about modern man have cited psychological characteristics such as alienation from selfhood (Fromm, 1941; Hoffer, 1951), latent dependency wishes (Meerloo, 1956), the need to submit to a strong authority (Adorno *et al.*, 1950), all of which lead, they feel, to longings to achieve harmony or a mystical union with a powerful group, great cause, or mass movement. Because the individual fails to find a personal identity or is dissatisfied with what he sees himself to be, he seeks a new identity by identifying with a mass movement. The stronger and more unanimous this movement, the stronger the sense of self which the individual gains by identifying with it.

Fromm, in his *Escape from Freedom* (1941), argues that modern man has a "feeling of insignificance in comparison with the overwhelming power of the world outside himself" (p. 185) and selects a "mechanism of escape" which meshes well with the totalitarian passion for unanimity:

This particular mechanism is the solution that the majority of normal individuals find in modern society. To put it briefly, the individual ceases to be himself; he adopts entirely the kind of personality offered to him by cultural patterns; and he therefore becomes exactly as all others are and as they expect him to be. The discrepancy between "I" and the world disappears and with it the conscious fear of aloneness and powerlessness. This mechanism can be compared with the protective coloring some animals assume. They look so similar to their surroundings that they are hardly distinguishable from them. The person who gives up his individual self and becomes an automaton, identical with millions of other automatons around him, need not feel alone and anxious any more. But the price he pays, however, is high; it is the loss of his self. [Fromm, 1941, pp. 185–86]

Hoffer, in his analysis of mass movements, develops this theme by noting that people do not want freedom but faith and unity (unanimity):

. . . They do not want freedom of conscience, but faith—blind authoritarian faith. They sweep away the old order not to create a society of free and independent men, but to establish uniformity, individual anonymity and a new structure of perfect unity. It is not the wickedness of the old regime they rise against but its weakness; not its oppression, but its failure to hammer them together into *one solid, mighty whole.* The persuasiveness of the intellectual demagogue consists not so much in convincing people of the vileness of the established order as in demonstrating its helpless incompetence. The immediate result of a mass movement usually corresponds to what the people want. They are not cheated in the process. [Hoffer, 1951, p. 141; italics added]

Hoffer, too, feels that the needs of the follower mesh well with the needs of totalitarian society.

The vigor of a mass movement stems from the propensity of its followers for united action and self-sacrifice. When we ascribe the success of a movement to its faith, doctrine, propaganda, leadership, ruthlessness and so on, we are but referring to instruments of unification and to means used to inculcate a readiness for self-sacrifice. [Hoffer, 1951, p. 57]

    . . . The same is true of religious and revolutionary organizations: whether or not they develop into mass movements depends less on the doctrine they preach and the program they project than on the degree of their preoccupation with unity and the readiness for self-sacrifice. [*Ibid.* p. 58]

    The total surrender of a distinct self is a prerequisite for the attainment of both unity and self-sacrifice; and there is probably no more direct way of realizing this surrender than by inculcating and extolling the habit of blind obedience. When Stalin forces scientists, writers and artists to crawl on their bellies and deny their individual intelligence, sense of beauty, and moral sense, he is not indulging a sadistic impulse but is solemnizing, in a most impressive way, the supreme virtue of blind obedience. All mass movements rank obedience with the highest virtues and put it on a level with faith: "union of minds requires not only a perfect accord in the One Faith, but complete submission and obedience of will to the Church and the Roman Pontiff as to God Himself." Obedience is not only the first law of God, but also the first tenet of a revolutionary party and of fervent nationalism. "Not to reason why" is considered by all mass movements the mark of a strong and generous spirit. [*Ibid.,* p. 115]

Some members of society probably have needs to lose themselves in a movement no matter what the circumstances. More importantly, all of us have such needs latently within us, but they become pre-potent only under certain conditions such as disillusionment with existing values or at the time of some kind of crisis. Hoffer (p. 138) feels that in the early stages of a revolution it is up to the "men of words" to stimulate such needs into prepotency by denigrating the existing social order and "creating a hunger for faith." A crisis situation can have similar effects:

The unavoidable conclusion seems to be that when the individual faces torture or annihilation, he cannot rely on the resources of his own individuality. His only source of strength is in not being himself but part of something mighty, glorious, and indestructible. Faith here is primarily a process of identification; the process by which the individual ceases to be himself and becomes part of something eternal. Faith in humanity, in posterity, in the destiny of one's religion, nation, race, party or family—what is it but the visualization of that eternal something to which we attach the self that is about to be annihilated? [Hoffer, 1951, p. 63]

It has also been observed that under the stress of crisis the individual tends increasingly to perceive and judge in terms of blacks and whites and to be increasingly unable to see the nuances of gray, a condition which, of course, makes black and white kinds of ideologies like Marxism-Leninism particularly effective. We need not document here the specific appeals of this ideology. Suffice it to say that it offers to remove the frustrations of most of those members of society who have visible external frustrations. The Communists add another dimension to the problem by providing both the disease and the cure, as Lifton has remarked in discussing the leniency phase of thought reform (Lifton, 1956b). If things are bad at home it is because of the American aggressors. How does one deal with the American aggressors? By reaffirming the faith and supporting Communism and, parenthetically, sacrificing a little bit more for the regime!

In addition to personality factors which are to a degree universal, and factors which relate to the nature of crisis or disillusionment, we must add, of course, the personal features deriving from national character or particular cultural themes. Such cultural themes have been noted both for China and Russia—the striving for complete harmony in Chinese culture, the yearning of the individual to become mystically merged with the group in the old Russia as painted by Dostoievski and a number of students of national character. It is beyond the scope of this chapter to give a detailed analysis of such themes as they apply to Russia and China. Suffice it to say that some observers are struck by the continuity between pre- and post-take-over Chinese culture. For example, Guillain writes:

The Communist system found one of its luckiest breaks in the very good will of the Chinese. It was able to transform their great enthusiasm for the public good into an immense submission. *It is an absurd illusion to think that the great majority of the Chinese have secretly and obstinately renounced the system and, in their hearts, are in perpetual revolt against the regime. It would be far nearer the truth to say that by and large the system has been accepted by the masses.* They have allowed themselves to be guided from the paths of rebellion to those of obedience. . . .

. . . The man of the people in China has never known political or economic liberty. He has always been *passive*. If at times he has violently rebelled against tyranny he has, above all, grown used to constant oppression and from time immemorial has tended to *rally to established authority*. . . .

. . . *We must not forget that to copy and act as the next man is a four-thousand-years-old tradition in China.* If you were a potter you plied your trade as your father and your grandfather did before you. If, on occasion, a genius produced something novel, this creator was immediately followed by a line of imitators. China is still under the weight of this tradition when the generation of great revolutionaries is followed by millions of small conformists. [Guillain, 1957, pp. 273–74]

. . . past centuries have endowed the Chinese with *infinite flexibility* and great *opportunism*. Ideology has too long been overshadowed in his case by the need to think of his bowl of rice. To obtain this, he has too often had to profess the ideas of his master, and to change his ideas when he changed masters. He is not the only man in Asia to follow this pattern of behavior. I have witnessed within a few years two incredible, truly historic reversals in Asian countries: the change of Japan toward the Americans after the capitulation of 1945, and that of China toward the Communists after the liberation of 1949. [*Ibid.*, p. 275]

A final point which should be noted about the followers in the movement is that the Communists have instilled in many members of the "New China" a true missionary zeal based on a mixture of nationalism, youthful exuberance, and genuine hostility toward Western exploitation. The recognition among the populace that China is becoming an important world power and that, to a degree, this status is a Communist accomplishment is one important theme in building nationalism, no doubt strongly reinforced by the successful stalemating of the Korean War. The regime's strong reliance on youth who can be counted on to fight against old burdening traditions with the enthusiasm of adolescent revolt is important in setting an example for the entire nation. Finally, the regime's fanning of anti-Western feeling is no doubt strongly stimulating the desire on the part of the Chinese to prove that the Asian way can also prove successful.

Thus unanimity can serve important functions for the follower as well as for the system as a whole or the leader, and it may not be as difficult to achieve complete unanimity under certain conditions as some aspects of our discussion have implied. When most of our detailed knowledge of the system comes from defectors who have not been able to make their peace with it, we are dealing with a strongly biased sample, and risk missing members of an army of cheerful and enthusiastic "true believers" (in Hoffer's sense) who take their place in the totalitarian system secure in the knowledge that they are part of something bigger than themselves.*

* Studies of the motivation of defectors usually show a variety of motives for initially joining the movement. Whiting (1955), in his study of Chinese Communist soldiers who refused repatriation after the Korean War, found (1) willingness to follow any authority which promised something better for China, (2) protest against the old way of life, and (3) sheer opportunism to be the major motives in that order of importance. Kracauer & Berkman (1955) report that Hungarian refugees see the following kinds of Communists as existing in

Hungary: (1) real or convinced Communists; (2) opportunists; (3) those who joined in order to keep their jobs and status; (4) those who joined because they were threatened with arrest, withdrawal of ration card, or some other penalty if they did not; and (5) disillusioned Communists who started out as idealists, became disaffected, but then could not get out of the party.

PART TWO *Coercive Persuasion:*

Its Structure, Effects, and

Determinants

THE ACTUAL experiences of prisoners arrested by the Chinese Communists varied widely. They varied according to the purposes of the arrest, according to the general political climate at the time of arrest, according to the available facilities and personnel in the particular area of China where the arrest took place, and according to the attitude of the prisoner. In describing these experiences, it is tempting to ignore the variations and seek the common themes on the assumption that the CCP was able to exert effective and centralized control over all of its operations. Indeed, many of the analyses of coercive persuasion or thought reform which have previously been published (e.g. Hunter, 1951; Lifton, 1956a, b; Hinkle and Wolff, 1956) have organized their material in terms of the explicit assumption of a common core of prison methodology. Our own early efforts were also oriented in this direction, but a close analysis of the cases forced us increasingly to the recognition that the variations in prison experiences and in pre-prison circumstances were as important for understanding the ultimate outcome (in terms of influence accomplished) as the common themes. Furthermore, one could not limit a description of experiences to those events which occurred in prison. A number of pre- and post-imprisonment experiences were crucial. To avoid theoretical prejudgment of which were the important experiences we constructed the following general outline:

111

A. Pre-imprisonment Experiences.
   1. S's General Situation in China.
      a. Motives for being in China and circumstances surrounding the decision to remain there.
      b. Occupation and activities in China.
      c. Length of time in China prior to imprisonment.
      d. Identification with the Chinese, degree of integration into China.
      e. Political sophistication of S, attitudes toward KMT and Communism.
   2. Perception of the Take-over
      a. Type of information to which S became exposed.
         (1) Reading and listening to reports of others.
         (2) Witnessing the liberation in a rural or urban area.
         (3) Length of exposure, e.g., exposure only to initial victory parades, demonstrations, etc., vs. exposure to gradual process of establishment of CCP policies and practices.
      b. Attitudes of others around S, both Chinese and Westerners.
      c. Perception of own situation vis-à-vis the CCP: does S see himself as being a friend, enemy, or neutral party and how does he think the CCP will view him?
      d. Type of CCP activity witnessed.
         (1) Honeymoon period activities.
         (2) Land reform.
         (3) Aspects of the terror: People's Courts, accusation meetings, expropriation of mission properties, etc.
   3. Situational Factors
      a. Geographical location in China.
      b. Nature of political situation in general and in that area in particular.
      c. Type and quality of CCP personnel operating in that area.
      d. Facilities available for imprisonment and reform.
      e. Attitudes of local populace toward S and toward the CCP.
      f. S's personal feelings: e.g., fear of arrest, confidence in self, etc.
   4. S's Personality: Specific Vulnerabilities or Strengths

B. Experience of Imprisonment
  1. Circumstances Surrounding the Arrest
  2. Type of Imprisonment
     a. House arrest.
     b. Detention prison.
     c. Regular civil prison.
  3. Nature of Prison Facilities and Prison Personnel
  4. Initial Contact with Judge or Interrogator
     a. Type and intensity of feeling stimulated in S.
     b. Manner of presentation of S's situation.
        (1) Description of "lenient policy."
        (2) Nature of accusation, if any.
        (3) Sincerity and skill of judge or interrogator.
        (4) Types of threats and physical pressures.
  5. Type of Cell
     a. Physical properties.
     b. Number of cellmates.
     c. Type of cellmates and their attitudes toward S.
        (1) Type of crime committed by them.
        (2) Degree to which they are reformed and committed to reforming S.
        (3) Similarity of cellmates to S in terms of occupation, "cultural" level, experiences with CCP, aspirations for future, etc.
        (4) Chinese vs. Westerner.
  6. Daily Regimen or Routine
     a. Bodily need management.
        (1) Food and drink.
        (2) Sleep.
        (3) Elimination.
        (4) Exercise.
        (5) Heat, cold, and light.
        (6) Washing and hygiene.
        (7) Medical care.
        (8) Sex.
        (9) Tobacco and other habits.
        (10) Pain.

      (11) Clothing and possessions.

      (12) Level and type of sensory input.

  b. Daily routine.

      (1) Distribution and timing of activities.

      (2) Prescriptions and proscriptions about use of time and space.

      (3) Degree of organization and integration of activities around stated prison objectives.

      (4) Type of work expected and demanded of prisoner.

  c. Degree and type of contact with others and with communication channels.

      (1) Prison authorities

         (a) Amount of contact.

         (b) Rules concerning contacts: degree of deference and type of demeanor required.

         (c) Ease or difficulty of communication.

      (2) Fellow prisoners.

         (a) Number of other prisoners with whom contact is allowed.

         (b) Type of contact allowed or demanded.

         (c) Ease or difficulty of communication.

      (3) Outsiders.

         (a) Formal channels of communication with outside.

            1—newspapers, radio, bulletin boards, loudspeakers, movies.

            2—mail.

            3—word of mouth.

         (b) Clandestine communication with outside.

         (c) Type of information contained.

  7. Discipline—Rewards and Punishments Utilized.

  8. Activities Pertaining to Goals of the Prison: Confession and Reform.

  a. Interrogation—confession extraction.

  b. Struggle—*tou cheng* in the cell.

  c. Study.

      (1) Autobiography: repeated writing.

(2) Diary writing.

(3) Group activity: *tou cheng,* study groups.

(4) Mutual and self criticism.

(5) Mutual surveillance and reporting to authorities.

(6) Emulation campaigns—competing among prisoners.

(7) Reading and discussion of Communist materials— rationalizing conclusions.

(8) Airing of grievances.

(9) Behavioral commitment through forced self-degradation, denunciation of others.

(10) Politicizing of all activities no matter how trivial.

(11) Reform through labor.

(12) Observation of other activities—People's Courts, etc.

(13) Promulgation of certain norms of conduct and certain points of view—the People's standpoint, abandonment of self-concerns, etc.

C. Post-imprisonment Experiences.

1. Nature of Initial Contacts with Non-Communist World.

2. Degree to Which Predictions Made by Communists Come True, or Degree of Confirmation of What Was Learned in Prison about Self and Others.

3. Type and Intensity of Emotional Relationships Which Develop in the New Environment.

4. Degree of Social Support Available for Point of View Learned in Prison.

5. Activities of U.S. and Communist China in the World Arena.

This outline is intended to include all possible variables which might be important for an understanding of coercive persuasion and to serve as a frame of reference for our subsequent analysis. In Chapter 4 a socio-psychological model of the process of coercive persuasion is presented. This model emphasizes the stages in the process of being influenced and attempts to show the relevance of the prisoners' experiences to these different stages. Chapter 5 explores one particular facet of the coercive persuasion process— the role of guilt—in somewhat greater detail because of its central importance. Chapter 6 describes the outcomes of coercive persuasion in terms of the degree and type of influence accomplished by the process, and Chapter 7 attempts to select and illustrate from the broad outline of prisoner experiences those which can be thought of as determinants of influence or resistance to influence.

4

A Socio-psychological Model for the Analysis of Coercive Persuasion

THE CONSTRUCTION of a model for the analysis of coercive persuasion has three basic purposes: to provide a theoretical structure which will permit the organization of the many and varied prisoner experiences into meaningful categories; to provide theoretical categories which will make it possible to understand the coercive persuasion process and its effects psychologically; and to provide some basic categories for a more general theory of social influence, which will permit a systematic comparison of coercive persuasion with other kinds of influence processes.

The model we have chosen to fulfill these purposes derives from Kurt Lewin (1947) and was originally designed to analyze change processes in groups or organizations. It is particularly applicable to the analysis of influence because the kinds of resistances to change which Lewin and his collaborators observed in groups and organizations have their counterparts in the individual if an attempt is made to influence his beliefs, attitudes, or values. In fact, it is a basic assumption of the model that the beliefs, attitudes, values, and behavior patterns of an individual tend to be integrated with each other and tend to be organized around the person's self-image or self-concept. This integration, even if imperfect, gives continuity and stability to the person and hence operates as a force against being influenced, unless the change which the influence implies is seen to be a change in the direction of greater integration.

A second assumption of the model is that the integration described above is not a static but a dynamic equilibrium which results from the interaction of a great many forces that are continuously acting on the individual. What we mean by "forces" is all those external or internal events which the person perceives at a conscious or semi-conscious level as pulling or pushing him in some direction: needs, motives, desires, impulses, restraints, demands, questions, orders, temptations, goals, etc. For present purposes it is not important to distinguish carefully between different classes of forces, though in principle one should distinguish, for example, between internal forces (needs and motives) and external forces (requests, etc., coming from others).

Individually the forces acting on a person change constantly, but in the usual situation of everyday life the variations are either too small to affect the equilibrium or the person uses compensatory mechanisms to preserve his stability. The need to maintain a consistent self-image and the need to reduce uncertainty in one's environment are, of course, additional forces toward stability which operate once any equilibrium level has been reached.

We can illustrate what we have said thus far by taking as a hypothetical example a person holding the belief that "in order to survive in this world one must always think first of oneself." Our model would hold that this belief can be thought of as a dynamic equilibrium between one set of forces which push toward holding it and another set of forces which push against holding it. Examples of the former might be: desire to be like one's father who held this belief, desire to identify with a group in which such a belief is the norm, pressure from a boss to be more self-seeking, past successes with selfishness and failures with generosity, desire to see oneself as tough, fear of being taken advantage of by others, and so on. Examples of the latter might be: fear of retaliation by others for one's selfishness, desire to be loved more, desires not to have to fight all the time, pressure from friends to be more generous, successes with generosity and failures with selfishness, guilt for hurting others, and so on.

As was stated above, the individual forces vary all the time, but the integration of the belief into the self-image, the general desire not to change and thereby increase uncertainty, and the individual's capacity to compensate (for example by rationalizing that the success of others who are generous really is luck, or the related belief that people will love one more if one is really tough and self-seeking) can and do operate to preserve the equilibrium where it is.

If one conceives of beliefs, attitudes, values, and behavior patterns as dynamic equilibria which tend to remain stable, it follows that one cannot influence the person unless one alters the balance of forces sufficiently to prevent compensation and thus forces a change in the equilibrium (a change in intensity of a belief, or its abandonment, or reinterpretation, etc.). If one thinks of the person's stability (his resistance to influence) as the result of an interaction of many forces, it follows that the strategy of influencing him can be manifold—altering the strength or direction of various forces on either side of the equilibrium. The utility of this model derives in part from this point—it focuses attention on the many forces which underlie beliefs, etc., and therefore on the manifold strategies which the agent of influence can and usually does apply. It thus serves to steer us away from oversimplified explanations of the influence process.

A second important feature of the model is that it suggests that the process of change or influence occurs over time and consists of several successive stages or steps. These stages can be labeled *unfreezing, changing,* and *refreezing,* and can be defined as follows:

UNFREEZING. An alteration by the agent of influence of the forces acting on the person such that the existing equilibrium is no longer stable. Subjectively one can think of this as the induction of a need or a motive to change; i.e., the person who has been unfrozen with respect to some belief desires to change or abandon that belief.

CHANGING. The provision by the agent of influence of information, arguments, models to be imitated or identified with, etc., which provide a direction of change toward a new equilibrium, usually by allowing the person to learn something new, redefine something old, re-evaluate or reintegrate other parts of his personality or belief system, etc. Subjectively this would be experiences as "seeing the light," having insight, seeing that the other fellow's viewpoint has a lot of merit, beginning to understand how someone else thinks about things, and so on.

REFREEZING. The facilitation by the agent of influence of the reintegration of the new equilibrium into the rest of the personality and into ongoing interpersonal relationships by the provision of reward and social support for any changes made by the person. Sometimes, however, it is not within the agent's power to determine whether the new belief will in fact fit into the rest of the personality or will be accepted by the person's significant others.* Subjectively this would be experienced as discovering that others shared one's new point of view, that they were pleased with the change, that the new belief was quite congenial with other parts of the self-image and other beliefs, etc.

Given that the goal of coercive persuasion is to produce a change in the prisoner's beliefs and attitudes about himself and the Communists, and that a key step toward this outcome is the making of a sincere confession based on a feeling of guilt, we can now consider the experiences of the prisoner in the context of the model.

UNFREEZING

Before a prisoner could confess in the manner desired of him by the Communists and before he could change his beliefs and attitudes about himself and the Communists, several sets of stable equilibria had to be unfrozen. One of the central ones was simply the unwillingness on the part of the prisoner to confess to something which was not true. The kinds of forces which were acting on the prisoner with respect to this unwillingness in a well-run reform prison are exemplified in Table 1. We are not implying that each

---

* By significant others we mean all those individuals with whom a person has a close enough emotional relationship to care deeply what they think of him, and whose opinions about himself he will therefore respect and attempt to live by.

prisoner had acting on him all the forces listed or that this force field exhausts all the varieties of forces which might have played a role. What we are implying is that the act of confessing was a function of the relative strengths of those forces which were in effect and of the manner in which the prison experiences tended to strengthen or weaken them.

TABLE 1

FORCES ACTING ON THE PRISONER IN REGARD TO HIS UNWILLINGNESS TO CONFESS

Toward Confessing	Against Confessing
Fear for self or others	Fear of violating one's own values
Desire to comply to another	Fear of behaving inconsistently with self-image
Desire to relieve pressure from cellmates	Fear of loss of integrity (giving in)
Desire to relieve pain	Inability to be intellectually dishonest
Desire to achieve relationship with cellmates	Fear of violating reference group norms
Need to rationalize anxiety resulting from unconscious guilt	Fear of future consequences
Desire to adapt, to achieve a sense of reality	Fear of being punished for untruth by authorities and cellmates
Desire to "settle case" and be released	Unwillingness to be coerced
Need to attach felt guilt to concrete behavior	
Others	Others

Unfreezing in this context then refers to those experiences or events which tended to strengthen forces toward confession and weaken forces against confession. For example, if the cellmates, interrogators, or judges (the *agents* of influence) increased their pressure on the prisoner to confess, the likelihood of confession was increased unless this pressure also strengthened a counter-force, such as unwillingness to be coerced or the fear of loss of integrity.

Or, if the cellmates offered the prisoner a convincing argument as to why confession would not be intellectually dishonest nor involve a loss of integrity they would also increase the likelihood of confession, unless they at the same time weakened one of the forces toward confession.

It should be noted that the more forces there are on each side and the more intensely these forces are brought to bear in the struggle between the prisoner and the agents, the greater will be the likelihood of confession. This is the case simply because of the exhaustion resulting from the continuing inner conflict in the prisoner (this exhaustion encourages confession by increasing the desire to relieve pain). In other words, the continuing inner conflict operates along with sleep deprivation and other physically exhausting devices to motivate the prisoner to accept the only solution permitted—confession. Psychologically the only other solution possible is to convert the situation into one permitting an "escape from the field." The prisoner may become psychotic or develop psychotic-like defenses; i.e., he may imagine that his impulse to confess is telepathically introduced into him by the authorities and therefore must be doubly intensively resisted, or he may become impervious to the accusations and humiliations imposed by the cellmates by psychologically not hearing them.

Confession was a behavioral commitment which was initially out of line with the prisoner's values or his image of himself, but the attitude change of the type which was demanded in thought reform was tantamount to a change in this very image of self. Such attitude change involved a more fundamental kind of unfreezing in that the person's perceptions of and attitudes toward himself are typically more stably organized and more widely integrated into the personality than other kinds of attitudes. One would expect even more resistance on the part of the prisoner, therefore, with respect to changing such attitudes than with respect to confessing. The kinds of forces which were acting on the prisoner with respect to this unwillingness are exemplified in Table 2.

Both those forces which preceded confession and those which succeeded confession are included because attitude change often began before confession and continued after it. In principle the psychological processes leading to a confession and the ones leading to attitude change are independent and can occur together or apart. In most of the actual cases known to us, the two processes were closely tied together, however; confession facilitated attitude change and vice versa; successful resistance to one often meant successful resistance to the other (though by no means always).

TABLE 2

FORCES ACTING ON THE PRISONER IN REGARD TO HIS UNWILLINGNESS
TO CHANGE HIS ATTITUDES

Toward Change	Against Change
Need to rationalize behavior (if confession or some other concession has been made)	Need to maintain integration of attitudes into total personality
Need to find justification for confessing (if confession has not been made but force toward it is great)	Need to maintain integration of attitudes into interpersonal relationships
Need to establish communication with cellmates and to relieve pressure from them	Unacceptability of new attitudes to values or principles held by the person
Need to handle anxiety and guilt	Unacceptability of new attitudes to other parts of person, or to significant others in the environment
Desire not to appear different	Need to assert self by resisting intrusion attempts by others
Need to have a viable self-image (identity)	Fear of loss of identity
Desire to adapt to inputs— achieve a sense of reality	
Others	Others

Again, it can be seen that the induction of a motive to change could involve a strengthening of forces toward change (e.g., getting the prisoner to denounce a close friend which set up strong needs to rationalize his behavior; humiliating the prisoner in public to destroy his image of himself, thus heightening his need for a new identity, etc.), or a weakening of forces against change (e.g., making certain significant emotional relationships inoperative by cutting or manipulating communication channels with the outside; showing the prisoner that the new attitudes are not, in fact, incompatible with his values or other parts of the personality by intensive discussion and the encouragement of self-analysis on his part, etc.), or both.

The personal characteristics of the prisoner enter into this model in determining which forces will be present and their size or strength. For example, the poorly integrated individual did not have as much initial resistance to redefining the self as the well-integrated one; the individual who was strongly integrated into a cause (i.e., had strong emotional attachments to others, actual or symbolic) was more resistant to attempts to undermine such relationships; the person who was prone to anxiety and guilt was more susceptible because of his need to justify such feelings to himself once they were stimulated; and so on. The actual experiences in prison tended not only to create new forces but also to strengthen or to weaken forces which were already present in the prisoner.

Tables 1 and 2 are intended to exemplify the nature of the unfreezing process to which the prisoner was exposed. They are not systematic or exhaustive, however, with respect to the actual forces which were present in the total prison milieu, nor do they cover the various levels of resistance which the prisoner exhibited. Table 3 attempts to provide a more exhaustive survey, listing in the left column the key forces which operated as resistance to change (either confession or attitude change), and in the right column the various experiences which operated as forces toward change. To the extent that the forces or experiences on the right hand side were too powerful to be compensated for, the prisoner was unfrozen, i.e., developed a need to confess and/or change his attitudes. The table does not list those personal factors in a prisoner which would lead to the interpretation that he was already unfrozen at the time of his imprisonment; rather, the table applies to those prisoners who entered prison with an attitude of resistance.

The predominant emphasis in the well-run prison was on those techniques which tended to undermine the individual's social and emotional supports (Sections 3, 4, and 5 of Table 3). Those parts

TABLE 3

ASPECTS OF IMPRISONMENT WHICH TENDED TO
UNFREEZE THE PRISONER

Type of Support Undermined or Type of Resistance Force	*Imprisonment Experiences Operating as Unfreezing Forces*
1. Desire to Resist Communists; initial attitude of non-co-operation	Communist control of information, prevention of unfavorable information about the CCP from reaching S
	Exposure to other Chinese or Westerners who were pro-Communist
	Exemplary behavior of Red Army and the appeal of their sincere, enthusiastic, positive solidarity
	Convincingness of interrogator's threats and statements of "lenient policy"
2. Physical strength	Strangeness and general inadequacy of diet in prison
	Loss of sleep due to intermittent and continuous interrogation or cellmate pressure
	Diseases like dysentery resulting from diet
	Lack of exercise
	Excessive cold in combination with inadequate clothing
	Physical pain induced by prolonged standing or squatting in cell or during interrogation
	Physical pain and injury due to wearing of manacles and chains
	Physical pain due to prevention by authorities of defecation except at two 2-minute intervals during the day
	Requirement that prisoner not shift position in cell except by permission of guard
	Cuffing and beating by cellmates, occasionally by interrogator

TABLE 3 (*continued*)

Type of Support Undermined or Type of Resistance Force	Imprisonment Experiences Operating as Unfreezing Forces
3. Social-emotional and cognitive support; validation of beliefs, attitudes, and values by appropriate information input regarding the feelings and beliefs of significant others, reference groups, prestige sources, etc.	Control of information, only pro-Communist mass media allowed Continuous repetition of one line, one type of information input Control of mail, either withheld completely or unfavorable mail only passed on No personal contact whatever with outsiders No close relationships permitted with anyone except in the context of reform; even clandestine communication with cellmates prohibited in some circumstances Introduction of testimonials by others in the form of confessions, etc., lauding the virtues of reform and the CCP Continuous and unanimous condemnation of groups with which S identifies or of values to which he adheres Creation of mutual distrust among cellmates by presence of informers Solitary confinement
4. Self-image, sense of identity, sense of integrity and inviolability	Humiliation, revilement, and brutalization by cellmates as part of "struggle" Complete prescription of use of time and space in prison in the direction of making prisoner feel completely dependent on authorities Identification of prisoner by number only Prohibition of any decision-making; every act no matter how trivial must be preceded by obtaining guard's permission

Type of Support Undermined or Type of Resistance Force	Imprisonment Experiences Operating as Unfreezing Forces
	Unanimous perception of S as reactionary and criminal; denial of professional or other roles
	Manacling and chaining S, making him dependent on cellmates for basic bodily need management or making him manage at a sub-human level—enforced self-derogation
	Seducing or forcing S into making concessions which arouse guilt, e.g., false confessions, denunciations, etc.
	Social-emotional rejection of S by cellmates
	Prevention of personal hygiene, demeaning punishments, insults and taunts
	Denial of even a moment of privacy —continuous scrutiny by cellmates or guards
5. Basic personality integration, intra-psychic defense mechanisms, basic values, super-ego	*Threats* of death, of non-repatriation, of endless isolation and interrogation, of torture and physical injury, of injury to family and loved ones—induction of *anxiety* and *despair*
	Rewards and indulgences used to tantalize and confuse (not typical, see Ch. 7)
	Failure by cellmates and authorities to accept as valid S's own values and morals, or failure to accept S's behavior as being consistent with his professed values and morals—induction of *guilt*
	Continual criticism and rejection of S by cellmates
	Continual projection of image that Communists are operating according to higher moral and ethical principles than S

TABLE 3 (continued)

Type of Support Undermined or Type of Resistance Force	Imprisonment Experiences Operating as Unfreezing Forces
	Induced and enforced self-analysis by requirements to write autobiography, engage in self-criticism, write diary, reflect and meditate, etc.
	Recognition by S that some cellmates are good people who are sincerely trying to reform themselves—*guilt* for feeling hostile toward them
	Recognition by S of his own class attitudes and prejudices—*guilt* for feeling superior or for sense of failing in accepted role in China
	Stimulation of unconscious guilt by enforced state of dependency, re-creation of childhood conflicts
	Chronic failure on the part of S to be able to live up to the avowed norms of the cell pertaining especially to basic bodily need management; e.g., taking up too much room while sleeping is given political significance and considered a symptom of a bad attitude on the part of S—*guilt*
	Constant accusation and exhortation to confess
	Self-analysis induced by need to find solution

of the prison regimen which tended to be physically debilitating were not as crucial to the unfreezing of existing attitudes as one might suppose and were not emphasized by the authorities. The aim of the authorities was not to reduce the prisoner *physically* to a nonentity. The aim was rather to reduce him *psychologically* to a nonentity, a procedure which was justified by the assumption that his existing identity was a reactionary and useless one from the Communist point of view. However, the identity components of the personality are not the whole personality; hence, the destruction of identity is not equivalent to making a person psychotic. In fact, the authorities were generally very careful to ease the pressures on anyone who seemed to be in danger of becoming psychotic, because they seemed to want genuine reform. Both cellmates and authorities were always careful to justify their harsh psychological approach by saying explicitly, or at least implying, that they were only attacking the prisoner's "reactionary self" not his whole person; they were exorcising the devils within him and expected him to co-operate in this process. The irony of it was, of course, that the prisoner could not co-operate initially because he could not recognize in himself what the others saw as the devils in him.

CHANGING

Once the prisoner was unfrozen with respect to some of his beliefs, attitudes, values, and behavior patterns, he was ready to change in order to re-establish an equilibrium, but he did not necessarily know in what direction to change. If the influence agent did not provide any guidance, the prisoner had to search for a solution by himself; if the agent provided information or models to be imitated, the prisoner could use these as guides for altering his beliefs. The mental process which was involved in locating a direction of change and actually making a change in the unfrozen attitude is what we have labeled in our model the step of *changing*.

Unfreezing can be thought of as being primarily a matter of what happened to the needs and motives of the prisoner as a result of the agent's interventions. The process of *changing* was concerned more with *cognitive* processes in the prisoner. Once he was willing to confess, he had to have information which told him what confession meant and what he was to confess to; once he was ready to re-examine his beliefs and attitudes he had to have information concerning alternative beliefs and attitudes which were available.

The kind of information source to which the prisoner began to pay attention of course varied with the nature of his unfreezing experiences and the kind of motive to change which had been stimulated. For example, the prisoner who became motivated to confess because he no longer feared future consequences (by becoming convinced that a false confession could later be repudiated and could not hurt the United States anyway) would then orient himself primarily to his interrogator and attempt to learn from him just what he was to confess to. On the other hand, the prisoner who became motivated to confess because he saw confession as the only way to re-establish a sense of identity and a relationship with his cellmates would attempt to re-examine his own past in a manner seen to be acceptable by the cellmates and adopt their point of view.

In the well-run reform prison the prisoner was usually in a severe dilemma because he was pressured and exhorted to confess and change his attitudes without however being able to discover information which led reliably to a diminution of this pressure. Usually a false confession was condemned by cellmates and interrogators alike; attempts to use the ubiquitous Communist propaganda were likely to fail because mostly it did not make sense or was seen as patently false by the prisoner. His basic problem then was to find some credible information source which, if used as a guide, would lead to an acceptable confession and attitude changes in line with the agent's demands.

The information sources available were the controlled mass media, the interrogator and/or judge, the cellmates, and the prisoner himself. With respect to the mass media we have already indicated that the prisoner usually could not see them as credible, though some prisoners attempted to obtain usable information by "reading between the lines" or learning some of the Communist jargon. If the prisoner was strongly motivated to make an acceptable yet false confession, he would attempt to use such information to determine what he could safely confess to, and would use jargon to make the confession sound more convincing. Only if there had already been some attitude change could the prisoner see the Communist mass media as reliable and understand them sufficiently to help himself in further analyzing his own case.

The most significant source of information, by contrast, was the prisoner's set of cellmates, usually a group of Chinese prisoners who had already made acceptable confessions and were themselves on the way to successful reform. These cellmates had the mission of convincing the Western prisoner of his guilt and the progress of the entire cell was contingent on their success. In Table 3 we indicated the many kinds of pressure they brought to bear on the recalcitrant prisoner. We wish to focus now on the relationship which developed between one or more of them and the Western prisoner once the unfreezing process was well under way.

The cellmates as sources of information assumed especial importance because the prisoner had usually been deprived of all other personal sources who could confirm his basic sense of identity. If the unfreezing experiences had undermined or destroyed the prisoner's self-image and basic sense of identity (as was often the case), he found himself with a fundamental psychological problem to solve—namely the re-establishment of a viable self.* In other words, the unfreezing process could precipitate or exacerbate an "identity crisis" (Erikson, 1956). The establishment of an identity then involved finding new beliefs and attitudes about the self which would be reinforced and confirmed by others. If the prisoner was in an environment in which the only reinforcements available were contingent upon his accepting a particular set of beliefs and attitudes about himself, it was likely that he would eventually accept such beliefs and attitudes.

By what cognitive mechanism does such acceptance come about? The descriptions given by the prisoners suggest that the process is best characterized as one of a growing *identification* with cellmates (and/or interrogators, or judges). This process psychologically transforms these individuals into highly credible information sources. Sequentially the process can be described in terms of the following steps:

1. Precipitation or exacerbation of an "identity crisis" as a result of an intensive unfreezing process.

2. The induction of a motive to find acceptable beliefs about the self in an environment in which the number of such acceptable be-

* We are assuming that any person needs a viable social self and if systematically deprived of a given social self will be strongly motivated to find another one (Schein, 1960).

liefs is sharply limited.

3. A search for information relevant to finding acceptable beliefs about the self.

4. The finding of an "other" whose identity is acceptable (whose beliefs about himself are accepted as correct by other prisoners, interrogators, etc.).

5. Identification with this "other," even if he was initially defined as an enemy.

6. The acceptance of things this "other" says and does as credible information about the prisoner's own self.

This process of coming to identify with another prisoner or one of the authorities was often aided by the "discovery" that the "other" was in many respects similar to the prisoner. He may have pursued the same occupation prior to imprisonment, or may have had similar experiences with the Communists, or may have been intellectually and culturally similar to the prisoner, or may have represented a social type about which the prisoner had always been ambivalent (e.g., a lower-class person vis-à-vis a prisoner whose own middle-class status rested on situational factors about which he had felt unconsciously guilty).

Once an identification process was begun and the behavior of the "other" began to be treated as credible information, the foundation was laid for extensive *cognitive re-definition* in the prisoner. The basic process in such redefinition was the learning of *new standards* for judging behavior and a *new set of semantic rules,* i.e., the adoption of a new frame of reference, commonly called "the people's standpoint."

Once the prisoner began to *listen* to his cellmates or to the authorities, in the sense of genuinely trying to understand their viewpoint, he began to see how his own past behavior and his past and present attitudes were "wrong." And once he began to understand this, he could suddenly see and understand what it was he was expected to confess to, and what attitudes he was expected to change. From merely having a strong motive to find a solution to all his problems he moved to a stage of actually seeing a solution, one which was apparently acceptable to the authorities and the cellmates.* He received extensive "help" in this redefining process by the examples of his cellmates, by their criticism of him, and by their continued espousal of the "correct attitude."

Thus far we have been analyzing the rather extensive changes occurring in prisoners in whom identity crises were created. For others, whose identity remained more intact, the cellmates or authorities also assumed importance as sources of information, particularly if they represented a completely unanimous social environment. Unanimity of outlook in terms of premises completely different from the prisoner's led inevitably to some shifting of the prisoner's own standards of judgment and frame of reference.† Such shifts would occur especially in entirely new situations in which it was completely unclear to the prisoner what standards of evaluation or judgment should apply. The main difference between this type of shift in frame of reference and the type described in connection with identity crisis lies in the object of evaluation. In the case of problems of identity, the object of evaluation was the self; if the prisoner re-evaluated the self this would produce a wide range of behavioral changes. In the present instance, the object of evaluation would more likely be an isolated event, item of behavior, or specific situation, and a re-evaluation of it would probably not be generalized very widely. For example, a prisoner might become convinced, because of the unanimity of his social environment, that the Communist approach to penal problems was very progressive (in comparison to what China had before), yet this might in no way influence his general attitude toward the CCP or his attitudes toward himself. The only way in which a prisoner could protect himself against the effects of unanimity was to discount completely *all* information sources, but this was difficult to do (short of relying on a psychotic defense mechanism) if the cellmates really were intent on getting the prisoner to confess and to change.

Those aspects of the imprisonment experience which pertained most directly to the process of changing are described in Table 4.

* Lifton (1956b) aptly terms this transition a "psychological unplugging of the environment."

† Experimental work by Helson, 1948, Schein, 1949, Asch, 1952 and others has demonstrated this type of influence effect, particularly in situations in which there is ambiguity about the task or the standards of judgment.

TABLE 4

ASPECTS OF THE IMPRISONMENT EXPERIENCE RELATING TO CHANGING

Aspects pertaining to information provided by the mass media

Type and quality of mass media available in terms of S's predispositions, e.g., his need for and dependence on newspapers, their intellectual level in comparison to a level which S respects and pays attention to, their idiom in terms of whether S could comprehend the message or not, etc.

Content of mass media in terms of S's perception of it as credible or not, e.g., internal consistency and logic, manifestness of propaganda aims, etc.

Sources to which content was attributed in terms of S's perception of them as credible or not, e.g., use of testimonials or confessions by members of S's reference groups (germ warfare confessions, for example, reprinted in entirety, or movies of the confessors), use of "impartial" observers like the International Commission which investigated the germ warfare charges, statements by Western observers, etc.

(We cannot draw definite conclusions about any of the above points because we have no clear evidence of any prison policy other than previously mentioned restrictions on non-Communist media. Whether any of the mass media affected the prisoner positively or negatively in terms of the above points seemed to depend more on the prisoner and his orientation toward mass media than on specific events which occurred within prison.)

Aspects pertaining to information provided by cellmates

Among a number of cellmates it was likely that S could find someone with whom he could identify.

The presence of several cellmates made possible the observation of their interaction and their relationships as a model of how S was expected to behave in reference to others.

The presence of several others who were all unanimous provided information of high potency by virtue of its unanimity.

The presence of others with whom S was living in very close contact made possible a coaching or tutoring relationship in which rapid feedback could be obtained by S concerning any provisional behavior he might engage in.

Living in enforced close contact with others made it likely that strong feelings (anxiety, guilt, dependency, and hostility) would be stimulated which would heighten the likelihood of an identification occurring, either defensively to avoid deeper conflict or as an aspect of growth and the solution of identity problems.

The presence of several cellmates increased the likelihood of there being among them at least one who would be able to "see through" and consequently expose any defensive maneuvers on the part of S to avoid taking them seriously.

Aspects pertaining to information provided by interrogator and/or judge

The interrogator was often the only person in the prison with whom S could identify because of his being the only one capable of fulfilling S's intellectual needs (i.e., to discuss his case rationally and unemotionally—this would pertain to S's who dealt with emotional problems by intellectualizing them).

The interrogator was often the only person with whom S could identify because he was the only one who was similar to S culturally and intellectually.

The interrogator was usually the person who was seen as responsible for many of the events which made S dependent and afraid, and hence the only one who could produce changes in S's condition; this circumstance heightened the probability of "identification with the aggressor" as a defense.

For some prisoners the amount of contact with the interrogator was far greater than with anyone else, including cellmates (e.g., the prisoner kept in isolation or in a prison in which cellmate contact was prohibited).

The interrogator, by virtue of being an official member of the government and by virtue of being in charge of S's case, was the primary audience for S's behavior and hence the one most closely attended to for cues as to what was expected of S.

Aspects pertaining to information discovered by prisoner from his own self-analysis

Discovery by S of beliefs, attitudes, values, or past behavior which, even by his old standards of evaluation justified his treatment—guilt regarding own past.

TABLE 4 (*continued*)

Discovery by S of identity components within himself which he wished to strengthen and which fitted in broadly with the ethical generalizations depicted in the "people's standpoint"; increased motivation to reform self further, might then result from S's recognition that cellmate pressure had allowed this "therapeutic" discovery to occur.

To summarize, the process of *changing* can be thought of as the mental operations which the prisoner went through in arriving at new beliefs, attitudes, values, and behavior patterns. These mental operations can be thought of as the adoption of a new frame of reference, of new standards for evaluating behavior, and of new semantic rules. The whole process was given its direction by the information which the influence agent provided to the prisoner. Before acceptable changes could occur, however, the prisoner had to learn to pay attention to the information. He usually learned to pay attention when he began to identify with his cellmates in the process of trying to re-establish a sense of identity in the hostile prison environment.

REFREEZING

If changes in beliefs are to remain stable, the new equilibrium of forces must be *refrozen*. This process implies that the new belief must be integrated into other parts of the person and must be supported and reinforced by the behavior of significant others. If it is not so integrated or supported, it will change once again when the original forces toward change have been removed. For example, if a prisoner has been physically coerced into making a confession, he will repudiate that confession once the physical pressure is lifted; or, if he has adopted pro-Communist attitudes only because of a desire to please a particular cellmate, he will drop these attitudes when his relationship with the cellmate is terminated. On the other hand, the repatriate will not repudiate the confession or drop the new attitude if in retrospect either response seems rational and logical from the standpoint of new premises which he now accepts. Similarly, if important others treat the confession as a laudable response and agree with the new attitudes, they will thereby give them stability, i.e., help to refreeze them.

If the beliefs and attitudes which are involved in the change process concern the person's self and his sense of identity, it is particularly important to consider the role which interpersonal confirmation plays as a refreezing force. We know our self primarily through others, hence attitudes toward self must be shared by at least those others who are most important to us. If these others do not support or confirm new attitudes, they are in effect forcing the person to change them once again by motivating him to find attitudes which they will confirm or support.

Many of the experiences in prison tended to refreeze whatever changes in the direction of Communist attitudes had occurred in the prisoner. At the emotional level the prisoner received the support and encouragement of his cellmates; at the intellectual level he had ample opportunity to study the Communist point of view and thus to rationalize thoroughly any changes he had undergone. But once he left prison he was deprived of this support. Whether the new attitudes then persisted or not depended on how well integrated they were with the rest of the repatriate's personality and on the likelihood that the repatriate would receive emotional support for the changes from others he regarded as important. These and other aspects of the total experience which relate most clearly to this process of refreezing are shown in Table 5.

TABLE 5

Aspects of the Imprisoment Experience Relating to Refreezing

Experiences within prison

Communist propaganda as reinforcement of and justification for confession and attitude change.

Study of Communist materials within cell, by small group discussion technique involving the following elements:

Reading of materials.

Analysis of materials in the presence of others.

Implicit and explicit competition among prisoners in analyzing theory and deriving practical implications.

TABLE 5 (*continued*)

Mutual criticism for incorrect analysis or incorrect attitude toward material.

Requirement to analyze material in reference to own case, show how theory applied to S's own daily behavior.

Rationalization and justification of conclusions presented in materials; generally the conclusions could not be questioned, only justified, e.g., "*Why* are the Americans imperialistic and warmongering?"

Showing how all activities, no matter how trivial, have political implications.

Further public self-analysis in reference to materials, often as part of elaborating and deepening the confession; referred to sometimes as "thought conclusions."

Rewarding aspects of having re-established comfortable emotional relationships with cellmates and interrogator.

Rewarding aspects of having found a frame of reference and semantic rules which made communication with others possible.

Lessening or complete removal of all those pressures described in reference to unfreezing.

Experiences after release from prison and after repatriation

Cognitive confirmation of predictions made by cellmates and authorities regarding events which would occur after repatriation.

Location of significant others who support changes made in prison.

Sense of personal integration, in the absence of prison supports and pressures.

By way of conclusion, we should like to point out that among the influenced repatriates we saw some individuals whose change did not persist very long after repatriation and some individuals who were able to find social, emotional, and informational support for their new beliefs and attitudes, and whose beliefs and attitudes therefore have persisted. It is this latter group which emphasizes the need to analyze coercive persuasion in terms of a general theory of influence rather than to see it as a peculiar, uncommon, or bizarre set of procedures designed to make man do something "against his will."

Our model of the influence process suggests that any influence is to a degree against the person's will because it involves the discomfort of giving up some stable equilibrium and finding something new. The person who comes to a situation ready to change has already been unfrozen and has therefore suffered this discomfort at some time in the past, but it logically should be included as part of the total influence process.

What distinguishes coercive persuasion from other kinds of influence processes is the degree to which the person who is to be influenced is physically or psychologically confined to a situation in which he must continue to expose himself to unfreezing pressures. Not only did the prison confine him physically, but the round-the-clock vigilance and pressure from cellmates confined the person psychologically to an environment in which unusually intense unfreezing pressures were present at all times. The success of coercive persuasion in those few cases where it was successful in producing lasting belief and attitude change can be related primarily to the intensity of this unfreezing.

5

The Special Role of Guilt in Coercive Persuasion

ONE OF the primary motives which leads the prisoner to begin a process of change (to begin to allow himself to be influenced) is *guilt,* which he comes to experience in various forms in the prison environment. This experience of guilt results from a combination of external pressures and internal predispositions. From the point of view of the interrogator or judge, criminal guilt is assumed once the prisoner has been arrested, but there are several different bases for such guilt. From the point of view of the prisoner there are a number of predispositions which lead to psychologically distinct types of guilt, though they may not be experienced as different. The purpose of this chapter is to explore these distinctions and thereby to show how the captor's presentation of the nature of guilt begins to unfreeze the prisoner by stimulating in him a sense of guilt, and how the type of guilt which he feels is related to the final outcome of the influence process.

THE CAPTOR'S VIEW OF GUILT

Once arrested, the prisoner must come to understand the following version of his predicament: he is in prison because the government considers him a criminal; his crime is obvious to everyone but to him; his first task is to understand the nature of his crime, and in this task the government will do its best to help him. Analysis of his past will show him how he has been guilty, how the ultimate consequences of his acts have been harmful to the Chinese people. If he is honest with himself he will discover his guilt more rapidly and proceed easily to what is expected of the criminal: admission of guilt by confession, subsequent repentance, and reform of the undesirable thoughts, attitudes, feelings, and actions.

From the moment of his arrival in prison the prisoner has urged upon him the rationale of the Chinese authorities by his interrogator, judge, and, most important, his cellmates. He may attempt to defend himself against the accusations of guilt by denying criminal acts or intents, by laughing at their absurdity, or simply by failing to take them seriously, but the total prison regimen as outlined in the previous chapters may convince him that his own concepts of guilt and innocence are incorrect or at least are not shared by the other prisoners or the authorities.

The bases for being judged guilty which he must come to appreciate are the following:

1. GUILT BY ASSOCIATION. The prisoner is guilty if he has associated with any others who are themselves guilty, even if he has not committed any acts "harmful to the Chinese people," or exhibited any intent to do so, or been aware of his association with other guilty parties.*

2. GUILT BY INTENTION. The prisoner is guilty if he exhibits motives which could and probably eventually would lead to actions which would harm the Chinese people; thus the prisoner is at least a potential criminal who must be made to feel his guilt and be punished as social prophylaxis.

3. GUILT FOR INCORRECT ATTITUDES. The prisoner is guilty if he takes a negative attitude toward the party or the government or questions any of their decisions, because such an attitude undermines the effectiveness of the "people's representatives" in their programs to help the people; questioning his own guilt or asserting his innocence can be, of course, a further instance of such a negative

---

* Since the guilt of the "others" rests on bases similar to those discussed here, it can be seen that the attribution of guilt to anyone is possible.

attitude, thereby proving the government's correctness in the first instance.

4. GUILT FOR INCORRECT THOUGHTS.   The prisoner is guilty if he exhibits thought patterns which reflect bourgeois premises and if he fails to appreciate the validity of Communist premises, even if he does not exhibit intentions or attitudes which could be harmful to the people; it is assumed that wrong thoughts would eventually lead to harmful acts.

5. GUILT FOR HAVING KNOWLEDGE.   The prisoner is guilty if he has knowledge about China which could in any conceivable way be used against the Chinese, no matter how vague or seemingly non-political it might be; if the prisoner is a foreigner such knowledge is particularly suspect because of the presumption that the only possible reason for his remaining in China after the take-over could be the gathering of "intelligence information"; thus activities such as research, casual questioning, and reading all become espionage.

6. GUILT FOR HARMFUL ACTION.   The prisoner is guilty if he has committed acts which are harmful to the Chinese people, even if he does not recognize having committed them or does not recognize that they were harmful; seemingly innocuous acts can be defined as seriously harmful by the authorities, e.g., going to a party at a Western embassy is "establishing contact with spies" or actually "passing on information to Western agents"; looking something up in easily available volumes in the library for an attaché at a Western embassy (something he could easily have done himself) is "aiding in espionage activities," and so on.

7. GUILT FOR FAILURE TO ACT.   The prisoner is guilty if he has *not* been active in his support of the party and the government, if he has failed to show his own desire for the welfare of the people, if he has failed to give willingly his own possessions, time, and efforts in behalf of the Communist cause; to stand aside is to condone and support the old *status quo*.

8. GUILT FOR HAVING A CHARACTERISTIC PERSONAL FAULT OR FAULTS.   The prisoner is judged guilty if he shows in his behavior in prison some fault, shortcoming, or character defect from the point of view of the idealized image of the "new man"; for example, the prisoner is constantly being shown evidence of his own selfishness,

lack of concern for others, class and/or racial prejudice, personal weakness, failure to live up to his own stated ideals, and so on; because the idealized "new man" is morally "perfect" from both a Communist and non-Communist point of view, it is likely that the kinds of faults for which the prisoner is criticized will be perceived by him as faults also.

9. GUILT FOR HAVING DANGEROUS SOCIAL ORIGINS. The prisoner is guilty if he was born into a bourgeois family, if his friends and/or relatives are capitalists, if he was educated under a capitalist system, or if he associated with others of dangerous social origins; it is assumed that various of the consequences described above—incorrect attitudes and thoughts, failure to support the Communist cause, characteristic personal faults, are all due to such social origins; hence incorrect social origins are a primary and incontestable basis for guilt. What makes matters worse for the prisoner is that he cannot deny these origins, they are a matter of fact; he can only deny their effects which is not likely to be convincing.

As one reviews these bases of guilt, one sees that they overlap to a considerable extent and are linked by the underlying assumption that *all situations must be judged by their "objective" results, by their ultimate consequences.* Thoughts, attitudes, intentions, personal characteristics, and even accidents of birth and status must be judged by what they *could* lead to, not by the actual actions they have led to in the past. Thus the person may be guilty without knowing it, and it is the prison's primary task to make the prisoner conscious of his guilt as the prelude to reform. This logic carried to its extreme makes the primary basis of guilt simply the objective fact of having been arrested; arrest is the just consequence of guilt and the presumptive evidence of it.*

In general, the agents of influence (judge, interrogator, cellmate) presume the guilt of their subject(s). They believe the subject would never have been arrested if he were not considered a threat to the "people." They may not know the precise reason for the subject's guilt nor which grounds are justifiably applicable to him. They may

---

* It is an interesting psychological fact that even some prisoners who thought they were arrested unjustly, who saw themselves as innocent, were convinced of the guilt of everyone else in the prison.

not even be convinced that the grounds on which they are arguing are justified. Nonetheless they are able to be persuasive because of their "obvious" sincerity in working for the welfare of the people and in their belief that if the subject had not been guilty of something he would not have been arrested. Mistakes are considered unlikely, and, in any case, must be made in favor of the system since it defines itself to be in a state of combat.

The frequent allegation that the interrogators, judges, and cell-mates are Machiavellian in their tactics is probably based on the prisoner's perception that the agent is willing to manipulate the nature of the accusation to suit the subject's particular vulnerability. Thus the judge may sincerely believe that in some general fashion the prisoner is guilty of harming the people but may not believe the specific charges that he is making against the prisoner. Under the pressure of his job he may end up trying to convince the subject of his guilt rather than trying to ascertain whether he is guilty; and he may be willing in this process to make accusation after accusation until some are found which the subject seems to find difficult to refute. In the end the judge will most likely accept any honest confession drawn from the subject's general sense of guilt, and he will no longer attempt to ascertain facts relevant to the matters confessed to even if some of the confessed facts are incongruous or absurd. If the judge senses, however, that the confession is dishonest, in the sense of being merely an attempt by the prisoner to please him, he will probably be genuinely outraged and continue his efforts to find some basis for guilt which will elicit from the prisoner a genuine confession.

THE PRISONER'S EXPERIENCE OF GUILT

We shall assume at the outset that all socialized people experience a substantial amount of guilt when their behavior, desires, or feelings conflict with the dictates of the moral code or value system they have adopted or when they have not fulfilled some of the expectations held by themselves or by others. Because of their personal history and/or culture some people have stronger drives or make stronger moral demands on themselves than others; they therefore experience sharper conflicts and are consequently more guilt-prone than others.

Feelings of guilt are stimulated in the prison situation, both intentionally and inadvertently, by the exacerbation of old conflicts or the creation of new ones. For example, the prison regimen, whether handcuffs and ankle chains are used or not, makes the adult as dependent as a child and arouses some of the childhood conflicts, particularly around problems of authority. Or weakly held values are strengthened by continual emphasis until they begin to conflict with other values, as in the case of the priest for whom the value of unselfishness was sharpened to such a degree that it began to conflict with all efforts on his part to express any self-interest in the service of survival.

The prisoner can come to accept guilt on any one or more of the bases argued "logically" by the agents because he does begin to experience guilt in some form. This guilt may be felt primarily as guilt-anxiety (Lifton, 1956a) in which case the feeling is present but no psychological basis for it is perceived by the prisoner; or it may be consciously perceived to be related to one or more of the following areas of psychological functioning:

1. SOCIAL GUILT. A recognition on the part of the prisoner that much of what he has had in life has not been earned but has been given to him by accident of birth; thus for a middle-class person to have prejudices against the members of the lower class arouses guilt when he discovers that, in a sense, he has not earned but merely been given his middle-class status.

2. EGO OR IDENTITY GUILT. A recognition on the part of the prisoner that he has failed to live up to his image of himself.

3. *Persona* GUILT. The feeling of guilt which comes from wearing a mask, from the discovery or recognition of having deliberately or involuntarily deceived another person about oneself, for example, by playing the role of a guilty person while holding reservations.

4. LOYALTY GUILT. A recognition on the part of the prisoner that he has failed in his service to a group with which he is strongly identified or has violated its norms or defiled its image by behaving in a manner not consistent with what is expected of members of that group.

5. SITUATIONAL GUILT. Guilt which is aroused by the magnification on the part of others of minor infractions or petty acts which

normally do not run counter to the prisoner's basic values or self-image, particularly when they are perceived to have been stimulated by great stress; feelings of guilt in reference to such acts imply that the prisoner has already accepted some of the norms and standards of evaluation of the cellmates and authorities.

These types of guilt are not logically discrete but are important to distinguish if one is to understand some of the psychological processes which characterized the influence process in our subjects. In the remainder of this chapter we shall attempt to illustrate each of these types of guilt by quoting or paraphrasing some of the statements made by our subjects concerning their prison experience.

Social Guilt

"Basically, I guess I always felt superior to the Negro. I didn't realize it before, but when I looked back on it from the prison-situation, I could see it clearly."

"I realized that I had never done anything for society."

"What I came for [to China] was not so much to study, but to have a good time with the embassy set. To go to parties, and to make my dollar count in a country where help and housing was cheap."

"About ten years ago I was full of ideas of social climbing. I wanted to do some outstanding work so that I might acquire a distinguished social position. I wished to be above other people."

"We've always lived entirely for ourselves—not for others."

These paraphrased statements, taken from recent interviews, illustrate most directly what we mean by social guilt. The Communists tried to convince their prisoners that they had actually "harmed the people," or intended harm to them, or had at some time in their lives, as members of a more privileged class, intentionally or unconsciously taken advantage of others, because of inferior "class" status. The struggle meetings, both group criticism and self-criticism sessions, were designed to recall instances of such guilty behavior.

In his recollections, one American repatriate mentions how all foreigners living in China had at least subconscious feelings of superiority to the Oriental. He cites instances where even the unpretentious missionary family from which he came felt itself superior and, despite its low standard of living (lower than that of other foreigners), exploited the Chinese. Today he describes with pleasure, but also with considerable guilt, the gay, luxurious life of the foreign students, the parties, the hobnobbing with the intellectual, social, and political elite of the city.

Even one of the least guilt-prone of our subjects eventually became vulnerable to a sense of social guilt. For two years he had been in prison resisting influence, although making certain behavioral concessions. He recounts how, no matter what the agents tried, he continued to feel no guilt until a general personality crisis was precipitated which led him to "recognize" and accept social guilt.

As I continued my analysis I realized even more how my egotism had slowly developed to where I was incapable of seeing anything which was not to my advantage and where I was oblivious to the plight of others. I remembered how . . . I had looked with revulsion on the poverty around us when I arrived in China. One morning in November, 1948, we had stepped out of the gate of a friend's house where we had spent the night, to find a man stretched out dead on the doorstep, obviously starved to death. It was a shock to both of us and had brought an ugly note into a bright morning. Reflecting on my attitude that day, I realized now that the little sympathy I had felt for the man had been more overshadowed by annoyance over my day being spoiled in such a way. My attitude toward the Korean War had shown the same brutal disregard for the lives of others on a much larger scale.

This subject did not accept "social" guilt before this crisis, not only because he was not particularly guilt-prone but also because he had come from an underdog family, whose sufferings during the depression had made a deep impression on him. As his self-analysis continued, he was led to see the "selfishness" flaw in his character, and thus became ready to accept "social" guilt.

Though never a spy in our terms, he said:

Not wanting to harm others was no excuse at all, since a person totally blinded by his own self-interest is incapable of thinking of others, to begin with. If I had not been so blind, I would have been able to see long ago the fallacy in my supposition that my espionage activities had been of service to my country.

Having one's innermost self brought out and dissected under the glaring light of self-criticism was a shattering experience, but the resulting recognition of myself made me determined to overcome the weaknesses in my character which had been the cause of those former mistakes. Thus began the struggle with myself which was to last throughout the rest of my stay in prison, and, indeed, goes on even today.

The creation and exploitation of social guilt were possible with almost every prisoner who had already been successfully weakened by other means, even if he was not initially guilt-prone. One reason, among others, is that some evidence of having felt superior can always be dug out and turned into such guilt. The intellectual is vulnerable to accusations such as "you don't mix with the common man, you don't even speak his language." The missionaries who went to China to bring Christianity to the people sometimes lived better than the masses "for whom they were supposed to be an example." If this argument was not convincing, it was pointed out to the missionary that he undoubtedly felt some superiority over the un-Christianized heathens.

Thus to have had a feeling of social guilt and to have acknowledged it was to accept some version of this argument: if I have shown a lack of social awareness and have taken no global social responsibility; if I have been prejudiced toward a minority group; if I have felt superior toward anyone because of class origin, in fact felt superior *at all*; if I have been so concerned with my own life as to be unaware of the interests of others or have been too concerned with my own status and ambitions to do things for others, I have been guilty of "a crime against the people."

Ego or Identity Guilt

". . . Once you have made a false confession you lose heart and self-confidence. If they get you to make another confession then that lowers resistance even more."

The interviewer asked him, "Why did you make a false confession?"
He said, "Because I thought I would get out if I gave them what they
wanted, I thought I would try it." (Apparently the first time he actually
tried this was about four months after his imprisonment.)

The interviewer asked what he had confessed to and he didn't want to
tell but later in the conversation it came up. His lie was that he named
some sort of organization, which he had made up, for which he had
worked. Then he discovered that they had lied to him by telling him
that if he made a confession he would get out; and then they didn't release him once they had gotten it. From that time on he decided he
was not going to make a false confession. But because he had once made
a false confession he began to lose faith in himself. "Why had I given in,
why had I lied?" he asked himself. . . . "There is something *degrading*
about lying about yourself."

Because this confession undermined this man's self-image of being
special, different, even heroic, it drastically lowered his self-esteem.
It undermined his self-esteem not only because he had lied but also
because he had been unable to resist. Each time he was forced to give
in again (he confessed and retracted three or four times), his guilt
increased. As his guilt increased, his self-esteem was lowered and his
ability to resist making false confessions and believing them became
increasingly undermined.

In his explanation of ego guilt he repeated, perhaps without realizing it, the theme: If only I had been what *I thought I was* I would
have been able to resist. After having fought so hard and long to
resist, and then having given in because he just wanted the pressure
to stop, he could not face the idea that he was so weak as to give in,
that he could be willing to lie "just" to relieve the discomfort. Perhaps he began to believe in his own guilt, as argued by the agent,
because it was more bearable to believe that he really was a spy
and had confessed justifiably than to believe that he was making
false confessions about himself just to relieve the unceasing pressures
of the agent. It was this man who said on release in Hong Kong:

I knew in the first place that I was guilty. In order to gain self-respect,
one has to confess.

Ego or identity guilt is thus produced by eliciting from the prisoner behavior which is inconsistent with his self-image, by degrading him and/or provoking him into degrading behavior. One priest's attempt to resist such pressure is indicated in the following statement:

"As soon as the door opens we file off quickly to the washing-room at the end of the corridor. With only six or seven places there, we have to wait for our turn. Soap may not be used. You just dip your towel in the trough and pass it over your face and hands. There's a time allowance of two minutes and no more for all the fifteen of us, since twenty-eight other cells on this floor have to get through their ablutions in the course of the hour. We come and go back to our cell with the bowed heads of sentenced criminals, though no one has been condemned. The Communist technique sets much store on the outward sign. By subjecting the body to the posture of guilt, the spirit is moulded and brought into a responsiveness indistinguishable from that of domestic animals. That's what's wanted of everyone in the Communist regime. But why does my good friend, Number 1052, bend down lower than the rest, and outdo all by the exaggerated abjection of his posture? It hurts me every time I see this. The line I have adopted is 'submissively nonconformist.' I keep my eyes cast down like a nun, so that it's impossible to accuse me of breaking the rules by looking about. But I simply won't bow my head. Yet, apart from an occasional 'telling-off,' I have been left alone in my obstinacy." [Bonnichon, 1955, p. 4]

The use of handcuffs and ankle chains as punishment for refusal to confess of course insures degradation and dependency and thereby strongly heightens the probability of ego guilt. The provocation of behavior inconsistent with a man's image of himself is also made easier by the fact that in the intimacy of cell life it is not difficult for cellmates to discover those points on which a fellow prisoner is vulnerable.

One of our subjects after a long period of resistance started to make "concessions" in the form of confessions but he did not believe in any of the behavior he had confessed to, i.e., did not feel he had committed any crimes by his own standards. The close relationships which developed in the group cell and the constant argument and harangue from the interrogator led gradually to an intellectual acceptance of the Chinese Communist semantics and to some identification with cellmates, expressed most clearly in his calling his cell "a sort of home." The cellmates were the first Chinese that the subject felt he had ever known intimately.

Identification with his cellmates made it easier for this man to accept the validity of their definitions of crime. Gradually the acceptance of their definitions led to a habit of conceptualizing his activities and thoughts in terms of them. Finally he came to accept the point of view that he had been guilty of espionage, but then discovered in a newspaper article that repatriated POW's from Korea who had allegedly been brainwashed had been sent to Valley Forge "mental hospital," and concluded that if he stuck to his confession of espionage he would spend the rest of his days following release in an American mental hospital. To avoid this future possibility he decided to rewrite his confession in such a way as to make it seem harmless from an American point of view, and then settled down to await its acceptance by the authorities. After he had waited two months he was called before the investigating judge, at which time he offered to rewrite the confession again in the hope of finding a compromise version which would both be acceptable to the Chinese and get him off the hook with the United States. He was met with "cold hostility" and an order to get back to his cell and was most upset by the loathing and disgust in the voice of the judge. He suddenly felt he had been caught red-handed; until then no one and no experience had presented him with direct "proof" of his flaws.

The feeling of having been dishonest with the Chinese made the subject wonder about the core of his character, whether he had any principles at all, and led to a determination to find the causes for his developing the way he had "or he would never have confidence in himself again." For this subject the crisis was precipitated by his acceptance of certain standards of honesty and sincerity *defined by the Chinese cellmates,* and it is these standards he had failed to live up to in his own eyes, in contrast to the first subject mentioned in this section to whom the false confession meant something entirely different. The subject was guilty because his motives for rewriting his confession were selfish, regardless of the truth or falsity of its contents, and because he was acting selfishly he was failing to live up to a self-image of helping "the people." This conflict at the surface must have made contact with a deeper conflict and must have elicited guilt which was attached to impulses and deeds stemming from his earlier life. We cannot guess what these were, but it is clear that the prisoner was able to use the crisis provoked in the prison situation to re-examine more fundamental aspects of his character and to "reform" some of them.

In conclusion, ego or identity guilt, if it was elicited by the imprisonment experience, could range from being relatively superficial to being quite deep and could be the basis for other guilt feelings such as social guilt. To the extent that basic identity components in the prisoner became involved in the intrapsychic conflict the experience of thought reform could lead to fundamental personality or character change.

Persona *or Face-to-Face Guilt*

"Isolation would have been heaven in that prison. . . . I dreaded it when the others would come [back to the cell] . . . because I knew I would have no peace. . . . Don't mention the word 'help' to me. I never want to hear that again. I had to watch myself, because they would jump on everything I said. But I couldn't avoid saying something, because I just couldn't sit back and withdraw. I'm just that way."

"I'd prepare some answer hours in advance so that I could use [it] if they asked me what I was thinking . . . and I'd feel guilty when I didn't reveal my true opinion, but used a phoney one to make them stop. . . . I'd feel miserable when, after really having made a sincere effort, they didn't believe me. . . . Of course everyone else was *playing a game* of accusation and self-criticism. . . . It was just because everyone was forced to do it. . . . I knew people were forced to play roles. . . . Still I'd feel guilty about playing my roles."

"You could never tell who was play-acting and who wasn't and you couldn't make any kind of a judgment. You didn't have any kind of a relationship with anyone . . . They were not speaking to *you*, they were speaking to *the confessed you* [the masked "you"]. . . . There was no one we could trust. And you always thought someone was going to inform. But there was one person—a cell mate—with whom I once talked . . . we spoke one night when everyone was asleep and he said to me. 'This is the first time I felt that someone didn't speak to me in a role.' He said, 'I am innocent, should I try to make up a crime, do you think it would be a good strategy if I confessed to something, then they will think I have confessed and they will let me go?' Then I answered him frankly and I said, 'You must not make any kind of false confession. You must stick to the truth, otherwise you are going to get all confused.' " This was the only honest conversation and the only private conversation he ever had with anyone in his three and one half years in prison.

Persona or face-to-face guilt is the feeling of guilt which comes from wearing a mask, or from deliberately playing a role which one is aware is not congruent with the self; in short, which comes from deceiving others about oneself. In prison, persona guilt most often resulted when the prisoner, in order to reduce the continued pressure to reform, deliberately began to act as if he were someone he was not, or pretended to opinions which were not his own. In the model reform prison specializing in group struggle meetings, all prisoners were forced initially to wear verbal masks.

This face-to-face deception was more bearable to some than to others. One subject to whom close personal relationships, even with the resented cellmates, were crucial, saw in this type of guilt one of the major stresses of imprisonment. Another subject refers merely to the "embarrassment" of having to manufacture beliefs he did not have. A third subject was hardly affected by this type of deception because he approached human relationships primarily on an intellectual plane: people to him were not really individuals but personified abstractions with whom one relates through ideas (words). In the prison situation, with all his companions hidden behind masks, he was doubly removed from them. Their verbal masks obliterated any clue to their true selves; they were not real people with whom one could have any relationships. Given this definition of the situation and relationships, this prisoner was quite impervious to the group struggle meetings and to cellmate pressures since the screaming, kicking, spitting, and verbal assault came from "ciphers," not real people.

Thus susceptibility to persona or face-to-face guilt depended on the meaning which deception had for the person, how significant others were for him as persons to be concerned about, and how important it was for the person to obtain confirmation of his "real" self from the others in the prison environment.

Loyalty Guilt

For an instant, as he stood there, looking out over the street from a window high in Loukawei Prison, there came to him without warning so great a desire to get out of prison that he almost cried out. It would be simple, really. All he had to do was say the word. One single word in answer to one single question and this whole dreadful nightmare existence would come to an end, so that he could walk down a street and be able to turn whichever way he wanted at the corner.

And then there arose in his mind the faces and names of people whom he knew and loved: priests and laymen who had calmly put their lives and freedom on the line, students who had with wide open eyes taken the deliberate step of depriving themselves of a career and the possibility of a decent livelihood, women who had stood dry-eyed and proud as their men, their sons, their brothers, had been marched off to jail, to slave labor camps, to the firing squad. He saw his Chinese fellow Jesuits boldly speaking out against the Red tyranny, knowing that when they went, they would not come back without breaking. "If I do come out, and say anything different from what I have said before and am saying now, have nothing to do with me. . . ."

Shaken and almost sick at the thought of how close he had come to betraying himself and his friends, Father Phillips turned away from the window and moved back toward the door. [Becker, 1958]

Loyalty guilt resulted from behavior, thoughts, or feelings which the prisoner felt to be a violation of the norms of important reference or membership groups or which would sully the image which others held of that group. Thus a priest felt guilty if he committed any actions which were unpriestlike, Marine POW's in Korea felt guilty if they committed un-Marinelike acts, imprisoned Communist sympathizers felt guilty if they were accused of harming rather than helping the people, cell members felt guilty if they violated the norms of the prison cell (assuming they had become identified with it) by refusing to reform themselves. Just as the prison situation could provoke behavior inconsistent with the person's image of himself, so it could provoke behavior inconsistent with his group membership (for example, provoking a priest into a fist fight over some cell privileges). Clearly loyalty guilt and ego guilt overlap to the extent that the person's image of himself to a large extent reflects his perceptions of group membership and identification. A distinction between the two is useful, however, because the subjects themselves distinguished quite sharply between the feelings which resulted from violation of self-image and those which resulted from letting down important others. Perhaps loyalty guilt can be thought of as ego guilt plus something more—a sense of failure in someone else's eyes as well as one's own.

Situational Guilt

All our subjects made some reference to their commission of "petty" acts which their cellmates would catch and exaggerate into an indication of a great bourgeois flaw. From every prison come stories of "great crimes" by Western prisoners—occasional slightly uneven distribution of food or blankets, petty stealing or cheating, accidental use of another's soap, inadvertent selfishness, and so on. This behavior was identified as serious signs of old bourgeois immorality which warranted the moral outrage and sharp attack of the entire cell group. A man who turned a little too far out of "his space" during sleep was told that he did not do so accidentally but because he was selfish. Any "error," even if it did not remotely involve a serious breach of major values, was not overlooked. It was caught, dwelt on, and exaggerated. Thus, no matter how much he tried to get along, the prisoner was likely to find himself being accused of one thing or another all day and night long. The entire prison environment was characterized by constant accusation, making it highly likely that some form of guilt would be stimulated even in the prisoner who was initially not very guilt-prone.

CONCLUSIONS

Regardless of its psychological basis, once guilt was felt the subject became more prone to accepting one or more of the many arguments of the agent concerning his *objective* guilt. The prisoner's subsequent willingness to confess then resulted from his need to attach his feelings of guilt to behavior or thoughts which the authorities sanctioned as crimes, not from having been "broken." In the case of social, persona, or situational guilt his subjectively felt shortcomings coincided with the objectively defined crimes; in the case of ego or loyalty guilt the subject may have been influenced because it was easier for him to accept psychologically the objective crimes he was accused of and the belief system which defined these as crimes than to face the weakness in himself which allowed the guilt-provoking behavior to occur in the first place. In the case of guilt-anxiety where the psychological conflict itself was unconscious, the same mechanism may of course have applied, in that the prisoner may have accepted objectively defined crimes and attached his guilt to them to prevent his unconscious conflicts from becoming conscious (Meerloo, 1956).

We have treated the topic of guilt as an unfreezing force in some detail because it was undoubtedly one of the central forces motivating the prisoner to change. We wish to reiterate, however, that guilt was not the only force acting on the prisoner tending to unfreeze him; other forces could also start an influence process. On the other hand, the degree of susceptibility to guilt varied sharply from prisoner to prisoner and many prisoners had effective defenses against guilt which tended to prevent guilt feelings from precipitating major behavior and/or belief changes. Not all prisoners who experienced guilt were unfrozen by it and subsequently influenced. Many of them, like Father Phillips, quoted at the beginning of the section on loyalty guilt, used the small quantity of guilt which the *thought* of giving in stimulated as a defense against actually giving in. Others defended themselves by the usual mechanisms of repression, denial, rationalization, etc., at the psychological level, and by logical argument, or simple refusal to listen at the level of interaction with the agents.

6

The Effects of Coercive Persuasion

WHAT KIND of influence was actually accomplished by the prison regimen and how was this related to Communist objectives? In looking at our cases we found that a simple categorization in terms of complete resistance, confession, or confession plus attitude change is quite inadequate. Prisoners made confessions which were in varying degrees useful to the Communists, in varying degrees damaging to the United States, and in varying degrees accurate in terms of the behavior the prisoner had actually engaged in prior to imprisonment. Similarly, attitude changes varied in the degree to which the change was toward unequivocal acceptance of Chinese Communism, toward the acceptance of broad ethical generalities which Communism shares with other ideologies, or merely toward a greater appreciation of what the Communists are allegedly trying to do for the Chinese people. Attitude changes also varied in their degree of permanence, in their degree of internal consistency, and in their significance for the repatriate's later adjustment to our society. Finally, there were changes produced in some prisoners which were quite irrelevant to Communist objectives yet which were clearly the result of the imprisonment and coercive persuasion experiences.

In order to describe and evaluate the patterns of influence in our subjects we have chosen as an appropriate frame of reference changes in the prisoner's behavior and attitudes which had meaning for his own long-run adjustment, disregarding the political *effects* of these changes in aiding or hindering the Communist cause or in fulfilling their immediate political objectives. For example, two subjects who made identical confessions and therefore fulfilled some Communist objectives in identical ways might represent instances of two very different kinds of influence. In one subject the confession might be the product of sheer opportunism, while in the other it might represent a far-reaching change in self-percept and the acceptance subjectively of the guilt which the confessed behavior implied. Similarly, two subjects who changed their attitude toward Communism and the CCP in identical fashion (in terms of their manifest behavior at the time of repatriation) might represent instances of very different influence processes. In one of them the new attitudes might represent a new integration of previously conflicting tendencies; in the other they might be new cognitive responses which produce new and chronic conflicts within him. In the latter case we might expect the new attitudes to drop away rather quickly, in the former case they might persist indefinitely. The main point is that these two cases would not represent merely differing *degrees* of influence, but also different *types* of influence as a result of seemingly similar coercive persuasion attempts.

We shall present prototypes of the different types and degrees of influence accomplished, recognizing that we are thereby implying a degree of generality which is hardly warranted by our small sample. The reader should once again remind himself that our stated conclusions are actually hypotheses to be tested against further observations.

TYPES AND DEGREES OF INFLUENCE

No Discernible Influence

No change perceived in self (except possibly in physical condition); no aid given to the Communists, witting or unwitting; complete refusal to make or sign any confession; and no attitude change except possibly increased hostility toward the Communists.

Repatriates fitting into this category presented nothing in their post-repatriation behavior that would be considered unusual or would obtain for them any special publicity except the fact of their unusual resistance. They would discuss in a calm, mature fashion the horror of the experience and the manner in which they had resisted Communist pressures, and would likely confirm for their audience the conviction that Communism in any form or guise has to be fought to the limit of anyone's ability. They would strike those who knew them well before their imprisonment as having undergone no significant change in their attitudes, though one might note an increased determination to combat Communism and would sense that the coercive persuasion experience had taken a great toll physically and emotionally. The number of cases falling into this category is extremely small since almost everyone who was released from the mainland made some sort of a confession. Among published accounts, the case of Father Phillips is the most enlightening and best presented (Becker, 1958).

Altered Psychological Functioning

Diffuse change perceived in self, but not in direction of Communist values; some compliance with Communist demands, but only minimal in willingness to confess to things actually done; successful avoidance of attitude change or more extensive compliance by development of defense mechanisms which psychically isolated the prisoner and made it possible for him to discount incoming information, but at some cost to his total psychological functioning.

Repatriates fitting into this category appeared upon repatriation to be somewhat confused, perhaps sick or psychotic, but did not seem to have accepted Communism to any degree. They fitted best the image of the person who was "broken" by the experience. Such a subject might admit having confessed to certain deeds and accept his own guilt for them, but the observer would not feel that he had deserved his punishment or that he had been well treated. The extent to which his psychological functioning had been influenced might not be assessable for a long time but he would seem to have been influenced somehow, without having been influenced toward Communism. For example, some subjects remained very tense, restless, and nervous for an indefinite period of time following repatriation; some became almost paranoid about Communism, seeing various fortuitous circumstances back home as carefully elaborated Communist plots directed at them; some reported a lengthy post-repatriation period of "indifference to tragedy," being unable to feel strongly about nearby emotional events (one subject reported being almost unmoved when told of the death of his brother); and so on. Of course, the psychological effects attendant upon the tremendous physical incapacitation which resulted in some subjects cannot be discounted either. Some subjects returned with TB, some had the after-effects of vitamin deficiencies, some suffered considerably from the after-effects of having worn manacles and chains, and so on; but they all felt the psychological tension and other psychological concomitants to be the more salient post-repatriation problem.*

Behavioral Compliance Without Attitude Change

MINIMAL BEHAVIORAL COMPLIANCE. Willingness to make and sign confession provided it was seen by prisoner not to be technically true (even if slightly exaggerated) and not to be compromising to himself or his important reference groups; no subjective sense of guilt nor any degree of sympathy for Communist position; increased hostility, following repatriation, toward the Communist regime but not toward the individual influence agents who were likely to be seen merely as having fulfilled their job.

Repatriates falling into this category are distinguished from the previous one only in that they appeared upon repatriation to have weathered the experience somewhat better. They gave the appearance of rationality and objectivity and clearly did not appear as if imprisonment had in any way "broken" them. They usually admitted having made some confessions under duress but pointed out that, first of all, they had avoided seriously compromising anyone by their confession and, secondly, that their trial had been a mockery of legal process and that in fact they were not the criminals the Communists had stated them to be. They did not seem to experience any guilt in reference to their confession, largely because they did not feel that they violated their self-image by the kind of confession they made.

---

* It is interesting to note that in a follow-up study of American POW's repatriated from Korean POW camps a similar pattern emerged. A very high percentage of the repatriates had physical difficulties from wounds, diseases, frostbite, torture, etc., yet a prevalent complaint which seemed much more debilitating to them was tension, nervousness, jumpiness, etc.

Most of them had resisted the pressures of imprisonment with great courage and were proud of their resistance rather than ashamed of their confession.

An excellent example of the kind of resistance which sustained the self-image was cited by Bonnichon (1955). Though the prison rules demanded that the prisoners had at all times to lower their eyes and bow their heads in an attitude of submission when in the presence of the guards, Bonnichon reported that he simply refused to bow his head and was not punished for this defiance. He states that keeping his feeling of dignity intact in this fashion was crucial for maintaining his general strength to resist.*

One gets the feeling about subjects in this category that they expected imprisonment under the Communists to be no more or less than what they actually experienced; that they felt it to be an inevitable outcome of a political system like Communism; and that they therefore did not specifically resent the treatment they received at the hands of the influence agents since most of these were seen to be merely low-level workers doing the job demanded of them. Cellmates were seen not as an important reference group but more often as poor misguided folk who needed above all else pity and proper guidance, which occasionally these prisoners tried to provide; in any case there was virtually no probability of coming to identify with them or treating their own reform as being anything other than a bill of goods that the authorities had sold them. These subjects seem to have been able to look at the experience from a very broad perspective and had such a strong inner sense of identity that they simply did not need confirmation from anyone in their immediate social environment. In the end they made their confessions as a rational adaptation to the total situation inasmuch as it appeared to them that some kind of confession really was a prerequisite for release.

The long-run effects on this group are hard to assess since in the first place it tends to include many of the older missionaries who

* The fact that the guards did not enforce the regulation in this case is an excellent example of our point that the variations in prison routine were important. A different kind of climate in the same prison might have elicited more compliance and possibly attitude change in a man like Bonnichon.

were ready to retire by the time they were released. On the whole it appears that those who did not retire either continued their careers essentially where they left off or else continued their work in a somewhat curtailed fashion.

Extensive Behavioral Compliance.   Willingness to make and sign confession which included material reflecting the agent's accusations but was clearly recognized by the prisoner as false, yet was confessed to in order to ease pressure and gain release from imprisonment; subjective sense of guilt attached particularly to self-perception of weakness for being unable to resist, combined with or resulting in tremendous hostility toward the agents who thus marred the prisoner's self-image; this hostility toward the Communists might be major long-run effect following release.

Repatriates falling into this category exhibited two types of responses after their repatriation. They either withdrew completely from any publicity and attempted to hide themselves away as quickly as possible, or they volubly and compulsively attempted to explain their behavior (their confession) to as many audiences as possible. The confessions of the subjects in this category were likely to have included more material of the type that the Communists demanded, material which the prisoner recognized as false and possibly as being quite compromising to himself and to others. In some cases more elaborate confessions resulted after a number of initial confessions followed by retractions, and were seen primarily as coerced responses about which the prisoner felt helpless. The prisoner was generally not confused about the truth or falsity of the confessed behavior, nor did he accept the Communist's semantics or standards of evaluation. The prisoner often erroneously believed, however, that a false confession would be easy to repudiate following repatriation and that it would not do the Chinese any good to get it.

Because the coerced compliance was for most of these prisoners so damaging to their self-image, they were motivated on the one hand to emphasize the coercive aspects of their imprisonment and on the other hand the evilness and duplicity of the captors. One of the major effects of imprisonment, then, was a sharp increase in hostility toward Communism, leading in some repatriates to the determination to launch lecture tours, organize special programs or drives, write books and pamphlets, and so on, to expose Communism.

Behavioral Compliance * Accompanied by Attitude Change

UNINTEGRATED ATTITUDE CHANGE. New pro-Communist attitudes grafted onto old attitude structure but not integrated into it; no real identity crisis stimulated.

Repatriates fitting into this category appeared at repatriation to be sick, somewhat confused, and somewhat distant; they immediately made statements to the press and to other available audiences citing their crimes, such as espionage and sabotage, lauding their Chinese captors for their leniency and the good treatment received in prison, and condemning the "imperialistic warmongering" nations of the West for their policies toward Communist China and their failure to understand what Communism was really doing for the people. The listener often got the impression of a broken record, a compulsive repetition of the same points, and a heavy use of Communist jargon and of such stock phrases as imperialist and warmonger. The listener also got the feeling that the repatriate was compulsively clinging to some kind of façade and was not showing his real self.

After a period of time ranging from a few weeks to one year, this kind of person began to re-evaluate his prison experience and to recognize that he had been forced to comply against his will, that he had accepted attitudes and information which were incompatible with other attitudes he had and with information he could now check. He might be overcome with guilt and with hostility toward the Communists for having forced him into something so alien to himself, and would end up having a fairly accurate view of the total experience and his role in it.

The number of repatriates falling into this category is very small but of considerable interest since they represent instances of one

---

* Behavioral compliance here implies a sincere effort to make a confession as well as willingness to engage in other reform activities like self-criticism and *hsuen hsi* (Group Study). The actual confession might be limited to items about which the prisoner actually felt guilty, but *in toto* his compliance would be more extensive than that of prisoners in the above category.

popular stereotype of brainwashing—the person who has been seemingly made to believe something alien to him and against his will.

PARTIALLY OR TOTALLY INTEGRATED ATTITUDE CHANGE. New attitudes either continue to exacerbate an identity crisis or tend to resolve it; in the latter case they become integrated into existing attitude structures and ongoing emotional relationships.

This group of repatriates, though very small in number, includes the cases of greatest interest in that the coercive persuasion experience for them produced long-run influence at a fairly basic personality and attitude level. Subjects who fall into this general category appeared at the time of repatriation much the same as those just discussed, but the listener had less of a sense that the repatriate was compulsively clinging to a façade and more of a sense that some fundamental change had occurred in the subject about which he felt quite secure. These subjects seemed more at peace with themselves, seemed to have a firmer and deeper conviction about what they were saying, relied less on clichés and jargon, and did not push their message as compulsively.

In the period following repatriation this group did not "discover" the falsity of points the Communists had made, but continued to use the new standards of evaluation and the new frame of reference learned in prison. The main difference between the partially and totally integrated groups was that in the former the new attitudes and frame of reference did not produce a satisfactory resolution of the identity crisis stimulated in prison, while in the latter they did. Thus subjects in the former group vacillated between seeing their imprisonment as a very beneficial and therapeutic experience (leading to pro-Chinese and pro-Communist points of view on many issues) and as a basically destructive horrible experience (leading to pro-American and anti-Communist points of view).

In terms of our influence model these subjects have been changed but not *refrozen*. We would predict that some resolution of their problems will come through the new social-emotional relationships they form back home and the kind of identity and attitudes these new significant others will support. If they can find others who will support the kind of value emphasis which they learned in prison (i.e., being unselfish or working for greater causes), they may become confirmed in their pro–Chinese Communist view of the experience; if they cannot, they may increasingly see the experience from an anti–Chinese Communist point of view. In either case it seems clear that something deep has been carried away from the prison experience which has for this group long-term effects. The core of this "something" appears to be a sense of deeper understanding of the Chinese people and their problems and a recognition of what class exploitation really means in terms of middle-class failure to understand or help worker- and lower-class people.

In some subjects the new attitudes were adequately refrozen by being integrated into the remainder of the personality, by providing key identity components, and by being confirmed in significant interpersonal relationships. For this group a genuine identity resolution seems to have occurred, at least in one segment of their lives, and they were able to use the experience to "find themselves" by finding a cause or an ethic to which to attach themselves—they experienced a "conversion to commitment." *

The very few cases who fall into this category have held on to most of the attitude changes they experienced, but the form in which the new attitudes have come to be part of their daily life is very different from the form it assumed at the time of their repatriation. In essence, they seem to have adopted some of the basic ethics which the Communist system shares with other systems, e.g., the "collective" view of life, trying unselfishly to work for the greater good of others rather than pursuing purely selfish goals, trying to increase understanding between Communist China and the United States, working for world peace.

As examples of the kind of behavior which occurred as a result of such attitude change we can cite the following: apologies by a subject for having a seemingly expensive apartment or for owning nonessential appliances like a TV set; guilt feelings over any self-

* This concept was suggested by Inge Schneier and reflects our feeling that the people in this group whom we met some years after their repatriation still exhibited a strong generalized sense of commitment and stated this to be one of the most important things they had learned in prison. It is as if they were saying that their greatest sin prior to thought reform was just not caring about the plight of man. The only good published account of this type of conversion is Rickett & Rickett, 1957.

indulgence like buying some prints or thinking about buying a house; worry about being able to "talk to the man in the street" because of heightened awareness in prison of snobbish attitudes; fear of "talking down"; rejection of former friends who were associated with a period of life which now seems frivolous and in the context of which the friends are seen as reactionary, selfish, ignorant, and unfair; greater involvement than before in moral issues and rejection of typical "bourgeois" values of ambition, success, money; concern with the underdog, the underprivileged, the needy, and so on.

While members of this group have been outspoken politically and highly critical of the United States' economic and political system, they have not as far as we could tell attached themselves to particular political groups and have thus far taken only an academic interest in such groups. As far as we could tell, there has not, even in this most influenced of groups, been any switch in basic loyalty toward the Communists in general or the Chinese Communists in particular, though there is clearly an increased commitment to the Chinese people as such.

Whether from the Chinese Communist point of view these cases would represent instances of successful thought reform is therefore very difficult to assess. The Chinese aim is to inculcate "correct" attitudes, unquestioning obedience, loyalty, commitment, and willingness to pursue Communist objectives. In a sense, none of these things have been accomplished by coercive persuasion in any of its American subjects. At most, the experience has produced some fundamental attitude changes which have then produced a reintegration in the person, leaving him perhaps somewhat to the left politically by our own standards, but certainly no more so than many leftists who have never undergone Chinese imprisonment.

7

The Determinants of Belief and Attitude Change

The purpose of this chapter is to discuss those factors in the prisoner and those aspects of the imprisonment experience which, in our opinion, are related to successful influence in the sense of lasting belief and attitude change. If we consider the extensive outline of personal factors and experiences that was presented in the introduction to Part II, we can identify a number of them as being related to final attitude change. These are not variables which are necessary and/or sufficient, but rather variables which interacted to increase the probability of attitude change. Since the number of cases on which our analysis is based is small, we cannot treat the ensuing discussion as a set of conclusions. Rather, they should be viewed as hypotheses to be tested against future data.

THE INITIAL PSYCHOLOGICAL STATE OF THE PRISONER-TO-BE AND SITUATIONAL FACTORS

Proneness to Social Guilt

If the prisoner-to-be was susceptible to social guilt he was particularly vulnerable to the pressure of the cellmates in a group cell and was thus particularly prone to being unfrozen in a fundamental fashion. As we have indicated in Chapter 5, there were many bases on which a prisoner could feel guilty, and general guilt-proneness certainly increased the likelihood of being unfrozen; however, being specifically susceptible to social guilt fed so well into Communist accusations and into the general theme of reform that it must be considered to be a more specifically relevant variable.

Lack of Commitment or Lack of Inner Directedness *

If the prisoner-to-be had not yet found a cause or a basic set of goals and values to which to attach himself, or had not yet found a group into which he could integrate himself, he was more likely to be influenced in prison. Such a person was still searching for meaning and for significant emotional relationships and was therefore likely to have a weak sense of identity and to be prone to seeking information from the outside concerning his identity.

On the level of basic personality organization a similar variable was a basic tendency to want to relate to and comply with others, especially if they were in a position of prestige or authority. Such a tendency made it harder for a prisoner to dismiss the demands made of him by the Chinese, and, of course, if he treated them as reasonable in any degree, he became susceptible to further appeal or pressure.

Lack of Political Sophistication

If the prisoner was unsophisticated about the realities of Communist operations (as contrasted with lack of sophistication about Communist ideology), he was more prone to influence. In other words, knowledge or lack of knowledge about political ideologies was less relevant to the outcome of coercive persuasion than the ability of the prisoner quickly to "size up" the situation, to make accurate guesses about the intentions of the captors and about the means they would be likely to use in fulfilling such intentions. For example, the unsophisticated prisoner might be quite prepared to accept the Communist self-definition as agrarian reformers who would help a backward country like China to achieve a high standard of living by essentially acceptable means (i.e., without excessive brutality). If he accepted the modernization of China as a goal he

* We are using inner directed in the sense of Riesman *et al.*, 1953.

would tend to co-operate with the Communists even in his own thought reform. The sophisticated prisoner would be not only skeptical about the Communist self-definition and hence initially resistant to change, but also more able to assess just how far the influence agents would go in accomplishing their goals. Thus he might see that his value to them was greater alive than dead and would resist in spite of threats of death.

Lack of Prolonged First-Hand Contact with CCP Operations

As has previously been pointed out (Chapter 2), the CCP was very careful to train its soldiers to behave in an exemplary fashion during the take-over of a city, town, or country area. If a prisoner-to-be witnessed only this phase of CCP operations and was generally unsophisticated politically, he was likely to be convinced that the Communists were only agrarian reformers who would genuinely help China and should therefore be supported or at least not opposed. On the other hand, if the prisoner-to-be witnessed CCP methods of consolidating their power and their program of land reform, he came away with strong negative feelings toward the Communists because of their brutality and their basic disregard for the welfare of the common people if this welfare clashed with broader organizational objectives (e.g., raising food production, industrialization, communization of rural areas, etc.). Typically such subjects became uncompromisingly hostile to anything and everything the Communists did, including all aspects of the prison regimen. The witnessing of a single act of brutality could almost "inoculate" the prisoner-to-be against being coercively persuaded, because no amount of subsequent experience could ever make the Communists a credible source of information for him.

Quality of CCP Personnel Encountered

The degree to which a prisoner was influenceable depended in large measure on his initial attitude toward imprisonment. If his arrest and subsequent investigation were handled by obviously competent and confident political officials, he was more likely to be frightened and subsequently susceptible to being unfrozen than if the authorities he encountered were obviously incompetent. To come to believe the Communist message required the prisoner to have some confidence that they did indeed have a message. If his initial encounter with the Communists proved them to be stupid and gullible, the prisoner would be more likely to continue to discredit anything they told him no matter how plausible or appealing.

The best example of stiffening resistance as a result of contact with low-level authorities occurred in a small town where a medical missionary was arrested by soldiers and charged with espionage on the "evidence" that some staplers he had in his house were telegraph keys and that his transformer was a radio transmitter. This person concluded that the Communists were hopeless, and nothing he encountered in prison could change his mind about them.

Of course, the contact prior to and during arrest was by no means the only important determinant. Subsequent experiences in interrogation and in the cell were probably more important. However, it often seemed to be the case that certain prisons in China, usually the ones farthest away from Peiping, had poor-quality personnel in all phases of their operation so that initial impressions were often reinforced by subsequent events.

Attitudes of the Local Populace Toward the
Prisoner-to-Be and the CCP

If the prisoner-to-be was arrested at a time when the local populace was negatively disposed toward him and positively disposed toward the CCP, he was more likely to be influenced later than if he felt that both he and the local populace had to hold the line against CCP domination. For example, if a doctor or priest who was very popular in his area was arrested at a time when the local populace was still giving him support and comfort, he would resist strongly in order to remain loyal to this group. If at a later time the CCP forced the local population to abandon or repudiate such a person publicly and convincingly (by a propaganda campaign against him or by outright threats that continued contact with and support of a "counter-revolutionary" or "foreign imperialist" would lead to suspicion of similar tendencies in the Chinese involved), he would lose a strong support in his own struggle with the authorities and would lose some sense of commitment to his cause.

For many of our cases this was not a major issue insofar as they had not been in China long enough to form close attachments to individual Chinese or their jobs did not call for local support. The attitudes they *perceived* in the population of course played some role in structuring their own, but it did not have the same significance when this population was essentially a mass of anonymous "others" without immediate emotional relevance to the person.

Type of Facilities Available for Detention

Some prisoners were detained indefinitely in their own home; some were herded into completely inadequate prison facilities; some were imprisoned in modern, well-run reform prisons. The facilities available usually were highly correlated with the presence or absence of a number of other factors pertaining to the imprisonment experience itself, which will be taken up in the next section. For the present, suffice it to say that only those prisoners who found themselves in a reasonably well-managed reform prison were at all likely to be influenced.

Knowledge of the Chinese Language

Knowledge of Chinese proved to be important to the extent that lengthy and intimate interaction with cellmates or interrogators was important as an influencing force. The better the prisoner knew Chinese, the more susceptible he was to many kinds of subtle pressures like being humiliated, reviled, accused, etc. One prisoner reported that he learned Chinese while in prison and that pressures on him grew much worse after he understood the language than they ever were before (Ford, 1957). Some prisoners "forgot" their Chinese as a way of protecting themselves from overinvolvement.

It is not surprising that this factor should be important, since so much of the unfreezing pressure lay in the interpersonal communications between agent and target. It is much harder to exacerbate an identity crisis in a situation in which the interpersonal cues emitted by the agent fail to be understood by the target than in a situation in which the target is highly sensitive to all aspects of the behavior of others around him. The insertion of a translator destroys much of the immediate potency of the interpersonal situation because of the untranslatability of the feelings which are generated in the inter-action among cellmates and the awkwardness and loss of time involved.

Youth

Age seemed to become a factor in several ways. On the one hand, it was the younger person who was more likely to lack commitment and political sophistication. On the other hand, the very old person was likely to command respect from his Chinese jailers in spite of Communist efforts to subvert this cultural tradition, and hence have less pressure put upon him to confess or change his attitudes. It is also probably true as a general principle that, other things being equal, the younger the person the more influenceable he is. With as small a sample of cases as we have, we certainly cannot make any sweeping statements about age, but we can note our impression that the very old prisoners seemed least likely to confess or to change their attitudes, prisoners of middle age (40–55) sometimes made confessions but seldom exhibited attitude change, while younger prisoners (25–35) showed the most of both confession and attitude change. It should, of course, be underlined that age by itself means nothing. We need to be able to identify what psycho-logical or experiential factors contributed to the fact that the younger prisoner was more likely to change his attitudes.

VARIABLES PERTAINING TO THE PRISON EXPERIENCE ITSELF

Initial Contact with Judge or Interrogator

Though it was not always apparent to the prisoner at the time, the nature of the initial contact with a judge or interrogator played a key role in determining certain of his attitudes later. In particular, it was the presentation of the Chinese Government's "lenient policy" which had this impact. If the prison was well run, the judge was likely to indicate to the prisoner that the government was very lenient with anyone who confessed sincerely, saw the error of his past behavior and attitudes, and made a sincere attempt to reform himself. He did not indicate what the charges against the prisoner were or indicate what he was to confess to; rather he created an atmosphere which was somewhat therapeutic in suggesting that the prisoner examine his own conscience and learn to see his crimes for himself. At the same time he would indicate that the evidence against the prisoner was quite clear-cut and that there was absolutely no doubt of his guilt. Hence the opportunity of reform was really leniency on the government's part.

If the prison was not well run, the judge or interrogator was likely to accuse the prisoner harshly, make dire threats concerning the consequences of not confessing, and generally underplay the leniency and reform aspects of imprisonment. In the accusation he was likely to demand that the prisoner confess to being a spy or saboteur without, however, giving any clues as to what he had in mind by way of the alleged behavior engaged in by the prisoner.

The lenient approach, emphasizing self-analysis and reform, had its biggest impact when the prisoner later became aware that other prisoners really accepted this premise, worked hard at reforming themselves (confessing and changing their attitudes), and were indeed rewarded by the authorities and given shorter sentences. One of our subjects stated that it was quite a shock to him to discover that this lenient policy really meant what it said, that the government really was serious about rehabilitating and reforming people. He had not believed the judge upon initial contact, but once he saw the system in operation he remembered very vividly the attitude that the judge had taken toward him. Of course, if the prison was not well run there was likely to be among the prisoners a preponderance of sheer opportunists or outrightly hostile (toward the CPP) types, in which case the whole concept of leniency became merely an academic matter.

One other aspect of the initial contact with prison authorities which was important was the type of threat they employed and the degree to which they were convincing in employing it. In particular, if the threat of permanent imprisonment was presented in a convincing manner, e.g., if the subject came to believe that there really was no way out of prison except through confession and reform, and that the Chinese really were prepared to hold on to him for twenty, thirty, or more years, he became more prone to being influenced. To achieve such a belief in the prisoner it seemed that a soft approach which stimulated fear was far more effective than a harsh accusing approach which stimulated hostility. Perhaps the crucial variable was whether the prisoner perceived his judge or interrogator to be an essentially rational person who was rationally pursuing certain goals (to obtain a confession, for example) or a highly emotional, capricious person whose very capriciousness might raise doubts in the prisoner's mind concerning the seriousness and permanence of his condition. In the former case it was probably much more difficult for the prisoner to tolerate physical stresses (such as being restrained by handcuffs and chains) than in the latter case, because in the latter case the prisoner could convince himself that it was the capricious sadism of the interrogator that resulted in his pain, whereas in the former case it was somehow his own failure to produce what the interrogator wanted which resulted in the physical pain. The rational interrogator would point out that only uncooperative prisoners were ever given chains and cuffs to wear, and that they would come off as soon as any evidence was forthcoming that the prisoner was really interested in "settling his case."

In terms of our influence model, the initial contact with the interrogator usually led to feelings which could operate as forces either toward confessing or against it in the unfreezing stage. Our hypothesis is that the generally rational, soft, lenient approach was effective in inducing fear of permanent imprisonment and perhaps desire to please the authorities, both of which can be thought of as forces toward confessing; on the other hand, the harsh emotional, hostile approach was effective in inducing counter-hostility which operated as a force against confessing.

The Debilitating Prison Regimen

The prison regimen needs to be mentioned only briefly because its effects varied markedly from prisoner to prisoner, and different prisoners picked out entirely different aspects of this regimen as being the ones which for them heightened the probability of being influenced. For example, if we consider the problems of bodily need management, the degree to which a particular prison routine became a source of stress to the individual varied markedly with his past history, his attitudes toward his body, and so on. For one prisoner the lack of opportunity to clean up properly was a major torture; for another it was a minor annoyance. For some prisoners the toilet restrictions which sometimes led to incontinence were a tremendous humiliation; others barely cared about having to urinate or defecate into their own clothes when not permitted to go to the toilet. For almost every one of the factors mentioned in Chapter 4, we could cite some prisoners who minded very much and others who barely minded at all.

The question then arises: Was the rather stressful prison regimen irrelevant to the occurrence of influence, or were there over-all effects that can be identified? It is our hypothesis that the *over-all* effect of the prison regimen was to weaken many of the supports upon which a prisoner might ordinarily rely in his daily life (see Table 3 in Chapter 4). To the extent that this regimen was physically stressful, it weakened the prisoner physically and generally lowered his ability to cope with whatever new stresses were introduced. To the extent that the regimen deprived the prisoner of his normal daily routine and, in fact, forced him into behavior which he might have thought very untypical of himself (such as soiling himself, or being unclean, or eating unpalatable food, etc.), it undermined his self-image or sense of identity. To the extent that the prison regimen forbade contacts with persons outside or with accustomed-to information sources, it undermined cognitive supports for the prisoner's beliefs and attitudes. To the extent that the prison regimen enforced certain patterns of deference and servility to guards and higher authorities, it heightened the prisoner's sense of dependency, lack of freedom, and lack of opportunity to express his own will. In a sense the prisoner was carefully being trained to be dependent by a totally inflexible environment dedicated to making him dependent.

The over-all effect of these separate forces was to make the prisoner sufficiently uncomfortable to want to get out of prison quite badly, and in this sense the prison regimen induced a strong force toward finding *some* solution to his problems. The recognition of needing to make a certain kind of confession as *the* solution might have come much later; but once the recognition came there were strong motives available to make the prisoner go through with it.

The retrospective perception of the prison environment and its regimen of course varied with the degree to which the prisoner was influenced. We have pointed out previously that influence could be thought of primarily as a shift in the frame of reference for evaluation. The perceptions of the prison experience illustrate this shift. Generally speaking, those prisoners who were most influenced were most likely to state later that prison life was really quite comfortable, and, in particular, to underline how much better life was in prison under the Communists than it would have been under the KMT. Where we would tend to compare the prison regimen with life outside of prison or with American prisons, the influenced subject, operating from the premise that he was guilty and therefore had to be imprisoned in China, judged the imprisonment in terms of the Chinese standard. He considered what might have happened to him if the Communists had not introduced the concept of reform and had not provided adequate food, clothing, and heat in their prisons. In other words, in terms of an old Chinese standard, the prison was in fact well run and well equipped.

The subjects found to have been influenced to a greater degree were for the most part incarcerated in prisons in or near Peiping. It was apparently true that these prisons were better equipped and better run than those in other cities or rural areas. The physically more comfortable regimen in these prisons supports our conclusion that physical stresses alone were not a crucial variable in determining the amount of influence. Many of the prisoners who resisted most were also in the most physically grueling situations. Many prisoners who were influenced most were physically pressed very little.

"Struggle" Meetings in Group Cells

One of the most provocative hypotheses which our study suggests is that a period of being "struggled" by cellmates in a group cell was a *necessary* condition of being influenced to confess and change attitudes. In other words, the induction of a motive to change, the actual facilitation of change, and the reward of changes accomplished were all carried out primarily in the context of the personal relationships existing between cellmates.

Most prisoners experienced both solitary confinement and confinement in groups ranging in size from two to twenty or more. It has often been assumed that the explanation of a prisoner's weakening was to be found in the periods of isolation and solitary confinement he suffered.* Our data support the opposite conclusion—that the major stress for prisoners was to survive psychologically in a group cell in which the prisoners were committed to reforming themselves and particularly their most backward member.

Not all group cells functioned as explicit influence agents. Prisons varied in the degree to which they utilized group cells for this purpose and in the sophistication with which they employed them. At one extreme we found the case exemplified by one of the Shanghai prisons in which the prisoner was put into a cell containing one other prisoner according to the criterion of whether the two men knew each other or not. If they did not, they were allowed to share a cell. The prison regulations explicitly forbade any communication between the prisoners and enforced these by clandestine spying on the prisoners followed by severe punishment if any cellmates were caught talking with each other. The authorities used this strategy to make each prisoner feel like a nonentity, a number, a case which was to be settled solely between him and his interrogator. This system failed in that prisoners, in spite of regulations, would start to talk to each other and in many cases discover that they shared strong feelings of hostility toward the authorities which gave them a common bond that markedly strengthened their capacity to resist. In this same prison Western prisoners were moved

* The impact of long periods of solitary confinement varied markedly with the personality of the prisoner and the location of this experience in the broader set of experiences. For example, priests who were used to leading a solitary life seemed to prefer solitary confinement to other forms of cell life. Similarly, individuals who had been subjected to very severe and traumatic group-cell pressure were much relieved to be placed in solitary confinement (though, of course, if the authorities anticipated this reaction they did not provide the opportunity for this kind of relief).

several times, often into cells containing other "reactionary" or resistive prisoners; and each successive experience with cellmates reinforced their will to resist the Communists because of the increasing sympathy which learning of each other's cases seemed to generate.

At the other extreme, in the Peiping prisons the Western prisoner was usually put deliberately in a cell with several Chinese prisoners who were on the way to reforming themselves (who had already made confessions or were working on them). In these cells the regulations sanctioned and, in fact, demanded communication between cellmates. Specifically, they were to "help" their one recalcitrant member see the error of his ways, get him to admit his guilt, and help him to construct his confession. Usually the cell had a leader and it was made known through his contact with the authorities that the progress of the entire cell was contingent on the performance of their least-reformed members.

It is not unlikely that the prisoner's cellmates believed in his guilt, in that they believed that the government did not arrest or manacle (if he was manacled) innocent people. From their point of view, therefore, the prisoner's refusal to acknowledge his guilt must have been seen as genuine perversity and have represented not only a great threat (that they would all be held back), but also a challenge to their own skill in reforming others.* The Peiping prisoners' accounts detail vividly the accusation, browbeating, humiliation, revilement, etc., which characterized the frequent "struggle" meetings as well as the daily routine in the cell. Apparently it was the intensity and continuity of these pressures that was particularly difficult to handle. There was no escape during the entire

* At one point in his imprisonment, one of our Shanghai cases was put into such a cell, but two things made the experience very different: one, the other cellmates were intellectually and professionally far inferior to the priest; and, two, to be put into such a cell after a year or more of successfully resisting and forming emotional ties with other prisoners who were also resisting made the experience lose its emotional impact. What happened in cases like this was usually that the Western prisoner began actively to try to undo the effects which the authorities had produced, to show the other cellmates that they were not really guilty and should not feel so guilty, that the government had duped them, etc. Often they were successful, resulting in their being returned to solitary confinement.

twenty-four-hour day, and "struggle" sometimes lasted for months.*

The effect of these experiences on the prisoner can be inferred from two kinds of data: the influenced prisoners themselves attribute much of the cause of their change to their group cell experiences; the uninfluenced prisoners usually report that of all the stresses they ever had to bear the group cell was the worst, or they report that they were never subjected to any struggle meetings in a group cell of more reformed prisoners.

It is difficult to determine whether the group cell and its activities were a unique kind of influence, or whether such group cell activities always accompanied a prison regimen which was *in toto* dedicated to reform. We found that those prisons which did not seem to be either very qualified for or interested in reform tended not to utilize this type of group cell; whereas those prisons, particularly the one in Peiping, which were heavily committed to successfully reforming their inmates and seemed to be staffed with more skilled personnel, always utilized group cells and struggle meetings. We do not know whether the use of such a group cell in a setting less committed to reform would still have had similar effects, or whether it was necessary that *all* of the aspects of the prison milieu and daily regimen reinforce each other to be successful in influencing inmates. Our guess is that a properly organized group is sufficient to produce influence but it may be difficult to organize such a group if the rest of the prison regimen does not support it.

Interrogation

We have previously mentioned the importance of the initial contact between the prisoner and the judge or interrogator. The nature of the continuing contact between them, usually in the context of repeated and prolonged interrogations which sometimes went on for the entire period of imprisonment, constituted a further variable of importance. Such contact was important in three ways:

1. If the interrogator was skilled and convincing, it reaffirmed

* The role of the group cell in unfreezing, changing, and refreezing has been discussed in greater detail in Chapter 4 where the special properties of the group which make it an effective change agent are listed in Table 4.

the prisoner's belief that the only way to get out of prison or to reduce discomfort or pain was to make some kind of confession.

2. If the prisoner's cellmates were culturally and intellectually very different from the prisoner himself, it was the interrogator who often became a model for the prisoner to identify with and hence the agent of influence. We heard this from our subjects most often in the following form. They had an increasing need to talk to someone without feeling that they were merely playing a role; this someone had to be similar to themselves and share some common interests with them; and in the prison group, it was the interrogator who was most likely to fulfill the qualifications for a subject who was fairly highly educated. If the interrogator encouraged such a relationship by being matter-of-fact, sincere, logical, and calm, he could gain the confidence of the prisoner and build a relationship which then could become a lever for exerting influence.*

3. The interrogator was one of the direct agents of pain and pressure, a person who threatened, exhorted, questioned, tortured, pleaded, rewarded, punished, and did all the other things usually described in accounts of sophisticated interrogation. One major difference between him and the classical interrogator in military affairs was that he was not interested in getting the prisoner to divulge specific military information, but rather was interested in getting the prisoner to confess, which led to long discussions of the past history of the subject and a detailed analysis of all his activities. Because of the interrogator's role as the controller of the prisoner's ultimate as well as daily fate, strong feelings toward and about him were generated and such feelings could sometimes be used by him to exert influence.

Interrogation facilitated unfreezing in that it focused the prisoner's attention on his own past activities and attitudes, and maximized the likelihood of his finding something in his past which provoked guilt and hence induced a motive to change. The repeated writing

* Actually such relationships developed only in the few instances in which the needs of the prisoner and the personality of the interrogator complemented each other. An interesting question about which we can only conjecture is whether the relationship with the interrogator was more likely to be a father-child relationship, while a relationship with a cellmate was more likely to be a sibling or a peer-group relationship.

of a long and detailed autobiography often led to a genuine soul-searching, particularly if the interrogator guided the prisoner's thinking along the lines most likely to reveal the inadequacies of his past or of the social system in which he had spent his life. Such inquiries into the past were engaged in with equal force by the members of the group cell; but the interrogator could follow a thread through carefully and sympathetically, as would a therapist, whereas the group was more likely to aim at a quick destruction of resistance. If the prisoner formed a close attachment to a cellmate, as often happened as a result of "struggle," such an individual would become even closer to the prisoner than the interrogator had, and would help him to see his past in a new perspective toward the aim of getting him to make his confession.

In summary, interrogation along with cellmate pressure was an important variable insofar as it could operate to convince the prisoner of the hopelessness of his situation and could provide the basis of an emotional relationship between prisoner and interrogator. The development of such a relationship might be facilitated because of the prisoner's total dependence on the interrogator, and could then be used as a lever for influence. It was not possible to determine very accurately what skills on the part of an interrogator worked toward this aim, except that calm, rational, non-hostile approaches always seemed to work better than excited, emotional, hostile ones.

The Use of Rewards and Punishments

The use of rewards and punishments cuts across all the other conditions which have been discussed. In a well-run reform prison, the authorities made adequate diagnoses of what would constitute significant rewards and punishments for a prisoner (or used trial and error to determine it), and, insofar as possible, organized the prison in such a manner as to maximize the punishment for not confessing or changing attitudes while maximizing the rewards for confession and change. If the whole prison regimen was organized in this fashion, if the prisoner could get *no* reward except by co-operation, this total inflexibility constituted a great pressure on him.

The effectiveness of reward or punishment depended on the

rapidity with which it was administered following some response by a prisoner that could be diagnosed as either an attempt to co-operate or an attempt to resist. It is a well-known principle of learning that the efficacy of reward and punishment decreases as the time lag between the response and the administration of reward or punishment increases. The use by the authorities of effective in-formation-gathering channels, and the use of cellmates as surrogates for the authorities, insured a minimum time lag in this sense. For example, a prisoner living in the midst of several others who were "struggling" him was subjected to constant evaluation and the other prisoners were highly sensitized to detect any changes in attitude in him. If he began to see a solution, e.g., to see what he was to con-fess to and how to do it, this usually manifested itself in a slight change of behavior, and such a slight change was immediately re-warded by the cellmates by a lightening of pressure on him and was followed by strong encouragement and guidance as to how he should proceed.

The moment such a change in attitude was communicated to the interrogator (usually through the cell leader), a variety of physical pressures on the prisoner were lifted (e.g., chains and manacles might have been removed). The moment there was a change in the other direction, from a co-operative attitude to one of stiffening resistance, such physical pressures were intensified and the cell-mates intensified their efforts to get the prisoner to change once again.

It is unlikely that the whole system operated with as much effectiveness as has been depicted, but one senses that the au-thorities were attempting to use rewards and punishments in the manner described above, and when they succeeded they were build-ing into the prison regimen strong forces toward producing changes in the prisoner. Failure of adequate diagnosis by given prisoners of what were significant rewards and punishments provided some of the tragi-comic incidents of imprisonment. This could happen when the prisoner was offered some privilege as a reward, yet failed com-pletely to understand it as a reward (e.g., some Chinese delicacy which he still found unpalatable); his failure to react favorably then often led to the interpretation on the part of the authorities that he was strongly reactionary after all, since he failed to appreciate what the Chinese people were doing for him (a brand new crime to be added to the list of old ones), and therefore deserved to be treated more harshly than ever.

A number of subjects have stated that the authorities also used kindness and specific rewards as a *manipulative device* to *induce* motivation to change, *whether an initially co-operative response had been made by the prisoner or not.* It is a general principle of learning that you cannot teach a person to make a new response by the method of reward unless that response occurs for the first time spontaneously. It is a question, therefore, whether such alleged manipulation, or "calculated leniency" as Lifton (1956b) calls it, actually operated to show the prisoner what life could be like *if* he made certain kinds of responses; whether the authorities were using such a manipulation without an adequate understanding of what they were doing; or whether co-operative responses were in fact sensed by the authorities prior to their giving the rewards, but the prisoners themselves do not remember it or report the sequence inaccurately. It is quite possible that the first alternative, to show the prisoner a way out, is the rationale underlying this use of reward, but it should be remembered that such a stratagem does not show the prisoner what he is to do. To be told that a bright future awaits you if you do the right thing, but not to be given further clues as to what constitutes the right thing, can only lead to further frustration. And we must not underestimate the degree to which authorities and cellmates alike insisted on sincere and honest confessions, something which the prisoner at first failed completely to comprehend. Most prisoners knew that a false confession would lead to more punishment than reward, hence were motivated toward somehow finding out what was really wanted of them. Calculated leniency could not help them to find the answer. But reward which followed swiftly some cognitive step in the right direction (some beginning of understanding of what the "people's standpoint" was) would strongly help to keep the person on the path that would lead to the ultimate answer.

As a final point, it should be mentioned that the indiscriminate use of reward and punishment is certainly a powerful way to disorganize an individual. If one wanted to "break" an individual in the sense of the popular concept of brainwashing, this could certainly be an effective way to do it. But we cannot underline strongly enough that this was not the Communists' aim in a reform prison. They had a clear conception of what constituted a crime, a clear image of how the criminal should behave in making his confession and reforming himself, and a clear goal of a reformed individual who had adopted the people's standpoint. At no point in this process would there be room for simply "breaking" the person.* Rather, the unfreezing phase, the weakening or destruction of supports to certain attitudes and responses, operated (in principle at least) to produce changes in a fully intact individual, and the new behavior and attitudes had to be built squarely on the foundation of old attitudes and behavior (but seen from a different perspective).

Our conclusion is, therefore, that the Communists did not utilize the administration of rewards and punishments simply as a manipulative device to break people, but had a rational program of punishing those responses which they felt signaled a lack of willingness on the part of the prisoner to reform himself and rewarding those responses which they felt signaled an attitude of willingness to reform himself.

Indoctrination: Study of the Communist Point of View

In the well-organized reform prison the prisoners were expected to spend a considerable amount of time on the study (*hsueh hsi*) of materials which were distributed by the authorities. The correct manner of conducting study was for each of the group members to read the material and then, in group discussion, to justify and rationalize the major conclusions of the material, as well as to indicate how the ideas in the material applied to his own case (see Table 5 in Chapter 4 and Appendix 2).

The success of such study, in the sense of influencing the prisoner

---

* The Communists were exceedingly proud of their civilized and progressive approach to the problem of prison management and it would only be the deviant jailer who had not assimilated the new Communist concepts who would rely on traditional methods of torture and attempt to extract a confession at literally "any price."

to accept the Communist point of view at anything more than a superficial level, depended on the manner in which it was integrated into the rest of the prison routine and on the individual prisoner's self-image and level of sophistication.

A prisoner who had already committed himself to co-operating with the authorities (by working on his confession or by genuinely trying to appreciate the CCP position) was likely to seek, in the written material handed out for study, justifications for the course of action upon which he had embarked. On the other hand, those prisoners who had resisted confession extraction or who had been exposed to somewhat crude and ineffective procedures treated the study as simply another regulation to which only lip service had to be given. Thus the timing of study was important in terms of the psychological state of the prisoner.

Where the timing was poor, it seemed primarily to be an artifact of generally unsophisticated methods of influencing the prisoners. The same personnel who were insensitive to the problems of how best to get confessions out of resistant prisoners were the ones who introduced study materials at arbitrarily chosen times, with a crude set of instructions, and without any clear notion of how they should really be used in aiding the reform process. An excellent example is given in the account of his imprisonment by a Chinese bishop (Huang, 1954). He describes how study materials were passed out by prison personnel who themselves did not understand them fully. When ideological questions arose in discussion which were not covered in the distributed materials, Bishop Huang would be asked to give his opinions on them because he could understand the ideology better in spite of his rejection of it. Thus he ended up in the incongruous position of "helping" his cellmates with their study though no one really took it seriously. In other words, if the prison was not well equipped for reform and the authorities did not basically care about reform, they introduced the study materials in much the same way as they might any set of routine instructions from higher authorities.

The relationship between the success of the study program and the prisoner's self-image and level of sophistication can be stated in the following manner. If the prisoner had an image of himself which allowed him to participate freely in the study program (either because he felt he would not be influenced, or because he felt that he could genuinely learn something about the Communist point of view), and if the prisoner was unsophisticated about the relationship between political realities and political theories, he was likely to be influenced. If his self-image would not allow him to become involved, even at the level of superficial compliance, or he was sophisticated enough to know that any level of involvement was dangerous, he was likely not to be influenced.

Many prisoners felt that they could not possibly participate in study activities because it would be sacrilege or blasphemy even to repeat certain Communist principles in a public situation (i.e., in front of other cellmates); others felt that the material presented was obvious nonsense in terms of what they knew to be the realities of Communist politics. If a prisoner could be appealed to to participate, (e.g., by being asked at least to consider the other side of the story, or because non-participation might brand him as stupid or uneducated, or because such participation was a much-needed relief from the boredom of the daily prison routine, etc.), he could often be convinced of the validity of the Communist standard of evaluation, at least in some areas, and thereby have his attitudes changed indirectly.

The use of a small discussion group for study tended to heighten involvement, encouraged the acceptance of membership roles, facilitated understanding by heightening mutual identification, and facilitated the overcoming of resistance because the resister could be unanimously condemned and criticized. Specific study techniques such as self-analysis, criticism (mutual and self), airing of grievances, etc., all tended to involve the person and heightened his sense of participation.

VARIABLES PERTAINING TO POST-IMPRISONMENT EXPERIENCES

This group of variables is somewhat more difficult to discuss because the action of any given variable depended very much on the degree to which the repatriate had been influenced. If we limit the discussion to those prisoners who showed a significant shift in attitudes, we can isolate a number of variables that seemed to be related to the *maintenance* of such attitude shifts. Our influence model indicated that for attitude shifts to maintain themselves the new equilibrium had to be re-frozen; that is, the new attitudes had to become integrated into other aspects of the personality and into ongoing social relationships in which they would receive support. If the repatriate's attitude shifts could be characterized as having been refrozen while he was still in prison, he could maintain such shifts so long as no new unfreezing or changing process was initiated. If they were not refrozen, the post-imprisonment experiences could operate to refreeze them or to undo them quickly by not supporting them. In isolating variables, then, we must seek those experiences following repatriation that would operate either as further supports for the new attitudes or as underminers of such attitudes.

Initial Contact with Representatives of the Non-Communist World

It is difficult to determine what were the crucial aspects of the initial contact between the repatriate and representatives of the government, mission, or other agency who met him and cared for him during the first few days of freedom; but almost all of our cases indicated that this initial contact was somehow very important.

One key aspect seemed to be the degree to which predictions made by the Communists in prison were confirmed or disconfirmed in these early contacts. If the Communists told a prisoner that the press would sensationalize his new attitudes, that he would be treated as a sick "brainwashed" person, that people would reject him, and that the American Government would treat him as a security risk and put him under surveillance, and any or all of these things actually happened, it would, of course, tend to lend further support to the new attitudes and fix them more firmly. Particularly crucial in this connection were the contacts with members of the United States Government. A number of the repatriates indicated to us their resentment of what they believed to be "planted agents" of the FBI or some other government agency whose job, they felt, was surreptitiously to spy on them. Since one of the key dimensions of their new attitude was increased sympathy for the Chinese Government and decreased sympathy for the United States Government (not the American people), such experiences seemed to strengthen anti-government attitudes.

Contacts with people who knew something about Communist China, even if they did not really understand the nature of thought reform, seemed to elicit less hostility from the repatriates than encounters with uninformed members of the press or interested onlookers who seemingly did not understand anything of what the prisoners had experienced. One of the strongest components of the repatriate's new attitudes was the feeling that he had acquired a genuine understanding of what were China's basic problems and what the CCP was trying to do about them. He felt that he knew perfectly well that the CCP operations were not perfect, but he was evaluating their efforts in terms of the KMT's ineffectiveness and in terms of the degree of need for reform which he perceived. With this understanding went the feeling that the West had conspicuously failed in its attempts to understand what the CCP was trying to do and had created a genuine information vacuum about Communist China. Given this feeling on the part of the repatriate, it is not difficult to see how a reporter trying to learn more or a bystander asking innocent questions could confirm precisely what the repatriate had come to believe—namely that there was no understanding on the part of Westerners of what was going on in China, especially of events such as those which he had experienced himself. And it became very easy for him to attribute this ignorance to the policies of the American government and thereby confirm for himself his attitudes toward it.

In summary, the important aspect of the repatriate's initial contact with non-Communists seemed to be the manner in which these contacts confirmed or disconfirmed Communist predictions and aspects of the repatriate's new attitude. Of particular importance seemed to be the fact that Communist predictions were of such a nature that they were likely to be confirmed, which resulted for several repatriates in a strengthening of their new attitudes following release, rather than a weakening of them simply by virtue of being out of prison.

Ongoing Relationships with Significant Others

As has previously been argued, a person's key support of attitudes pertaining to self or the sense of identity comes from his emotional relationships with "significant others." It is the informational cues that these significant others provide which serve to reinforce or destroy identity, and which therefore are the crucial determinants of attitude and identity change (Schein, 1960). A repatriate could only maintain his new attitudes if he could embed them successfully in a significant emotional relationship, i.e., find some person with whom he was very close and who would support the new attitudes in the sense of accepting them and agreeing with them. If the repatriate could find no one who would fulfill this role, and if, in fact, the significant people in his life all failed to confirm the new identity and did not accept and agree with the new attitudes, he would again be influenced toward some new integration of beliefs and attitudes.

In our follow-up studies we have found instances of both types. Some repatriates found very secure emotional relationships which supported the attitudes learned in prison—these cases have maintained most of their new attitudes and have integrated them into their daily existence in this country. Other repatriates found themselves in emotional relationships which did not support the attitudes learned in prison—these cases have abandoned their new attitudes and have again found new integrations, or are still seeking them. Finally, a few cases have found themselves in the situation of having available both kinds of such relationships and have vacillated between commitment to some who would support the attitudes learned in prison and commitment to others who would demand the abandonment of such attitudes.

Situational Factors

A number of additional variables should be mentioned which derive their main importance from the fact that they seem to have further confirmed what the Communists had predicted, and that they determined the kinds of new emotional relationships that would be facilitated and made probable.

For example, the ongoing foreign policy of the United States vis-à-vis China was watched closely by most of the repatriates for evidence of the truth or falsity of Communist claims concerning our imperialistic and aggressive intentions and our policy of remaining ignorant of Chinese mainland affairs. To the extent that they perceived in this policy a confirmation of CCP claims, it of course confirmed and strengthened their new attitudes. Similarly, the repatriates might infer from their direct contact with our economic system (via their own efforts to find suitable jobs and places to live) whether Communist claims about this economic system are supportable or not. Obviously the conclusion drawn by any given repatriate would here be a function of an immense number of essentially fortuitous factors.

The nature of the contact which the repatriate had with different strata of American society was also a significant situational factor. There is some evidence to support the conclusion that contact with working-class members of this society operated to disconfirm the repatriate's new attitudes while contact with upper middle-class members or members of underprivileged groups served to confirm them. To the extent that members of the working class (who "earn" their position by their direct contribution, rather than by family origin, according to Communist doctrine) became a significant reference group for the repatriate, the discovery by him of their strong support of American traditions and their lack of support for Chinese Communist methods of control and organization became a strong disconfirming force for the new attitudes. On the other hand, seeing social injustice at first hand by having primary contact with members of society whose contribution was seen to be questionable by the repatriate (the rich businessman) or who were the failures and rejects of society (the slum-dwellers) would, of course, reinforce Communist attitudes concerning social class and the social ills which capitalistic economic organization allegedly breeds. To a large extent the kind of contact the repatriate had was a function of his decisions as to where to go and what to do, but for some of them, fortuitous factors entered, such as having to go to a hospital for prolonged treatment of TB, having friends and relatives who lived in a certain kind of surroundings, or being asked to participate in political activities, etc.

Becoming involved in activities that have political significance was particularly important in that it elicited behavioral commitment which would require further justification and further alignment of attitudes with behavior. The pro-Communist repatriate who was asked to speak to leftist groups about his experiences had his attitudes reinforced just as much by this activity as did the strongly anti-Communist repatriate who was asked to speak to anti-Communist groups. In turn, such activities made available ranges of people with whom the repatriate could form relationships and who would support whatever attitudes he brought from prison.

The main point is that we cannot assume that mere re-entry into our society will guarantee a discarding of anti-American and pro-Communist attitudes, nor can we assume that individuals who do not drop such attitudes now constitute a hard corps of Communists ready to destroy democratic society. Rather the evidence from the very small number of cases for whom such attitude changes were significant points clearly to a complex embedding of the new attitudes in the ongoing personality and social relationships of the person concerned, and the new integration seems to have as many different basic features as there were different personalities and different sets of experiences involved.

CONCLUSIONS

In this section we have attempted to delineate those features of the total experience of our cases which seem to constitute crucial variables for determining the degree to which they were influenced. We have stated in many places that these variables interacted strongly with each other, which makes it very difficult to isolate a few of them as the necessary and sufficient conditions of attitude change. Our hypothesis is that the occurrence of influence in the direction of the acceptance of pro-Communist attitudes (i.e., using the "people's standpoint" as a new frame of reference for evaluating the self, the United States, the CCP, and the prison experiences) is made most probable if:

1. The prisoner is prone to social guilt or guilt regarding the Chinese "people."

2. The prisoner lacks a sense of commitment to some cause or group and is not strongly inner directed.

3. The prisoner is not sophisticated about politics (Communist politics in particular).

4. The prisoner has not had first-hand contact with CCP operations during the phase of consolidating their power and initiating their programs such as Land Reform.

5. The prisoner has contact with high caliber CCP personnel during all phases of his imprisonment.

6. The prisoner (if he has attachments among the Chinese) loses the support of Chinese to whom he feels committed.

7. The prisoner finds himself in a well-organized, physically adequate prison.

8. The prisoner knows the Chinese language.

9. The prisoner is relatively young.

10. Initial contacts with the judge or interrogator lead the prisoner to believe in the sincerity of the Chinese Government concerning their leniency to those who are willing to reform themselves.

11. The prison regimen operates to weaken the prisoner and remove his usual social and psychological supports.

12. Struggle meetings are held in cells in which the cellmates are well on the way to becoming reformed and are highly motivated to reform their new member.

13. A relationship forms between the interrogator and the prisoner which can be exploited by the interrogator.

14. Rewards and punishments are used consistently to reinforce co-operation with the authorities.

15. Study of Communist materials by group discussion is correctly timed and worked into the prison regimen.

16. Contacts following repatriation tend to confirm predictions made by the Communists.

17. Emotional relationships support whatever changes have occurred in prison.

18. Events in this society and types of groups encountered rein-

force and confirm what the Communists had predicted and the new attitudes.

In looking down this list it becomes quite apparent that some of the later variables can only operate if some of the earlier conditions have been met. A given influence technique like group study could only be effective if the prisoner had already been partially influenced. American foreign policy could only be seen as confirming pro-Communist perceptions if those perceptions were actually there. This is one kind of interaction between the variables. Another kind which we have repeatedly mentioned is that some prisons seemed to be effective in all of their operations while others were ineffective in all of them. Similarly, some prisoners, perhaps those whom the Communists diagnosed early as likely to be influenceable, were subjected to a regimen very likely to produce influence, while others were essentially left alone. These factors make it difficult to state with any more precision than we have which variable of the above long list is really any more crucial than which other variable. The only one about which we have a strong hunch is "struggle" meetings in a group cell. All the evidence supports the conclusion that "struggle" in group cells was the single most effective device used to influence the prisoner.

PART THREE *Theories of Coercive Persuasion*

A NUMBER OF specific theories have been proposed to explain how and why changes occurred in the beliefs, attitudes, values, and behavior patterns of prisoners. Most of these theories postulate a particular mechanism as *the* explanation for the outcomes observed (e.g., Pavlovian conditioning, hypnosis, dissonance reduction, transfer of guilt-anxiety, identity change, social conformity pressure, etc.). As Chapter 4 has attempted to explain, we view the influence process as a fairly complex sequence of events involving the three major phases of *unfreezing, changing,* and *refreezing*; we feel further that each of the psychological mechanisms which are suggested in the various one-factor explanations is important for understanding some part of the total change sequence. We do not feel that any one of them alone can explain the outcomes observed in the different phases, nor do we feel that any one can be dispensed with as irrelevant. Our job in the next two chapters, then, is to show where various psychological mechanisms are relevant and where we feel the limits of their utility lie.

For the most part we have considered only theories which have explicitly attempted to explain "brainwashing." We have not, except in the sections of Chapter 9 on the social psychology of influence, treated works which could explain some of the outcomes of coercive persuasion unless their authors themselves made the attempt. Our purpose is not to show how one could relate different theories to coercive persuasion, but rather, to evaluate existing explanatory attempts and to develop a conceptual scheme which can encompass coercive persuasion as well as other types of influence processes.

The major criterion for the utility of such a scheme (and the major criterion by which we shall evaluate the theories to be presented below) is its capacity to organize a wide range of observed data into meaningful categories (variables) and to state causal relationships between these variables. The degree to which the variables developed are also conceptually pure, operationally definable, and easily measurable will only be considered secondarily in our evaluation.

Theoretical mechanisms which have been suggested as explanations for coercive persuasion fall into a number of general categories. First, we have a number of explanations based largely on *psycho-physiological stress* mechanisms. We include here Sargant's (1957) use of Pavlovian conditioning (he emphasizes the physiological aspects of conditioning particularly) and Hunter (1953); Hinkle and Wolff's (1956) analysis of the debilitating effects of various psychological and physiological stresses; and theories about the effects of drugs, implanted electrodes, and other esoteric methods of allegedly producing specific involuntary behaviors (Miller, 1957; Huxley, 1958). Second, we have a series of explanations deriving from *traditional learning theory*, using either a Pavlovian or an instrumental conditioning model (Farber *et al.*, 1957; Winokur, 1955; Santucci & Winokur, 1955; Meerloo, 1954). Third, we have a series of explanations based on *psycho-analytic formulations* which emphasize in particular the vicissitudes of guilt and guilt-anxiety in the coercive persuasion process (Meerloo, 1956; Moloney, 1955; Lifton, 1956). These three theoretical positions will be treated in Chapter 8.

In Chapter 9 we shall consider explanations which are more socio-psychological. Thus a fourth type of explanation combines psychoanalytic theory with sociological formulations around the problem of *identity* (Lifton, 1956; Biderman, 1957; Schein, 1956, 1960; Goffman, 1957, 1959; Strauss, 1959). A fifth type of explanation puts emphasis on *cognitive processes* such as shifts in frame of reference and learning new semantic rules (Lifton, 1956b; Schein, 1956, 1960; Biderman, 1956). Finally, a number of formulations will be discussed which deal specifically with the *psychology of social influence* (Festinger, 1957; Kelman, 1958; Asch, 1951, 1952; Hovland *et al.*, 1953). Logically one should also include in this section those authors who feel that hypnosis or pseudo-hypnosis offers an explanation (Hunter, 1951; Meerloo, 1956; Huxley, 1958). However, these authors tend to see hypnosis as an esoteric technique of the kind referred to in our first category, rather than as a complex interpersonal influence process, and hence will be treated only in the former context.

Because most of the theories to be discussed are technical and rely in varying degrees on terminology, Part III will be generally more technical in nature. We shall examine each of the theories from the point of view of the psychology of influence; a reading of this part therefore presumes some familiarity with the technical vocabulary of psychology.

8

Theories of Coercive Persuasion I:
Stress, Learning, and
Psychoanalytic Theories

PSYCHO-PHYSIOLOGICAL STRESS

ONE OF THE most comprehensive and, we feel, most adequate descriptive accounts of the total coercive persuasion process is provided by Hinkle and Wolff (1956). They attribute the changes observed in the prisoner primarily to a state of mental and physical exhaustion resulting both from the combination of fatigue, pain, and physiological stress due to disease and malnutrition and from the psychological strain due to isolation, total dependency, and humiliation. According to Hinkle and Wolff, the prisoner then complies to his captors' bidding and accepts their beliefs as his own, even if his own are in contradiction to them, because his state of exhaustion results in his being confused, uncritical, and highly suggestible. Once the pressures are lifted and the prisoner is allowed to regain his physical and emotional energy he is said to recognize how he had been deceived, to revert to former behavior patterns and beliefs, and to repudiate his prison experience as having been basically a horrible ordeal. The stimulation of anxiety and guilt, the various social pressures, and the interpersonal contacts with cellmates and interrogators are seen primarily as contributing to the ultimate state of psycho-physiological exhaustion.

Hinkle and Wolff explicitly deny the relevance of Pavlovian mechanisms to an understanding of coercive persuasion (primarily because the Pavlovian formulations as used by Hunter, Meerloo, Sargant, and Huxley are such oversimplifications), but their own theory closely resembles the Pavlovian formulations in the emphasis they put upon psycho-physiological collapse. Sargant (1957) has made a vigorous, if somewhat loosely reasoned, argument for the analogy between the collapse which Pavlov saw in his experimentally induced neuroses in dogs and the collapse seen in various kinds of human conversion processes, of which he feels "brainwashing" is a good case in point. Specifically, he alleges that the brain (whether human or animal) will go into a state of severe "inhibition" if stimulated by unusually powerful stresses and emotional stimuli ("unusually powerful" stimuli being defined as stimuli well beyond the capacity of the organism to cope with by normal habitual means), and in this state will become highly suggestible and capable of a complete reversal of values. According to Sargant, such a state of inhibition is evidenced in the human by emotional collapse such as that seen in revival meetings, under the effects of barbiturates, under shock treatments of various sorts, in very severe and traumatic initiation rites, and so on. The fact that sharp changes in belief and value occur in all of these situations leads Sargant to the hypothesis that it is the emotional collapse and subsequent brain inhibition which, via the state of increased suggestibility, explains the change.

Hunter (1951, 1956) is less explicit in postulating specific theoretical mechanisms, but the burden of his argument is similar to the above two. By systematic pressure at the physical and psychological level a person is reduced to a state of confusion * in which he can no longer clearly distinguish what he believes and how he should act.

* Hunter gives the following definition of brainwashing: Brainwashing . . . is an effort to put a man's mind into a fog so that he will mistake what is true for what is untrue, what is right for what is wrong, and come to believe what did not happen actually had happened, until he ultimately becomes a robot for the Communist manipulator. (Hunter, 1956, p. 67)

The feature which these theories have in common is evident—that the change in the victim of coercive persuasion is to be explained by a systematically created state of psycho-physiological exhaustion, in which state the victim cannot think clearly enough and does not have will enough to avoid accepting beliefs and engaging in behavior which he would ordinarily resist strongly. A key assumption upon which such a formulation rests is that a state of high suggestibility and uncriticalness results from such exhaustion. The assumption is crucial because only in such a psychological state might one expect a person to accept beliefs that are in flat contradiction to other beliefs he holds. In this argument lies a second assumption, however, which must be made explicit. All these formulations accept as given that coercive persuasion involves the acceptance of beliefs which are in contradiction to other beliefs or values the person holds, that these new beliefs are somehow *added* to the personality rather than being integrated into it, and that these new beliefs will be given up as soon as psychophysiological equilibrium has once again been reached (i.e., when the captor's pressure is lifted). The implication is that the victim and captor are always in a situation of total conflict with each other.

Miller (1957), in conjecturing about possible future developments, extends this line of thought by noting the potentialities of sensory deprivation, new kinds of tranquilizing pharmaceuticals, electrodes implanted in the brain, etc., for eliciting behavior which the prisoner would not ordinarily engage in. Again, the key assumption is that the new behavior is totally unthinkable for the prisoner, hence some means must be found to get him to produce it involuntarily, whether this be by Pavlovian conditioned reflexes or some other esoteric means.

Critique

1. Our study of those cases in whom any attitude change was accomplished by the Chinese suggests that the psycho-physiological stress explanation applies only to limited portions of the total imprisonment experience, and that very few, if any, special physiological stress-producing devices were ever consciously employed by the captor. In other words, even in those cases where

physical and physiological stress was fairly extreme, both the prisoner's and captor's attention was on the *psychological* facts about the prisoner which were implied by his debilitated condition, and it is these psychological facts which constituted the greater pressure in our opinion. For example, the wearing of handcuffs and ankle chains was intensely painful and debilitating, but worse, it was perceived by the prisoner's cellmates as the symbol of his recalcitrance and unwillingness to reform himself and thus served as the justification for further humiliation, revilement, and brutalization.

The psycho-physiological stresses entered into the unfreezing process in generally lowering the prisoner's resistance, but the assumption is not tenable, in our opinion, that such lowering of resistance is equivalent to the production of a state of uncriticalness and high suggestibility. The most that could be said is that these stresses facilitated unfreezing and the induction of a motive to change. But the prisoner could not be said at this time to have been mentally incapable of exercising critical judgment (though it might have seemed that way to him retrospectively). On the contrary, in some cases the prisoner gained in such a crisis situation some very clear notions and insights concerning himself and his total situation.

2. The assumption that coercive persuasion is fundamentally a process of an omnipotent captor finding a way to convince an impotent prisoner of something that the prisoner would not ordinarily accept, i.e., the assumption that the captor-induced beliefs are completely in conflict with the prisoner's, may be applicable to a few cases but certainly is not an accurate description of the situation of those cases who were influenced by the process. The psycho-physiological exhaustion explanation is basically irrelevant to those cases in which influence resulted from a gradual shifting of the cognitive frame of reference, the adoption of new standards of evaluation, and the discovery of new perceptions of self and others (none of which were necessarily in fundamental conflict with the person's own value system). As in other influence processes like psychotherapy, very drastic measures may be utilized to create a state in which the patient or prisoner is "ready" to have new

perceptions or conceptions, but these new perceptions or conceptions are not necessarily completely alien ones to him; rather they are likely to draw on portions of his personality which have hitherto remained unconscious or which he could not consider before.

3. The postulation of increased suggestibility or decreased capacity to think critically as the key change mechanism evades the basic issue of how change is actually produced. This evasion is reminiscent of the conflict within social psychology concerning the explanation of certain experiments in which people's judgments were influenced by knowledge of others' judgments (Asch, 1948). The issue was whether a behavioral change represented a new evaluation of the same stimulus object (the suggestibility theory), or whether the stimulus object was perceived differently as a result of learning how someone else judged it, and hence evaluated differently. Asch argued very persuasively for the latter position and his cognitive formulation certainly fits the facts of coercive persuasion better than a straightforward reliance on the suggestibility explanation. This argument, as applied to coercive persuasion, would be similar to the one we have previously stated. The prisoner learns new evaluations of self and others by first identifying with another prisoner, then by seeing various objects in his social world from this perspective, then by shifting his frame of reference and his standards of evaluation, and finally by applying these new standards to the social objects including his self. One can certainly assert that all of these cognitive processes involve a state of suggestibility. Our main argument against such an assertion is that basically it does not explain anything.

4. The above arguments apply primarily to the theoretical position of Hinkle and Wolff. The Sargant, Hunter, and Miller theories emphasize more heavily than do those of Hinkle and Wolff the involuntary changes produced by psycho-physiological interventions like drugs, conditioning, etc. The main argument against this position is that there is little evidence that any prisoner actually had experiences of the kind described by these authors, or if he had symptoms which implied such experiences, that they were in fact due to them. To produce involuntary changes simply is not what the Communists appeared to be interested in; in fact as we have

repeatedly stated, they leaned over backward to produce changes which were self-initiated. They wanted the prisoner to see and feel his guilt, not just be willing to sign a piece of paper. False confessions were usually rejected by the interrogator, not as a diabolical strategy, but because the interrogator was interested in proving the prisoner's guilt by at least a locally acceptable legal process.

The question remains whether during straight military interrogation for key information the captor might be willing to use devices like truth serums and whether he would have success if he did so. From the little definite evidence available on the point,* one would infer that most good interrogators do not need to rely on such devices and, in fact, would prefer not to because the data produced by them tend to be highly unreliable anyway (Kubis, 1957; Orne, 1960). With respect to Pavlovian conditioning as a technique, it has been pointed out (Bauer, 1957, Schein, 1959) that no evidence exists of the use of Pavlovian methods in thought reform operations and that, in any case, coercive persuasion as a process of influence could not possibly be explained by such a simple basic mechanism. In fact, the whole applicability of Pavlovian conditioning formulations to adult human behavior has not yet been convincingly demonstrated.†

5. Perhaps the most serious deficiency of the debilitation-suggestibility explanation is that it fails to take note of the fact that the judge or interrogator did not define for the prisoner what he was to do (or what he was to believe) in any manner which the prisoner initially could understand. Hence, even if he wanted to comply or was suggestible to the point of complying, there would not have been available a ready model of what he was to do. A number of prisoners, as we have mentioned, tried to evade the issue by making false confessions which involved guesses as to what the captors wanted, only to find themselves being punished further for insincerity and unco-operativeness. The only thing the prisoner could be sure of was that he was in some manner guilty of some crimes, but

---

* For a recent comprehensive evaluation of the problem of interrogation, see Biderman, 1960.
† See the next section for a more detailed analysis of learning theory formulations.

the nature of the crimes and the feelings of guilt were things he had to locate for himself out of a reanalysis of his own experiences.

In summary, the psycho-physiological exhaustion explanation may be quite applicable to those parts of the process which we have called unfreezing, i.e., in creating a desire on the part of the prisoner to find some solution to his problems. But this explanation does not provide a plausible mechanism for the subsequent process of changing, of learning how to comply and to what to comply.

THEORIES EMPHASIZING TRADITIONAL LEARNING MODELS

We find in this group of formulations some which emphasize Pavlovian conditioning as an explanation (e.g., Meerloo, 1954), some which emphasize Pavlov's work on experimental neurosis and the production and consequences of conflict (Sargant, 1957), and some which combine Pavlovian learning principles with those of drive reduction or instrumental conditioning (Santucci & Winokur, 1955; Farber *et al.*, 1957). The only one of these that we shall examine in detail is the theory which combines both Pavlovian and drive reduction formulations. In the context of this examination it will become evident, we hope, why a purely Pavlovian conditioning model could not possibly be adequate. In fairness to Meerloo and others who argue strongly for the Pavlovian explanation (e.g., Hunter, 1951), we should state that these authors themselves do not stick to a purely Pavlovian model. They present a variety of explanations for "brainwashing" which go well beyond Pavlov, but label these as Pavlovian. We shall not include them in this section because we feel they have mislabeled their own theory.

Basically the learning theory analysis states that the prisoner is initially coerced to engage in behavior which strongly conflicts with beliefs and values he holds. This conflict arouses anxiety and guilt which act as drive states and lead to a search for responses which would reduce such guilt and anxiety. However, the only response which can reduce the anxiety and guilt is a cognitive change in the prisoner, namely, the adoption of beliefs and values which justify the elicited behavior. Changes in beliefs and values in the direction of those of the captor are reinforced because they reduce anxiety and guilt, and because they lead to extrinsic rewards in the form of praise and improved material conditions from the captor.

Pavlovian conditioning enters into this learning process at two points: (1) The anxiety and guilt come to be conditioned (by the avoidance conditioning paradigm) to the threats and punishments which initially produced the complying behavior, and thus come to be elicited by fewer and fewer cues on the part of the captor; such a mechanism would be important in explaining the continued co-operation of the prisoner with his captor in the seeming absence of severe threat or punishment; (2) Once verbal behavior consistent with the captors' ideology has been elicited and learned by being reinforced, it could then be transferred to other cues or stimuli by a Pavlovian conditioning mechanism; thus behavior initially elicited by a complex shaping process (i.e., the prisoner having to learn what was wanted of him at the level of belief and value) could become conditioned to a variety of simple cues with which it has been paired (e.g., the mere presence of an interrogator or a verbal signal like "imperialism"); the extensive repetition of slogans, singing of songs, and reciting of dogma could be paired with appropriate emotional responses elicited by some other means leading to the conditioning of these emotions to the slogans, songs, etc.

Another formulation which is similar to the one presented above is stated by Farber and others. They feel that the Communist control techniques as manifested in their handling of POW's in Korea can be thought to produce a motivational state—which they call DDD for its three basic components: debility, dependency, and dread. The reader should have no difficulty in seeing how the kinds of circumstances previously described can be categorized into a DDD classification. Farber *et al.* feel that occasional indulgences and unpredictably administered rewards have the effect of conditioning (Pavlovian) the prisoner's "expectancy" of relief. It is the intermittent reinforcement which tends to maintain expectancy at a high level and renders it less susceptible to extinction. ". . . this process serves to keep hope alive, permitting some degree of adaptive behavior, and inhibiting self-destructive tendencies, which would frustrate the enemy's purpose." (Farber *et al.*, 1957, p. 276)

At the same time, instrumental conditioning enters the picture in that certain kinds of verbal and other behaviors are reinforced selectively by the alleviation of the DDD syndrome. The fact that the alleviation is intermittent and unpredictable leads to particularly high rates of emission of the conditioned behavior and makes it particularly difficult to extinguish (Skinner, 1938). How it is that the correct verbal and other behavior is elicited in the first place is not dealt with by Farber, except to note that most humans have already learned to emit various kinds of verbal behavior when in a motivational state like DDD.

Critique

1. The basic virtue of a learning theory analysis is that it brings the phenomenon of coercive persuasion into a realm of psychology which is reasonably well understood and which allows, therefore, the formulation of specific predictions about the outcome of the process. A second virtue is that it provides an actual mechanism of change; i.e., it offers an explanation of how a new response comes to be learned and states principles which govern the strength or stability of that new response. As stated in the preceding section, it is the failure to provide such a mechanism which is the main weakness of the psycho-physiological stress analyses. Thus, *if* learning theory applies to coercive persuasion this is a tremendous theoretical gain. The question is, to what extent and how fruitfully does it apply?

2. The basic problem with the application of learning theory to the phenomena of coercive persuasion is that it explains too little and at the same time too much. There is little doubt that both Pavlovian and instrumental conditioning enter into the process at some points, but such a statement would be true for virtually any situation that one might conceive of. It is in this sense that learning theory explains too much. It is of such a level of generality that its applicability can almost always be demonstrated.

At the same time, this level of generality results in analyses which are somewhat sterile in that they do not explain the phenomenon at a level at which it "makes sense" or at a level at which differential predictions about outcomes can be reliably made. For example, it is undeniably valid, as far as all available experimental evidence is con-

concerned, to state that the prisoner *learns* to make certain kinds of verbal and cognitive responses because: (a) he is in a *motivational state* in which learning is likely to take place; and (b) he is selectively *reinforced*. If we cannot go beyond this, however, and describe the nature of the motivation and the nature of the reinforcement we have contributed relatively little to the understanding of the outcome.

At this point, most learning theorists are willing to become circular in their definitions and rely on an empirical criterion of what sorts of stimuli constitute reinforcements for a given individual, and what kinds of motivational states are of particular importance to him. There is nothing in the theory itself, however, which would offer to predict what would be motivating and what would be reinforcing. The limit of the theory would be the suggestion to examine empirically the subject's previous history for clues as to what kinds of motives had been learned and by what kinds of reinforcers.

The utility of various other theories such as those based on psychoanalytic and those based on sociological considerations lies precisely in their attempt to make refinements in the concepts that learning theory has left unrefined. These theories offer concrete hypotheses about the kinds of motivations that will be important in an adult human under given conditions of stimulation, and about the kinds of reinforcing states of affairs for which the adult human typically strives. As Farber *et al.* (1957) themselves note in paraphrasing Spence: ". . . the view that principles derived from conditioning might apply to more complex behavior does not at all imply that complex behavior can be explained solely in terms of the variables affecting conditioning." (p. 274)

3. Learning formulations such as those described above tend to leave unexplained the *induction* of motivational states which predispose the subject to learn something new. By "leaving unexplained" I mean that the theorist is not able to use the learning theory itself to explain why or how, for example, a state of DDD is induced. For this explanation he relies on general stress theory similar to that used by Hinkle and Wolff, or simply describes the observed conditions which are *assumed* to have a certain predictable effect (e.g., withholding sleep is assumed to produce mental con-

fusion). Yet there is a legitimate area for theoretical analysis in these phenomena which is left largely unexplored.

It is only recently, for example, that physical and social isolation as motivation-inducing conditions have become the objects of systematic study. The need for such study is signaled not only by the diversity of definitions which have been given for a state such as *isolation* (ranging from "solitary confinement with guards present and available for some human contact" to experimental conditions such as described by Bexton *et al.*, 1954, or Lilly, 1956a, in which the subject is cut off from as much sensory input as is physically possible), but also by the diversity of initial findings of the effects of isolation (ranging from dramatic reports of psychotic-like states produced in a few hours to reports of subjects being able to perform in a manner indistinguishable from normal after several days of isolation). Recently, as a result of the study of data from Chinese Communist prisons, more attention has been given to *social* isolation, a state in which the subject may be in the midst of others but feel himself completely isolated from them. The effects of such a condition are at present only reportable anecdotally, there being little theory and less experimental data available to throw light on them.

Studies of sleep deprivation (Fisher & Rubinstein, 1955) are quite equivocal concerning the degree to which heightened suggestibility can be demonstrated. Similarly, there is ample evidence that physical torture may stiffen resistance in some people while weakening it in others. Thus it is descriptively correct to state that Korean POW's suffered from a state of DDD, but we certainly cannot derive from learning theory alone just why this state occurred. The same arguments apply, of course, to the explanation of motivational conditions which were present in the prisons in which coercive persuasion took place.

4. Learning formulations are as yet weak on the problem of how new behavior is initially elicited and thus made available for reinforcement. Skinnerian formulations emphasize a process called "shaping" the behavior, which consists of reinforcing any partial response which is in the direction of or part of the final response that is wanted. Pavlovian formulations apply only to situations in which a stimulus-response connection already exists. Thorndikean instru-

mental conditioning formulations rely on the occurrence of "trial and error" behavior, by which is meant that in a suitable state of motivation the organism will emit various kinds of behavior until some is found which leads to reinforcement. Response hierarchies are postulated in terms of the probability of occurrence of given responses, but no good theoretical explanation is offered for the actual placement of given responses on the hierarchy.

Critics of "trial and error" learning have noted that the animal certainly does not respond at random, but that there seems to be some cognitive component to its behavior which makes for some degree of "calculated guessing" or "hypothesis testing" even in a low-level organism. We feel that this kind of cognitive component is crucial in the adult human and needs detailed analysis if human learning situations are to be understood. For example, in Chapter 4 we noted the complex manner in which prisoners seemed to find ways of orienting themselves to their social and informational environment which permitted them to determine what kinds of responses were wanted of them. A key point in this connection was the failure of the interrogator or judge to reveal to the prisoner specifically what was wanted except in very generalized terms such as "You must confess, you must admit your crimes." The crux of the matter was that the prisoner had to learn *how to find out* what he was to learn.

The general prison routine favored high response productivity in some areas by enforcing active participation in all kinds of activities, ranging from the trivial (e.g., singing Communist songs at certain specified times) to the psychologically highly significant (e.g., taking part in criticism and self-criticism in the cell). However, the production of ideologically correct responses, ones that would be reinforced, depended, we feel, upon a certain amount of insight on the part of the prisoner concerning what was wanted. Hence, enforced participation could not automatically guarantee that reinforcible responses would occur.

5. With regard to the specific formulations presented, for example, by Santucci and Winokur, the main flaw in the analysis lies in the assumption that the captor can routinely elicit certain kinds of collaborative behavior which then produce conflict and subsequent

learning of new beliefs. There is ample evidence that the captor cannot routinely coerce certain kinds of behavior; i.e., that many prisoners resist such coercion to the hilt, or that the captor's demands are too unclear to allow the prisoner to determine what behavior is wanted. It is probably true that for POW's, upon which the Santucci and Winokur analysis is based, there were fairly clear demands such as to sign petitions, inform on fellow POW's, etc. But it would be quite erroneous to identify what these authors label as "brainwashing" as being equivalent to what we have tried to describe as coercive persuasion. Learning theory analysis may have limited practical applicability to the POW situation, and can be applied in principle to the coercive persuasion situation, but we should not mistakenly overgeneralize from one of these situations to the other.

PSYCHOANALYTIC FORMULATIONS

One of the most interesting formulations using psychoanalytic theory is the one proposed by Moloney (1955). He argues that in certain individuals there exists a particularly authoritarian, demanding superego which requires continual neutralization by the ego lest the individual be swamped by his superego and become a "carbon copy" of what the superego wants. If such an individual is put through a physically and emotionally exhausting experience he may be unable to sustain his war against the superego, or its surrogate in a present relationship, and may experience a "psychic emptying" of himself which actually reflects a process of abandoning the self to the authority of the superego. Moloney notes that such a process can be seen in religious conversion and training (particularly in Zen Buddhism), in creative or inspirational experiences of problem solving, in the origin of schizophrenic processes, and in reactions to Communist interrogation methods. If the individual does *not* have a powerful authoritarian superego opposing an insecure ego he will hold out much longer before confessing or will attempt to escape the situation physically by avoiding capture initially, by trying to escape at any cost if captured, or by committing suicide.

The key elements in the formulation then are: (1) a personality predisposition; (2) a process of becoming physically and emotionally exhausted (here Moloney agrees with Sargant); (3) an authority figure like an interrogator or judge who comes to be the surrogate or representative of the superego in the prison situation; (4) an eventual abandonment by the prisoner of his self-strivings and a total "giving in" to the superego surrogate, which in this case means the interrogator.*

A second psychoanalytic formulation is Meerloo's analysis of the transfer of guilt.† Meerloo asserts that there are both external and internal motivating factors involved in confessing and becoming converted. The external factors are the various prison experiences which weaken the ego's resistance by exhausting it physically and emotionally. The internal forces are the conscious desire to remove pain and threat and the unconscious dependency needs and child-hood hostilities, both of which produce great quantities of guilt. The childhood feelings and needs are stimulated by the actual depend-ency of the prisoner on his captor and the accusing environment which treats the prisoner like a child who has done something bad.

Submission to the authority and identification with him then solves a number of the prisoner's problems: (1) it removes the external threat and pain; (2) it permits the unconscious guilt to be attached to some concrete behavior (e.g., making a confession) and thus releases the individual from having to face his own unconscious unacceptable impulses which stimulated the guilt in the first place; (3) it permits a giving in to dependency longings (this latter ap-pears to be similar to Moloney's "self-abandonment"); and (4) it

---

* An interesting additional point is that the prisoner then has available to him the resistance patterns which were originally used against the inroads of the compulsive authoritarian parents, e.g., slavish following of orders while sabotaging the spirit of the venture, various kinds of passive resistance, refusal to take any responsibility, etc. The degree to which such resistance patterns were used might be a reflection of the degree of self-striving which had to be abandoned; i.e., the person with a stronger ego being forced to abandon self because of unusual stresses might be expected to fall back on more resistance devices of the kind cited.

† Meerloo in giving his analysis has unfortunately muddled his own theory by stating that these processes are also explainable by Pavlovian conditioning and that they involved essentially hypnotic techniques. We do not see how these three models can be made readily consistent with each other; perhaps Meerloo can. In his writings on the subject of "menticide" he has not stated a clear position, however, hence we have taken the liberty of stating his separate theories in the separate parts of this chapter (see Meerloo, 1951, 1954, 1956).

permits some gratification by magical means in that the prisoner's submission "annihilates" the interrogator by removing the reason for his existence. Since the environment fails to fulfill all of the dependency needs of the prisoner even if he submits (e.g., he is still asked to be "responsible" for his own re-education), a further psychological defense, that of identification with the aggressor, is necessary. Presumably much of the motivation for learning the captor's ideology comes from such defensive identification.

The formulation given by Lifton (1956a) is considerably broader than the previous two, not only in relying on a wider range of psychoanalytic theory, but also in adding some sociological formulations. Basically, however, Lifton's explanation of why change occurs is psychoanalytic; hence we shall treat his theory primarily in the present section.

Lifton divides the experience of coercive persuasion into four basic stages:

1. THE EMOTIONAL ASSAULTS which have the effect of (a) destroying the prisoner's feelings of individual identity; (b) mobilizing within the prisoner powerful guilt anxiety; and (c) making him feel in total conflict with an inflexible environment.

2. LENIENCY: A sudden shift on the part of the authorities to seemingly kind treatment,* which has the effect of showing the prisoner the possibility of an adaptational solution and enlists his aid in reforming himself.

3. CONFESSION: "The constant accusations and demands for atonement and conformity with the prison group create both a universal and a personal confession compulsion. Guilt anxiety is channeled into specific areas which the Communists make use of in guiding the prisoner towards his final confession or coercive confabulation." (Lifton, 1956a, pp. 2–3)

4. RE-EDUCATION: "Through a unique and thorough 'group therapy'—utilizing mutual study, criticism, self-criticism, exposure of

---

* In Chapter 7 we questioned whether there was adequate evidence of manipulation of the sort which this stage implies. The point is crucial because according to Lifton it is the authorities' leniency which starts the change process in motion. According to our formulation, some change must already have occurred in the prisoner if the authorities suddenly became kind, even if only a subtle change in attitude or motivation.

'wrong thoughts,' and 'depth interpretations'—the Communists seek to change the prisoner's political and ethical beliefs, and alter his personal and group loyalties." He goes on to say:

> There is a broadening of guilt to his entire previous pattern of existence; there are adaptational rewards or emotional appeals such as group participation, self-surrender, catharsis, problem-solving, and super-morality; there is a "working through" by means of repetition and continuous application of oneself to the doctrine; and there is finally a recoding of reality, an acquisition of a new world view, and a new personal relationship to the world.
>
> We can see that the process represents a symbolic "death and rebirth" —and that it uses in powerful combination, techniques which resemble hypnosis, induced religious conversion, and a coercive form of psychotherapy. [Lifton, 1956a, p. 3]

As can be seen from the above quotes, Lifton sees the process as consisting of a number of separable stages and implies that different mechanisms may be operating at different stages. The core of Lifton's formulation is his analysis of guilt anxiety. He feels that the total environmental control "quickly and inevitably" produces guilt anxiety (which is guilt which the prisoner *feels,* though its true basis may remain unconscious, and which produces generalized feelings of being sinful and deserving of punishment). Because the basis of the guilt remains unconscious, the prisoner experiences the guilt as freefloating until he is able, in his confession, to attach it to concrete pieces of behavior he may have committed or fantasied committing. In this stage is involved the cognitive operation of adopting the "people's standpoint." "Channeling of guilt" is, as far as we can tell, the same process which Meerloo describes as a transfer of guilt, and serves a similar function: to save the prisoner from further pressure and to save him, at the same time, from his own unconscious.

In the next stage the guilt is broadened to include not only the specific acts cited in the confession, but basic elements of the prisoner's identity. He learns that "his entire past life has been in the service of evil." In the stage of emotional assaults the prisoner had already found it impossible to sustain his normal social and occupa-

tional roles, thus destroying or at least undermining major portions
of his identity. Now he learns that this identity was actually an evil
one to be gotten rid of, and embarks upon the process of finding a
new one. In this process a variety of group forces and further cognitive reorganization play the major role in completing the "rebirth"
of the prisoner. These are steps eight to eleven in Lifton's (1956b)
"steps" of reform:

Re-education—the rebirth

8. *The broadening of guilt.* The prisoner's guilt, which has earlier
been channeled into specific categories, is now expanded to include the
major elements of his basic identity. He "learns" that—as a "messenger
of imperialist conquerors"—his entire life has been in the service of evil.
He feels in need of thorough personal "reform."

9. *Adaptational rewards.* His "progress" brings meaningful psychological rewards. Following the unbearable pain of the early period,
these can assume immense meaning to him. During the latter months
of imprisonment, when he has adjusted to the "academic routine" of
"re-education," he experiences the "togetherness" of intimate group living, suffering, and "reform"; the rewards of self-surrender—of merging
with an all-powerful force and sharing its strength; the satisfaction of
problem-solving, in which nothing remains unanswered; the rewards of
uncovering—the catharsis of personal confession and the satisfactions of
"frankness"; the increased prestige and improved treatment that go with
being a "progressive"; and finally, the moral satisfaction of participating
in a great crusade of redeeming oneself and others—and, on a mass
mystical level, of joining the "struggle for peace," the "human brotherhood," the "fight for equality," and the "great Communist future."

10. *The "working-through."* The prisoner must express, act upon,
and *live* the principles of "thought reform"—that is, in Communist
terminology, he must "combine theory with practice." He may at first do
this only outwardly, and then ritualistically—as if reciting a catechism;
but through his interminable "group therapy" he eventually finds himself
thinking and *feeling* in terms of these "truths." He must constantly
"analyze" his alleged deficiencies, his "thought problems," and his "resistances." "Depth interpretations" are available for all varieties of non-
conformity. Everything is reducible to the "insights" of the Marxist

doctrine: he "works through" every barrier to "reform."

11. *The recoding of reality.* Finally, he approaches the ultimate attainment of "thought reform"—the acquisition of a new view of the world, and of a new personal relationship to the world. He reconstructs his communication techniques, shifts his role behavior, and alters his values and his identity. He has accomplished this vast recoding chiefly through a two-step reinterpretation of his own past and present status: from kind missionary, or teacher, to evil spy, and from evil spy to repentant sinner. And he applies a similar reinterpretation to all spheres of thought and behavior: the Communist world, formerly considered aggressive and totalitarian, is now seen to be peace-loving and democratic. He identifies himself fully with his captors. He is happy in his faith. He has been reborn. [Lifton, 1956b, pp. 190–91]

Lifton's analysis is deliberately descriptive, because he mistrusts the process of Western observers imposing their own theoretical formulations on processes which derive from different cultural origins.

Critique

1. As can be seen, the theoretical sections described thus far tend to build on and supplement each other rather than to offer competing hypotheses. The main thing to be said for learning theory is that it provides a change mechanism where general stress theory only says "something" will happen. The main thing to be said for the psychoanalytic formulations is that they fill in some of the places where learning theory has little to say, without being in any major way inconsistent with learning theory. Thus, as we build up our theoretical discussion, the total picture becomes more and more complete, and the individual theoretical positions become less and less vulnerable so long as they admit of the need for supplementation by others.

The psychoanalytic formulation supplements a learning theory and stress theory analysis at the following crucial points:

a. It provides a concrete set of hypotheses about guilt-anxiety as a motivating force demanding of the individual some change or new learning.

b. It brings in unconscious factors and offers hypotheses concerning their relationship to the prison experience and its outcome.

c. In the concept of identification it offers a mechanism to explain how the prisoner learns what sorts of responses are wanted of him, i.e., what to do to get reward and alleviate punishment.

d. In the concept of transfer of guilt there is offered a hypothesis which could explain the basis for the different lengths of time which expire before a given prisoner makes a confession; i.e., the implicit hypothesis is that the prisoner becomes ready to change—to make a confession—when his ego's capacity to defend itself against the unacceptable wishes or feelings (which are the basis of the guilt) begins to weaken dangerously. Coercive persuasion involves self-analysis at many points and one might expect that such self-analysis in a punitive environment would be especially guilt-provoking; handling this guilt would be one of the prisoner's main problems (see Chapter 5 for an analysis of the kinds of guilt which become relevant in coercive persuasion).

e. The psychoanalytic formulation, particularly as espoused by Moloney, offers a clear-cut and testable hypothesis concerning proneness to being coercively persuaded—that the individual with a powerful and authoritarian superego opposing a relatively less powerful ego will be the most likely to give in to his interrogator or judge and attempt to become precisely what the authorities want him to become.

f. Meerloo's formulation, in particular, puts considerable emphasis on the role of dependency wishes which make the prisoner *want* to comply; most theories too glibly assume that any sane prisoner would resist and only resist. It is particularly important in analyzing individual predisposition to seek out those factors which not only weaken the prisoner's capacity to resist, but also those which strengthen his desires to comply, e.g., desire to identify with a powerful authority or social movement, desire to help the Chinese people, desire to be taken care of completely, etc.

g. Finally, the psychoanalytic formulations partially fill in the large gap left by stress and learning theory where these fail to analyze the interpersonal process which is involved in coercive persuasion. Much of what is crucial about this process occurs between people, and the psychoanalytic formulations give much needed attention to the authority and dependency relationship between prisoner and captor.

2. The social relationship which is analyzed by psychoanalytic formulations is that between the prisoner and his interrogator—a relationship which simulates in many respects the parent-child relationship. A number of analyses of extreme situations (e.g., concentration camps, POW camps, and prisons) have noted the importance of the relationship between prisoner and authorities. The applicability of psychoanalytic theory to such situations is, of course, not accidental inasmuch as child-parent relationships as prototypes of authority relationships are the main object of analysis in the theory. The shortcoming of the theory lies in its failure to give adequate attention to other kinds of social relationships which develop as the adult becomes integrated into society. In our opinion, peer-group relationships (i.e., the relationship of prisoner to prisoner) were particularly crucial in coercive persuasion, yet little attention is given to such relationships in the psychoanalytic formulations discussed. Part of the reason seems to be that the theory itself is not well developed for handling peer-group relationships and group phenomena.* Another reason is that psychoanalytically oriented individuals who have attempted to analyze Communist techniques of imprisonment (with the exception of Lifton) have taken as their model the Russian case, and it happens that in Russian prisoner-handling the relationship between prisoner and interrogator is indeed made paramount. Typically the prisoner saw no one except his guard and/or interrogator for his entire imprisonment. The Chinese, by placing prisoners in group cells with others who more "reformed" than they, have introduced a new and crucial circumstance which demands theoretical analysis. Lifton describes well the kinds of situations which arise in such groups but offers little theoretical clarification of their origins or outcomes.

3. A final point, which applies to most psychoanalytic explanations, is that the theory often offers explanations at too complex or too deep a level. Where a simple explanation in terms of contemporary events would suffice, the psychoanalytic theory offers an ex-

---

* Some of the writings of Freud (1922) and Redl (1942) are relevant to any attempt to formulate psychoanalytic hypotheses about peer-group relationships in a prison setting. However, the only explicit attempt to make such an analysis is Lifton's (1957b) account of emerging leadership patterns in one particular group of European prisoners.

planation which involves the person's entire psycho-social history and a host of unconscious factors. One argument against such theorizing is its basic untestability at this stage of our knowledge of experimentation. If no other theory will fit, then it is appropriate to try one that will fit even if it is untestable, and find ways to test it. But if another and more testable theory fits, it should certainly have priority. A good example is the guilt analysis offered by Meerloo and Lifton. Both of them make the assumption that the guilt is founded on some unconscious basis and that change takes place in the prisoner in order to prevent this unconscious factor from becoming conscious. The evidence for this position derives from subsequent "insights" which prisoners have had concerning personal flaws which they had hidden from themselves, and the motivating force of which they could subsequently recognize.* Perhaps this was true, but is it not equally possible that the prison situation stimulated or elicited behavior (as the learning theorists suggest) which directly conflicted with certain values the individual held (and which he consciously recognized) and thus produced guilt directly (guilt being the feeling which signaled the conflict which the learning theorist pins his analysis on)? We feel that the prison environment, particularly the necessity of living in close quarters with a number of other human beings, stimulated a great many feelings which became the motivators for change. A number of these could quite correctly be described as guilt (see Chapter 5), but some of them did not depend on unconscious factors for their potency. At most they were preconscious insofar as the individual did not recognize them until they were pointed out to him; but once pointed out they were readily perceived.

If our argument is correct that there are many bases for guilt, some of which lie in the person's peer-group relations, it is necessary to broaden the hypothesis about the sources of individual vulnerability to coercive persuasion. It may be true that the "strong-superego, weak-ego" type of character is vulnerable; but there will be other

---

* An intriguing hypothesis is that the generalized sense of guilt which seems to reflect unconscious historical factors occurs *after* the prisoner has been influenced and repatriated as a *response* to his recognition of having complied rather than being a *cause* of the compliance.

types who are vulnerable as well, e.g., the individual with multiple reference groups, the person in transition from one commitment to another, the as yet uncommitted person, etc. In terms of the content of Communist coercive persuasion, the person born into a well-to-do middle-class family who found himself in China because of a "tourist's curiosity" might be vulnerable because of the ease of eliciting in him "social guilt" about his class status, i.e., his failure to have earned by his own labors the social position he then occupied. Of course any hypothesis about vulnerability is on shaky ground because of the fact that the Communists exercised their own selection criteria of whom to put special pressure on, and there is little question that amount of pressure is at least as important a variable as personal vulnerability in determining the amount of influence accomplished.

In summary, the psychoanalytic formulations contribute to the theoretical analysis some hypotheses about the nature of the motives which are stimulated in the unfreezing process and about the kinds of individuals who might be prone to influence. They also suggest some mechanisms like self-abandonment, identification, and transfer of guilt which can explain change, and help to clarify the role of interpersonal processes between the prisoner and the authorities.

9

Theories of Coercive Persuasion II:
Socio-psychological Theories

IDENTITY THEORY

IT IS DIFFICULT to find a single proponent of all the elements which go into this theoretical conception. Much of it comes from Lifton's analysis of ego-identity change; much of it comes from the sociological analyses and observations of Goffman (1956, 1957a, 1959); a number of the points come from the detailed account of interrogation by Biderman (1957, 1960). Others who have discussed coercive persuasion from this point of view are Strauss (1959), Erikson (1958), and Leites and Bernaut (1954). Our own formulation would fall primarily into this section, though, as we have pointed out, we feel a number of mechanisms are necessary to clarify all the events of coercive persuasion.

We may take as a starting point Lifton's analysis of the Communists' "assault on the prisoner's ego-identity" and supplement it with some of our own conceptions. Basically what is involved for the prisoner is that his professional and personal roles are denied explicitly by the cellmates and the interrogator, while the role of "spy," "saboteur," or "criminal" is the only one which is accepted. If we define a person's self or his identity to be largely his conscious and unconscious perceptions of himself in his various roles, it becomes clear that a denial of certain roles by others constitutes an undermining of the individual's self or sense of identity. Another way to put it is to say that we know ourselves largely through what we do; when we are prevented from doing what we are accustomed to, our self-knowledge begins to be undermined. For example, it may be difficult for a doctor to continue to see himself as a doctor if he is prevented from practicing. The denial of role, then, is one way in which the prison environment operated to undermine sense of identity.

A second and perhaps more fundamental threat resided in the fact that the prisoner's cellmates typically refused to confirm *any* of his self-perceptions which were in any way predicated on assumptions of innocence or blamelessness. We are assuming that any sense of self depends upon constant confirmation by others (Goffman, 1955; Schein, 1960). If we see ourselves as "intelligent" or "handsome," yet significant others fail to confirm the perception by withholding deference or compliments, it becomes more difficult to continue to hold on to the self-perception. As we have detailed in our previous descriptive material, it was the humiliation, revilement, harassment, etc., by the cellmates which served primarily to deny to the prisoner any role or sense of self other than that of the "guilty criminal." This statement means that the prisoner could not get *any* positive response (i.e., approval or even sustained attention) from another prisoner unless he was willing to assume the "guilty criminal" role.

To further the self-destruction process, various supports of self were undermined. We have assumed that the sense of self depends to a large extent on emotional relationships with significant others, on membership in and identification with certain groups or professions, on information about others who have some relationship to self, and so on (Schein, 1960). The cutting and manipulation of information channels undermined each of these supports with a resulting loss of sense of self or identity in the case of many prisoners. One interesting hypothesis in this connection would be that the mental confusion noted by those analysts who are most concerned about psycho-physiological stresses (e.g., Hinkle & Wolff) does not include all cognitive functioning, but only those areas of cognitive functioning which pertain to the prisoner's identity. A further hypothesis which we favor would hold that the psycho-physiological stresses have their greatest impact on the prisoner via their destruction of even his bodily self-image and his physical sense of selfhood. We would assume that for the prisoner *to see himself* as unable to function normally, forced to live like an animal, and in danger of permanent injury and impairment represents fundamentally a greater stress than the physiological concomitants of the actual debilitation and physical trauma.

The denial of role and identity operates, in our terminology, to unfreeze resistances and induce a motive to change, i.e., to find an acceptable role and identity. A basic theoretical assumption which is implicit in this formulation is that any adult human must have some sort of viable role and identity which permits him to organize his own behavior and make meaningful contact with others in his social environment. One may conjecture that this assumption is but an extension of a general principle in psychology which is receiving increasing support—namely, that the nervous system functions in such a manner as to organize the perceptual world; i.e., that random stimulation is intolerable (produces basic anxiety) and either must be organized by the nervous system itself or avoided by the organism. Recent studies of sensory deprivation have shown that minimum levels of stimulation are also a requirement of healthy functioning. If such minimum levels are not maintained the organism generates its own stimuli in the form of hallucinations, though such a process is obviously only a temporary expedient, and continued deprivation produces irreparable damage (Bexton *et al.*, 1954).

We would hypothesize that the need for an optimal level of stimulation and for organized consistent input is just as important in the area of social cues, e.g., those cues emitted by other people in reference to oneself, as it is in the area of physical cues. In fact, it is possible that personality damage can occur in the same sense in which nervous system damage can occur, if levels of social stimulation or confirmation are inadequate.

Most of the studies of sensory deprivation have dealt with understimulation, though it is quite likely that *over*stimulation might have comparably disorganizing results. In the case of social cues, we can identify in the Russian interrogation methods a tendency to rely on understimulation (keeping the prisoner in solitary confinement), while the Chinese rely on overstimulation (preventing the individual from having any privacy whatsover). The disorganizing effects of the latter condition, quite apart from the content of the specific attacks made by the cellmates, have been described by Goffman (1957, 1959). He argues that our social self is a "constructed object" which requires for its successful maintenance that the individual can periodically "step out of role" to "compose himself," etc., which, of course, requires privacy or what Goffman calls an available "backstage" area. For most individuals the maintenance of a "constructed self" is impossible if no privacy whatsoever is permitted them (e.g., if the input of social cues is higher than the person can handle and still remain organized). This line of reasoning leads to the conclusion that the disorganization and destruction of identity can be more effectively accomplished by social *over*stimulation than by understimulation.*

The amount of social stimulation which the individual is receiving and its degree of randomness does not depend on the specific number of people who are present. We should hypothesize, instead, that:

1. A given social self or identity requires reinforcement and support from only *one* significant other.

2. If the individual has the support of one significant other, this is a sufficient level for him to tolerate large quantities of *dis*confirming information which may come from others (in the realm of perceptual judgment this effect has been demonstrated conclusively by Asch, 1952).

3. If the individual does not have the support of anyone in the immediate face-to-face situation, he can rely to a certain extent on self-administered symbolic reinforcement; but in this condition he

---

* An interesting hypothesis might be that the emotional collapse which is described by Sargant as characterizing war neuroses, religious conversions, initiations, etc., is in fact an identity collapse produced by social overstimulation. It is true that such a collapse is often induced by physiological means, e.g., drugs, but it is equally true that it can be produced by continual unabated social pressure, e.g., the haranguing arguments of a revivalist preacher or interrogator. The advantage of the identity collapse theory is that it can make differential predictions based on different initial roles and identities which individuals have. Sargant's emotional collapse theory cannot deal well with individual differences in susceptibility, except to fall back on a crude typology of temperaments which are difficult to define operationally.

does become vulnerable to disconfirming information, and the disconfirming information gains potency as a function of the number of others who are unanimous in the cues they provide (though there is evidence from perceptual studies that the impact of a unanimous majority which stands in disagreement with a lone individual reaches its maximum effect when it is three against one; e.g. Asch found that even 15 against 1 produced little more effect than 3 against 1).

4. The problem of over- and under-stimulation refers not to the number of people who confirm or disconfirm a given self, but to the degree to which the person can regulate the amount of information which others can get about him to react to. If he is in complete solitary confinement, nothing he does by way of presenting himself as any given kind of person makes any difference (unless the person has the capacity to administer significant reactions to himself—herein may lie the answer to the riddle of why prisoners who compulsively maintain certain rituals of shaving, going to the toilet, etc., seem to survive better than those who abandon these rituals). If he is confined with others twenty-four hours a day of every day, the others get too much information about the person to react to, which makes it impossible for him to present himself in any given pattern, and to deal with all the incoming reactions.

5. The degree of stress which over- or under-stimulation represents may be related to the individual's personality and to the type of identity he has. At the level of his personality, one may expect a person whose ego is highly autonomous from the id and superego to be able to stand understimulation better, while one whose ego is highly autonomous from external reality may be able to stand overstimulation better (Rapaport, 1951). At the level of identity, one might expect persons with identities which require relatively less routine confirmation (e.g., religious persons, intellectuals, etc.) to be able to stand overstimulation of a disconfirming nature better than those persons whose identities do require routine confirmation (e.g., salesmen, politicians, etc.).*

* Of course, all identities require some kind of confirmation. Identities can be distinguished, however, in terms of the amount of confirmation they require, from whom it is required, in what kinds of forms (symbolic vs. direct) and in what kinds of time intervals it is required.

Thus far we have confined our analysis to the destruction of identity. We have stated our conclusion that the intense social environment in the prison was capable of destroying the prisoner's sense of identity and thus could induce a motive to find a new identity. Before discussing this finding of a new identity we must briefly consider, however, how one can best characterize the psychological state in which the prisoner finds himself when his old role and sense of identity has been destroyed. There are basically two alternative conceptions: (1) the prisoner is in a state of complete confusion, strongly motivated to find something with which he can identify himself in order to regain some sense of self, and to find a role which will be an acceptable adjustment to the prison; or (2) the prisoner drops the unacceptable role but falls back on other role patterns and self-images which still allow survival; e.g., if he is forced into a state of complete dependency he can still take the role of the dependent person or child and use this role-conception as a way of saving a sense of self.

Much of the resistance behavior of POW's fits the latter conception (Biderman, personal communication). Biderman argues that the POW found himself in a situation in which the most adaptive role was that of "schoolboy"—this was the role which the Chinese demanded and were willing to reward. However, within the context of this role there were still extensive measures that the prisoner could use to undermine the indoctrination program, measures deriving from his own schoolboy history—not paying attention, needing to go to the bathroom frequently, pretending not to understand, forming gangs or coalitions to mock the teacher (e.g., the "Crazy Week" affair in which numbers of prisoners pretended to be crazy), etc. We have previously referred to this kind of role behavior in reference to Moloney's analysis of the ego abandoning itself entirely to superego authority (Chapter 8). This abandonment produces compliance, but only of a very passive sort which might be quite unsatisfactory to a captor.

Assigning our own cases to these categories is complicated by several problems. First, only some cases could be described as genuine cases of identity destruction. Second, in a number of these cases we do not know through what psychological stages the prisoner went. Third, some cases seem clearly to illustrate a desperate switching from role to role (with mounting guilt for the role-playing itself). Others illustrate what would seem to be a temporary state of complete identity diffusion. Lifton (1956) implies in his analysis that most of his cases reached such a point of diffusion.

This issue is crucial in terms of any conception of resistance to coercive persuasion. If the prisoner can find a role which is acceptable to his cellmates and interrogators without complying or being strongly influenced, he has found a powerful way to resist coercive persuasion. Perhaps the crucial variable is the sophistication of the cellmates in identifying and rejecting roles which are not consistent with the reform aims of the prison; i.e., their skill in identifying the individual who is managing to withhold personal involvement or is successfully playing the role of the penitent criminal without really believing in his guilt. We have said in another context that a cell should be more effective in locating such "role deception" than an isolated interrogator might be, because there will be a greater likelihood that among a number of individuals there will be at least one whose own personal style gives him the capacity to see through whatever the prisoner is trying to do, to expose him, and thus to force him into more "honest" change.

Turning now to the problem of finding and accepting a new role and identity, there seems to be agreement that this occurs through the prisoner's finding a model in a cellmate or in the interrogator and identifying with him. Here again the group cell heightens the probability of successful relearning because of the increased likelihood that the prisoner can find someone among his cellmates with whom to identify, and because the intimate cell life permits the administration of immediate reward once a step in the right direction is taken by the prisoner. According to Lifton the sequence then consists of moving from the role of "guilty criminal" (during which the confession is constructed) to the role of "repentant sinner," the latter shift involving extensive self-re-evaluation and the formulation of a conception of self based on premises more acceptable to Communism. Such a shift is largely accomplished through the identification with someone who has already accepted such premises about himself. The prisoner thus acquires a new frame of reference and new reference groups in terms of which to make judgments.

The depth and permanence of identity changes will depend, as we have detailed in Chapters 4, 6, and 7, on the experiences of the repatriate following his release. If his new identity finds support, it will be sustained; if it fails to be supported, the person will be forced into still another influence process. Support need not be limited to reinforcement by significant others. If elements of the new identity come to be integrated into and play important functions in the individual's total personality, they will be more or less permanent and the experience may retrospectively be viewed by the subject as having been a therapeutic one.

Critique

1. The most important thing to be said about the kind of theory presented above is that it applies especially to those prisoners who were influenced at the level of their beliefs and attitudes. The theory is important, then, to the extent that our aim is to explain those cases which involved belief and attitude change, not to explain all possible reactions to imprisonment.

2. This kind of theory is complex in that it involves many complex variables, the precise or reliable measurement of which is far from easy. It is therefore difficult to test, just as the psychoanalytic formulations are difficult to test. On the other hand, the theory's complexity also gives it greater explanatory power in that it makes possible the explanation of many separate cases of coercive persuasion in which the outcome in terms of influence was very different.

3. One of the chief virtues of this kind of theoretical conception, we feel, lies in its making the self or identity a central concept and point of reference. Insofar as coercive persuasion involves attempts to change central beliefs and attitudes, and insofar as such beliefs and attitudes tend to be organized around the self-conception, it stands to reason that this self-conception must become a central target of influence. The Communists, of course, use the language of self, identity, and role as the idiom in which to communicate their political conceptions and to describe what the prisoner is expected to accomplish in his "thought reform."

If one takes the self as a point of reference, a great many other theoretical positions can be fitted comfortably into a broad model of change. For example, the theorizing about self-conception tends to refine and supplement the learning theory formulations at several points:

a. A concrete motive is suggested, need for sense of self, which drives forward the learning process, and conditions are stated in terms of environmental manipulations which allow for the estimation of the strength of the motive in a given prisoner at a given time.

b. A concrete definition of reinforcement is suggested, i.e., that the significant reinforcers for the prisoner are self-confirming cues from cellmates and interrogator, reductions of personal and physical threat, and material rewards like medicine and food if specific deprivations exist (though it should be emphasized again that for many prisoners the latter reinforcer was not very signicant because they were not sick or underfed).

c. A concrete mechanism is suggested by which new behavioral and cognitive responses are initially learned, i.e., identification with cellmates or interrogator.

d. The suggestion is made that learning via cellmates can be very effective because reinforcement follows very closely the emission of a response.

The identity change conception is, of course, also quite consistent with previously cited psychoanalytic formulations, but goes beyond them at a number of points:

a. While unconsciously-based guilt may be a key motive in some individuals, identity theory provides other possible motives which would produce change in the individual; even with respect to guilt, the evidence suggests that many kinds of guilt can be aroused in coercive persuasion of which some of the most significant are guilt feelings pertaining to failure to live up to one's self-image (ego-ideal) or failure to remain loyal to groups with which one is identified (these kinds of guilt may be stimulable in a wider variety of individuals than guilt based upon unresolved childhood conflicts).*

* A simpler change mechanism which we have not discussed in detail is, of course, adopting new beliefs and values which fit better with an existing identity, wherein this identity never comes under direct attack. The cellmates certainly

b. Identity change conceptions refine the crucial area of prisoner relations with other prisoners, an area which we felt is insufficiently analyzed by psychoanalytic formulations. The same point can be made with respect to the prisoner's integration into various kinds of groups, his current emotional commitments, and his reference groups.

c. By noting that identification can occur with a cellmate, the suggestion is made that there may be two basic types of influence which can occur through identification: "resocialization" occurring primarily through identification with a parent figure like the interrogator; and "reinitiation" or forced integration into a group, which occurs primarily through identification with other incumbents for the status and role of group member.*

The relationship between psycho-physiological stress theory and identity-change theory is somewhat more difficult to unravel. In some sense these theories stand in opposition in that the former states the sufficiency of psycho-physiological stresses to explain prisoner compliance, while the latter argues that only certain kinds of psychological stresses can explain prisoner compliance, specifically, those directed at the prisoner's sense of identity. Part of the problem lies in the different aims of the theories. Hinkle & Wolff, for example, set out to explain the reactions of all types of prisoners to all types of stresses under both Russion and Chinese handling. This aim would, of necessity, lead to a broader and less refined kind of theory. Our aim is to explain the small number of cases of belief and attitude change, and what we are asserting is that *in those cases* the psycho-physiological factors, as broadly outlined by Hinkle & Wolff, offer insufficient explanation and overemphasize the role of pain and

---

were not sparing in their utilization of accusations that the person was not even living up to his own stated ideals, but such pressure seemed to act more as an unfreezing force than a force toward change.

* The whole psychology of adolescent and adult initiation has, in our opinion, been insufficiently analyzed. It is quite possible that one would find in the passage of an adult from one key position to another coercive persuasion processes which are not too dissimilar to ones we have described here. In a sense coercive persuasion can be best understood if one regards it as a particularly intensive initiation rite geared to prepare prisoners to become productive members of Chinese Communist society, as this concept is defined by them (see Chapter 2).

debilitation.

The crux of the issue lies in the concept of "the breaking point." There has been much discussion of this concept: whether every man has one, how one should determine its location, whether its location can be altered by suitable training and indoctrination, etc. In all of the conceptions the assumption is implicit, however, that the breaking point has something to do with the individual's ability to tolerate *physical pain* in some absolute sense. Lip service is usually paid to the fact that fear of pain is more painful than the actual physical sensation, and that psychological factors can influence the perception of pain in many ways; but the final implication is seldom drawn that "breaking point" may not have anything to do with physical pain whatsover, but may be primarily a *psychological* process in which self-conception plays a central role.

We have to distinguish two points: (a) a point of physiological breakdown where the pain has produced sufficient trauma of one sort or another that the prisoner faints or in some other way defends himself at a basic physiological level; and (b) a point of psychological giving-in which may be thought of as the point where the prisoner *sees himself* as having reached a level of pain or trauma where his physical self is about to be destroyed or where some fundamental damage is about to be done to his self-concept; he may be far from the point of physiological breakdown when he has the perception of having reached his limit (a response like fainting may, of course, also occur here but for psychological reasons).

It is our contention that very few, if any, prisoners could be expected to behave in terms of the first conception of a breaking point. Such behavior would require that the individual had reached a point of ceasing to care about his body as a significant portion of his self, ceasing to care how much pain and trauma he could observe himself tolerating, and being quite unanxious about the physical sensations involved. Without specific training to assume such a role (i.e., by means of yoga or certain kinds of religious training), it would not be possible for a person readily to cease caring, though some prisoners apparently reach such a point of not caring if they have been repeatedly subjected to physical pain. The upshot of this argument is that the psycho-physiological theory needs to concern itself explicitly with the individual's self-conception in order to make any reliable prediction concerning the effects of psycho-physiological stresses.

Our argument has an important implication for resistance training. If it is true that the breaking point comes for most people far short of their physiological limit of endurance, it is possible by suitable training to increase their capacity to resist physical pressure by teaching them to tolerate greater levels of physical pain. Such training would have to be aimed at showing the potential prisoner that the amount of damage to body and self which is actually done by certain kinds of traumas is perhaps less than he believes in terms of his self-conception. For example, one wonders how many prisoners were aware that even if fingernails were pulled out that they would grow back normally. The prisoner also needs the information that certain physiological stresses may produce permanent damage yet be avoidable. The best example concerned the dietary problems of POW's in Korea. One wonders how many POW's were aware of the fact that by not eating everything which was in any way edible they were risking permanent damage to their eyes and other organs and in many cases their life. If preservation of psychological and bodily self is to be maximized, information about the effects of different kinds of psycho-physiological stresses must be maximized.

Given this psychological concept of "breaking point," what are the psychological consequences of "giving in"? A prisoner may give in at a point where he believes he can no longer tolerate pain, only to discover that he has not really suffered much damage. Then he may feel guilty for not resisting more strongly and must cope with the guilt in addition to the captor's pressures. If he can be made aware that such giving-in short of the physiological limit is the normal response, that it does not constitute personal failure, and that physiologically he still has many resources, his capacity to resist should be sharply increased.

4. The chief shortcoming of the "Identity Theory," as well as of the theoretical conceptions discussed in the earlier sections, is its failure to deal explicitly with the problem of how change in belief or self-conception actually comes about. What actually happens at the level of the person's cognitions which can account for some of the dramatic changes in verbal behavior which repatriates have ex-

hibited?

In summary, what we have somewhat loosely labeled "Identity Theory" contributes some further refinements to the theoretical analysis:

1. The placement of the "self-image" or "identity" at the center of the conceptual scheme.

2. A depiction of the unfreezing, changing, and refreezing processes as being primarily socio-psychological and concerned with interpersonal forces.

3. Emphasis on interpersonal communication and peer-group relations.

4. A specification of the role of social cues and a consideration of the possible impact of over- as well as under-stimulation.

5. A definition of the breaking point as essentially a function of the subject's self-image.

6. The suggestion that identification with peers represents a different kind of influence process from identification with authority figures.

7. The hypothesis that guilt-anxiety is only one of several possible motives for changing.

COGNITIVE THEORY

The cognitive formulation below is a combination of our own ideas and those of Lifton, and was developed to explain the events which occur during the phase of coercive persuasion which we have previously labeled "changing." Given a prisoner with some readiness to change, how does the change actually occur *at a cognitive level* and how does it lead to new behavior and beliefs?

The primary effect of unfreezing is that it makes the prisoner seek information which will guide him in finding an adaptational solution to his problems. Such information can be gotten to some extent from the propaganda input to him via the mass media, lectures, loud-speakers, etc., but more likely is obtained from cellmates or interrogators who begin to be models of how to adapt successfully. The prisoner who has been unfrozen begins to treat the interpersonal cues he obtains from them as credible and valid, and begins to take their point of view seriously, where previously he may have paid no attention to it or even discounted it. The unfreezing stage, then, can be thought of as making available to the prisoner some channels of information input, or rather, making the prisoner open himself to certain kinds of information input.

The information to which the prisoner begins to pay attention contains the following kinds of data: (1) Data about himself; i.e., the prisoner begins to see how his cellmates actually perceive him, and to become aware of the fact that they actually believe him to be guilty of crimes which he is "obstinately" refusing to admit. (2) Data about his cellmates; i.e., the prisoner begins to see how some of his cellmates (the more reformed ones) view the world, the kinds of assumptions they make, the way they reason and draw conclusions, what they believe in, and by what standards of evaluation they operate; he also learns something of their past history and the experiences they have had which clarify for him some of their current perceptions, feelings, and beliefs. (3) Data about China, its history and political development, the rise of Communism and its role in the China of today, the manner in which Communism defines its relationship to the rest of the world (e.g., its unceasing struggle against real or imagined enemies or reactionary attitudes, etc.; see Chapter 3 for further elaborations of this point), the position of the foreigner in Communist China during the Korean hostilities, etc.*

The key process of reorganization which then occurred involved the recognition on the part of the prisoner that certain of the premises held by his cellmates, certain of their standards of evaluation, and certain of their feelings deriving from their acceptance of Communist premises did indeed make him guilty in their eyes. For example, he might recognize that if his Chinese cellmates believed themselves to be in an economic and psychological struggle with America, and if they perceived America's intervention in the Korean War to have been an act of hostility as a prelude to invading China, then indeed they would be justified in regarding with great suspicion

---

* Of course, when we speak of data here, we mean data only in the sense of what was accepted by the interrogators and the cellmates as factual. When we say that the prisoner began to pay attention to such data, we do not mean that he began to believe what his cellmates believed, but only that he began to attempt to understand their position by trying intellectually to see the world through their eyes.

any Westerner who remained in China after the outbreak of hostilities and continued to communicate various kinds of information to the outside. Furthermore, the Western prisoner could see that his Chinese cellmates were justified in holding the opinion that the new government was fair and lenient if they had had concrete experience with KMT police methods, and if they felt that the standard of living in the prison was much higher than ever before, and if they wanted a chance for a decent future life. The fact that he had no adequate trial might not mean anything to him since he might not have had any under the KMT either. Perhaps the greatest shock to the prisoner was the recognition that, from the standpoint of certain premises which his cellmates accepted, the conclusions they drew and the evaluations they made were quite rational and defensible. If he had built, as so many prisoners had, defenses around the notion that the system was irrational and merely devoted to getting him to "break," it could be a great shock to be confronted by a point of view which was different but quite reasonable and quite sincerely held.

The disagreement between the point of view of the prisoner and that of his cellmates was then discovered to be primarily a matter of how certain key concepts were defined and how certain "facts" of human behavior were theorized about. The prisoner began to see that *guilt* and *crime* had an entirely different meaning in the Communist frame of reference (see Chapter 5) and that the causes of crime were defined quite differently in this frame of reference. Aiding this process was the discovery by the prisoner that some of his strongly held convictions about what captivity would be like were not valid—the prisoner found that his expectations of torture and Communist malevolence were erroneous, that their "leniency" and willingness to reform the prisoner were sincere (the cellmates' view of their experience being the evidence). Though the treatment he received was bad from an absolute point of view, it was often not as bad as he had expected.

The acceptance of the new frame of reference, the new semantics, the new standards of evaluation, and the new theory of human behavior then probably resulted from three forces: (1) the need to be able to explain meaningfully the events of imprisonment; (2) the need to find a cognitive mechanism which would make further adap-

tation to the prison situation possible; e.g., once the prisoner had discovered how crime was defined and evaluated, he could locate those
behaviors in his own past which constituted crime from this point of
view and construct the confession which was wanted; (3) the need
to get social reinforcement from his cellmates; i.e., any degree of
understanding on the prisoner's part of his cellmates' point of view
would presumably be perceived by the cellmates as a change of
attitude which they would strongly reward as being a fundamental
step toward reform.

It is important that this process not be confused with a process of
merely granting to someone with whom one is in conflict his definition of terms. The process we have described above involves much
more—the genuine understanding of how the other person thinks
about his world, the recognition that such a way of thinking has
validity for him, the recognition that it is fair under the circumstances for the other to expect the prisoner to think the same way
he does, and finally the application of this way of thinking by the
prisoner to his own behavior. The degree to which genuine reorganization was involved could be surmised from the ease with
which the prisoner began to be able to remember pieces of behavior
which now fitted together into a pattern of crime. Having adopted
the "people's standpoint" he could construct his confession and recognize his guilt.

Having recognized the criminality of certain of his past behaviors,
the next step was for the prisoner to apply the general theory of
crime to himself, the step which Lifton calls "the broadening of
guilt." The prisoner must recognize that his crimes were an inevitable result of his class origins and that he is in fact guilty simply
because of these origins and the attitudes which go with them. His
own guilt, i.e., the "wrongness" of his attitudes, is demonstrated to
him over and over again in the crowded life of the cell through the
criticism of his cellmates—the prisoner is told he is selfish, he does
not have appropriate concern for the working classes, he does not
appreciate the "excellent" food that the prison dispenses or the high
quality of the accommodations, and so on. Again, these criticisms
have a real impact only after the prisoner begins to understand that
the cellmates really feel this way, and that for them the prison really

is "a good deal," that the food really is good, that they are lucky to have heat in their cells, and so on.

The constant exhortation to examine himself and criticize himself focuses the prisoner on his own identity in a manner calculated to reveal whatever faults he might believe himself to have, in addition to the ones pointed out by the cellmates. If he has adopted an orientation of trying genuinely to understand himself from his new perspective, he will likely find many things to feel guilty about in his relations to others. That is, the conception of political crime now may generalize as a concept of crime being "any relationship to the Chinese people which he exploited for personal gain." Failure to understand the "real feelings" of the Chinese people would, of course, be one of the biggest crimes he would perceive, especially if his life in China had consisted of contacts with the diplomatic set and a small number of middle- and upper-class Chinese. The prisoner could readily generalize this perception further to include his relationships with people as a whole, and if this process occurred he might attempt to make changes in himself which would have long-run consequences in areas quite separated from politics. It was this kind of experience which, we believe, led some repatriates to report some years after the repatriation that imprisonment was genuinely therapeutic for them and made them "better people."

An excellent example of this process can be given from one of the cases quoted by Lifton, that of a European priest:

"And now, like a monster from out of the abyss, the most fearful realization dawns: You, the missionary, the herald of the gospel, are not you a messenger of the imperialist conquerors, their pioneer, on account of your ethnological and industrial reports on your missionland? And after the occupation of your missionland you go on rendering the conquerors many different services. And take your mission work as a whole: Does it not now prove as a big, long and heavy sin? And the question whether your mission activity has been of more harm or good to the people answers itself. But because you grew up in imperialistic ideologies, it has never until now occurred to you how much you have been of help in the enslaving and the exploitation of a people which formerly enjoyed liberty. Yes, the scope of your corrupting activity is enlarged: what you do, your colleagues do. Thus you cannot escape the fact that your society and your mission are to be regarded as spy centers, sending out reports to both headquarters, and that Rome becomes the world center, from where imperialist governments draw their perverting information.

"As proof that you now condemn this process you must at once give full information about the spy activities of your society, of your mission, and of Rome. By doing this you acquire the mentality of the new regime, which alone will make you realize the sins of your past life and those of your comrades. Only this mentality will give you true guidance for your future work. With that, the chances for your pardon are greatly enhanced." [Lifton, 1956b, p. 188]

A crucial question is, of course, how much of what we have called cognitive reorganization is built on false logic and cognitive distortion. The logic of Communism is beyond the scope of this analysis, but some comments can be made which may clarify the issue.

Cognitive distortion probably plays a larger role in that phase of coercive persuasion which we have called unfreezing than it does in the change process which has just been described. It is in his initial dealings with the interrogator and cellmates that the prisoner finds himself being trapped into conclusions which he cannot accept or into making confessions which he later repudiates. He recognizes the logic as false and sees the attempt of the captor to distort facts because he does not as yet see all the steps and all the premises from which the captor is operating. From the interrogator's point of view this process is one of probing for the weaknesses in the criminal's defense. He is pretty sure in terms of his dossier that the prisoner is guilty, but he is not completely sure about the specific crimes, hence will test out various possibilities by trying to get the prisoner to confess to many different things. The prisoner who does not go beyond this stage of conflict with his captors is not influenced at the level of attitude or belief, hence has not really been coercively persuaded of anything.

On the other hand, the prisoner who identifies with cellmates or interrogator as a way of adapting to the situation, one who has been unfrozen and is ready to change, finds in the logic of his models a series of cognitive steps which are reasonable and plausible. The question still remains: Are these steps of thinking really logical or only seemingly so? We believe that they are as logical as any set of reasons ever are for holding certain attitudes, which means that they probably would not stand up under detailed formal analysis but that they are entirely plausible given the premises and experiences of the person who holds them. Thus, if one is influenced through the process of identification, that is, through the process of adopting new attitudes by seeing the world through one's model's eyes, one accepts the "psycho-logic" of the model and treats it as entirely rational.* Probably the initial question is somewhat beside the point. There is always a certain amount of distortion, sharpening, leveling, and false logic in the beliefs and attitudes which other people acquire. Because people are ambivalent on many issues it is easy to play up some "facts" and play down others when our value position or feeling changes. Coercive persuasion involves no more or less of such distortion than other kinds of influence, but our popular image of "brainwashing" suggests that somehow the process consists of extensive self-delusion and excessive distortion. We feel that this image is a false one; it is based on our lack of familiarity with or knowledge about the process and the fact that so much publicity was given to the political influence which resulted in a few cases.

In summary, the change process viewed as a series of cognitive steps can be described as follows:

1. Learning to pay attention to a certain class of information which is available in the environment.

2. Learning a new frame of reference for organizing and evaluation behavior and the self, which involves: (a) new basic premises to reason from; (b) new semantics, i.e., new denotative and connotative definitions of certain key concepts like "crime" and "guilt"; (c) new standards of evaluation or judgment, i.e., new anchors or neutral points for the dimensions on which evaluations are to be made which shift the ranges of stimuli judged to be, for example,

---

* In a recent unpublished paper Garfinkel (1958) has shown brilliantly the many conceptions which sociologically define the term "rationality." When we say that someone has acted rationally this can mean any of a great variety of things, including such things as "taking into account alternatives," "considering the future consequences of a piece of behavior or a belief," "keeping one's personal feelings or desires out of consideration," etc.

"good" or "bad," "O.K." or "not O.K.," "fair" or "not fair."

3. Applying this frame of reference to one's own behavior and discovering why one was "guilty" in the Communists' eyes.

4. Applying basic premises about the causes of guilt to one's basic self and recognizing aspects of this self which deserved condemnation and required change.

5. Using the new frame of reference, or portions of it, after repatriation to evaluate behavior, both own and others, producing judgments and evaluations which appear to others to represent dramatic shifts in belief and attitude which cannot be understood.

Critique

1. The biggest problem with the cognitive type of explanation is its complexity and the difficulty of specifying exactly what is meant operationally. Whether this is inherent in the terminology or represents a lack of theoretical clarity on our part is difficult to judge. On the positive side, we feel it to be essential to refine the area which is usually covered by such loose terms as "changing your mind," "becoming converted," "having insight," "changing your beliefs and attitudes," etc. The problem lies in spelling out the relationships between overt non-verbal behavior, overt verbal behavior, covert symbolic behavior (thinking), and various processes such as those described above—learning new definitions for old concepts, broadening the range of perceptions which are classified into a given concept, shifting one's scales of judgment, shifting the anchors in new and old scales of judgment, and so on.

2. Cognitive formulations like the present one cannot, of course, be divorced from motivational analyses like those presented in the four preceding sections. These formulations supplement each other and each is necessary. In fact the relationship between motivation and cognition remains one of the most interesting areas of psychology to unravel. It seems quite clear from the study of coercive persuasion that one cannot equate information available in the environment with information which will be perceived by the prisoner. The motivational side of the experience concerns the problem of creating "perceptual readiness" for certain kinds of information, partly by destroying or undermining certain perceptual defenses.

3. The cognitive formulation puts heavy emphasis on the assumption that the prisoner is at all times engaged in organizing and evaluating his information input, that he is at no point in his experience simply an empty organism into which the captor can pour conceptions, beliefs, and attitudes.

In conclusion, we feel that only with a cognitive conception such as the one presented above is it possible to understand fully how some prisoners could undergo what would be described by most observers as a "conversion" to Communism. That phase of the influence process which we have called changing cannot be understood without a cognitive sequence being specified.

SOCIAL-INFLUENCE AND ATTITUDE-CHANGE THEORIES AND EXPERIMENTS

It would stand to reason that the fields of psychology which have devoted themselves to studying the problems of social influence and attitude change would have the most to contribute to an understanding of coercive persuasion. There is, however, an important reason why they probably cannot claim such a position—namely, there has been in this field a tradition of doing basic experimental work with humans, and such work has typically precluded: (1) working with beliefs and values which are fundamental to the person; (2) working at motivational levels which could produce severe trauma; and (3) creating experimental conditions which could produce extensive and irreversible changes in the subject. Experiments have generally been limited by what the experimental subjects and our cultural norms would tolerate. It is possible that in adapting to such limitations we have missed not only some crucial facts about attitude change but also some good theories. In the present section we shall review some of the theories and findings that are available and test their applicability to coercive persuasion. We cannot undertake a complete review of the field because of its size and the questionable relevance of many of the studies.

Dissonance Reduction

In a recent book, Festinger (1957) has proposed a theory of cognitive change which he feels explains the kind of influence pro-

duced by coercive persuasion.* Festinger's basic assumption is that
when two or more cognitions (thoughts, perceptions, implications of
behavior engaged in, etc.) are inconsistent with each other, this
inconsistency creates a state of "dissonance" and such a state motivates the individual to do something which will reduce the dissonance; i.e., dissonance acts as a powerful motive. Festinger feels
that one of the most common causes of a state of dissonance is the
performance by a person of an action that is inconsistent with
some value or belief he holds. The action may take place on impulse
without having been thought through, it may have been elicited by
a trick or goad of another person, it may have occurred under the
influence of alcohol, or have been coerced, etc., but the fact remains that its commission implies certain things about the person
which he now must bring into line with his values, beliefs, and self-
image.

The dissonance between the implications of the behavior and the
person's values, beliefs, and/or self-image can be reduced either by
"undoing" the behavior, i.e., changing its implications, or by changing the beliefs, values, or self-image. Festinger asserts that the undoing of the implications of behavior is by far the more difficult
thing to do, hence belief, value, or self-image change will more
likely occur. That is, the overt behavior usually constitutes a more
final commitment in that it involves others, is very salient, may
have set into motion consequences for the originator and others, and
so on. The privately held belief may have less of such commitment
attached to it, hence may be more changeable.

The implication of this point of view for the analysis of coercive
persuasion is clear—if the prisoner commits acts, for whatever
reason, which have certain kinds of consequences or implications
he produces dissonance which then must be dealt with. Such behavior might be a confession which the prisoner is aware will hurt
some group or his country, a denunciation of a loved one, an act
of informing on a fellow prisoner, or any behavior which violates
important values held (e.g., a priest acting ungenerously to a fel-

* These ideas were communicated to E. Schein by Festinger in a series of
conversations and do not appear in his book. Our apologies if we have mis-
quoted him.

low prisoner). Its committing aspect may be that it is witnessed by others, becomes public through the mass media, or simply is witnessed by the person himself.

Once the behavior has occurred and the dissonance been created, the prisoner has the following alternatives: (1) to tolerate the dissonance; (2) to reduce the dissonance by rationalizing that his behavior was coerced (by "rationalizing" we mean here simply choosing a certain reason from among several as the dominant one; for example, some behavior may or may not in fact have been coerced from the point of view of an outside observer, but this is irrelevant to the choosing of coercion as a reason for the behavior); (3) to try to undo the committing aspects of the behavior (e.g., repudiate the confession, though this may produce further dissonance in that the prisoner now must see himself as the sort of person who would make and then repudiate a confession); (4) to find reasons why the behavior was justifiable on grounds other than that it was coerced. It is the last of these alternatives which then cognitively produces a change of belief (e.g., the confession was made because, so the prisoner believes, the acts alleged in the confession actually occurred, or actually had the implications alleged in the confession). Of course, this kind of mechanism would be greatly aided by the presence in the informational environment of ample justifications for the behavior which was wanted, e.g., the whole set of ideological premises which justify confession.

The only check on this kind of belief change would be the danger of creating even greater dissonance by changing isolated portions of the total belief system. It might be tempting to rationalize a confession in terms of some Communist premise, but then it might be discovered by the prisoner that this premise leads to another which is in even greater conflict with other basic values which the prisoner is not prepared to change. A good example might be a priest confessing and coming to believe that the confession was justifiable because it was helping the Chinese people, only to discover that such help also involved completely repudiating the role of the Church in China, something he might be unwilling to do.

As evidence for the applicability of his theory, Festinger cites the fact that confession almost always preceded attitude change (at least as far as one could surmise from prisoner accounts); i.e., that the typical coercive persuasion sequence was to get a behavioral commitment which then produced dissonance, the reduction of which then produced the belief change.

Critique

1. Festinger's theory of dissonance reduction is very similar to those learning formulations which state that coerced behavior produces conflict, the reduction of which acts as a reinforcer for any cognitive response which reduces it. Its main value lies in the explicit analysis which is made of belief changes in a variety of situations and in the careful spelling out of the relationships which obtain between overt behavioral commitment and covert "private" beliefs. In his book, Festinger gives considerable experimental evidence to show that beliefs are indeed quite responsive to overt commitments which have been made, and that the adult human will change his cognitions drastically to preserve a sense of inner harmony, i.e., to avoid dissonance. This is not to say that beliefs are more malleable than behavior. Rather, because behavior is more malleable, it must, in a sense, be changed before beliefs can be expected to change. In general, he asserts, that if one wants to change beliefs or attitudes one should change the overt behavior first because this is generally easier to do than to attack the beliefs and values directly. This point would be especially true in those situations in which the consequences of a given behavior are not immediately obvious, e.g., making a concession in an argument on an early premise which seems trivial, signing an innocuous-sounding peace petition in POW camp, etc.

2. The problems of applying Festinger's formulation are, however, serious ones. First of all, as we have previously stated, the captor did not have an easy time at all in eliciting behavior which would produce dissonance. Especially with regard to the matter of making a confession, it seemed as if a prolonged unfreezing had to occur before behavioral commitments were made by the prisoner. Festinger would probably argue that the unfreezing process itself consisted of a series of minor behavioral commitments which could only be justified by going farther along the path of confession and

attitude change, but such a formulation would leave out of the picture the effects which have been observed to result from psycho-physiological stresses which debilitate the person (i.e., great suggestibility which, in turn, should make the subject more tolerant of dissonance—Orwell's "double-think" would be a good example), the problems of dealing with guilt, and the problems of trying to maintain a viable self-image. Each of these problems could probably be translated into dissonance terms as they can be into learning theory terms, but then our criticism would be the same for both—they are both too general and too unrefined to be fruitful analytical tools.

3. The dissonance formulation seems to oversimplify cognitive operations. For example, a prisoner who committed himself behaviorally by confessing and who then accepted the justifying beliefs which the environment offered him found himself under pressure immediately to prove the "sincerity" of his acceptance of the beliefs and attitudes by showing willingness to engage in more extreme behaviors such as denouncing loved ones or highly valued groups. To prevent himself from getting into such a vicious cycle the prisoner often simply tolerated the dissonance.* The whole question of specifying the conditions under which dissonance can be tolerated must be explored before the theory becomes fruitfully applicable.

4. It is often true that any of a number of belief and attitude changes could reduce dissonance by adequately rationalizing the behavior engaged in. The particular rationalization chosen will depend, of course, on its acceptability and the degree to which it leads to reinforcement from significant others in the situation. If, however, the reference group of significant others shifts, and the new group does not accept the first group's rationalizations, one would expect a new shift to occur in order to reduce the new dissonance. For example, while in POW camp, the prisoners who collaborated might have been expected to rationalize their behavior by accepting certain Communist premises; after repatriation such

---

* From the point of view of dissonance theory the only way the person could stop being influenced is if some behavior is demanded of him which lies on a dimension qualitatively different from the one he has been concerned with. Such qualitative change would be assumed to occur when certain strongly held values are suddenly encountered.

rationalizations would make the individual a deviant, but other rationalizations would be available—namely that the collaborative behavior had been coerced or that the individual had been "brainwashed." Such flexibility poses the problem of being able to state some conditions under which belief change will be stable, even if the reference group shifts. The postulation of identification as a mechanism of change overcomes this difficulty in that the emotional relationhip can survive even if the parties to it are physically separated, or if reference groups shift.

5. Experimental evidence is widely available pertaining to belief and attitude changes which follow forced compliance or behavioral commitment. Such evidence goes all the way back to the observations of World War I that in literacy training for illiterate troops the writing out of certain statements (as part of the process of learning how to write) led to the acceptance of attitudes which were reflected in the statements themselves. In his book Festinger cites data from a variety of carefully controlled experiments which demonstrate, for example, that: (1) following a decision there will be an active seeking out of information which produces cognitions consonant with the action taken; (2) following a choice between alternatives there will be an increase in the attractiveness of the chosen alternative and a decrease of the unchosen one; (3) following a forced public statement of opinion (if different from subject's own) there is a significant shift in the subject's private opinion; (4) if subjects are exposed to information which would produce dissonance they are able to misperceive, fail to pay attention, or distort it in a manner calculated to minimize dissonance, etc.

Strong support for the conception that active participation and behavioral commitment is a key device for producing attitude change also comes from several experiments carried out at Yale by Janis and King (Janis & King, 1954; King & Janis, 1956), from studies in which attitude change resulting from role shifts was measured (Lieberman, 1956), etc. In the Janis and King studies it was shown that subjects would shift toward an opinion different from their own original one if they were put into the position of having to deliver a speech which argued for the new opinion. Lieberman showed that workers promoted to foreman would change their attitudes in the direction of prevailing foreman attitudes within a matter of months, and if demoted (as happened in sufficient numbers to observe the same subjects through *two* role shifts) readopted the prevailing attitudes of the worker group.

In all these experimental situations the position to be accepted was highly visible. The problem of how the prisoner finds what beliefs and values to acquire, how he comes to learn to pay attention to his cellmates, is not illuminated by this line of research.

Compliance, Identification, and Internalization

Experiments on influence and attitude change have traditionally paid little attention to the mechanisms which underlie the change, concentrating instead on isolating the variables in the communication source, in the communication content, and in the nature of the receiver of the communication which predict actually observed change. Recently, however, a number of formulations have appeared which imply that the change process may occur by any of several mechanisms, and that the degree, depth, and permanence of change are crucially affected by which mechanism is operating. We shall not discuss all of these models in the present chapter, concentrating instead on Kelman's (1958), because it is an excellent synthesis of several of the others, and has been experimentally supported.

Kelman argues that overt change of behavior can reflect any one of three underlying processes:

1. COMPLIANCE: In which the S changes his behavior in order to obtain some reward or avoid some punishment; i.e., he is trying to control the social effects of his behavior.

2. IDENTIFICATION: In which the S changes because he wants to maintain or establish a satisfying self-defining relationship to another person or group; S believes in the induced behavior but its actual content is irrelevant to him; it is the act of conforming (of maintaining the relationship) which is satisfying.

3. INTERNALIZATION: In which the S changes because he recognizes the content of the new behavior to be intrinsically rewarding; i.e., it serves to provide a solution to a perceived problem or fulfills a personal need.

The kind of influence process which is likely to occur will depend, according to Kelman, on the kind of power the influence agent possesses. If he can control the S's basic fate and the means of accomplishing his goals, the influence is likely to be compliance and to be in evidence only when the agent is present. If the agent's basis of power is his attractiveness for the S, the influence will take the form of identification and will be in evidence so long as the relationship persists or is salient. If the agent's basis of power is his expertness with respect to solving problems of a type which S has and perceives, the influence will take the form of internalization and will be in evidence whenever conditions are relevant regardless of the amount of surveillance or attractiveness of the agent.

In an experiment dealing with different influence sources to which different kinds of power were attributed it was demonstrated by Kelman that the theory could predict the extent and permanence of attitude changes.

Critique

1. Kelman's typology of influence processes is highly relevant to our analysis in that it sharpens the distinctions between the various kinds of outcomes which we have attributed to coercive persuasion. Clearly some of the prisoners only complied with their captors, showing the effects of influence only during the time that they were under surveillance. Some prisoners, as we have indicated, came to identify with their interrogator or cellmate and were influenced in the more fundamental fashion which identification implies. Finally, some prisoners found in the Communist attitudes some solutions to personal problems and internalized these solutions.

2. The main problem with the applicability of the Kelman formulation is that the interaction among the processes of compliance, identification, and internalization has not as yet been spelled out. To what extent will compliance lead to identification, or identification lead to internalization? Can and do these processes overlap? We have previously argued against the glib explanation of influence as a process of rationalizing behavior elicited by compliance, on the grounds that compliance could not readily be predicted for any given prisoner. Therefore, it is not of major concern to us whether

compliance leads to identification or internalization (though this is an interesting theoretical problem in its own right). We are more concerned about the relationship of identification to internalization insofar as it is our contention that the crucial influence step is the one where the prisoner begins to identify with cellmate or interrogator. Two kinds of connection between identification and internalization can be spelled out:

a. Through identifying with a cellmate or interrogator the prisoner may discover a way of viewing the world which exposes to him some personal problems he has and which he can solve by being influenced; that is, the influence agent may, in effect, provide both the problem and the solution, which implies that internalization can logically follow identification. A good example would be the case of the prisoner who discovers by seeing the world through his reformed cellmate's eyes that his own relationships to people fail to satisfy deeper values he accepts and that the Communist values pertaining to interpersonal relationships are likely to solve this interpersonal need which now has become salient.

b. For many prisoners the problem of psycho-social survival was how to find out what was wanted by the authorities. As we have pointed out, identification with a cellmate often proved to be the mechanism by which information became available that enabled the prisoner to satisfy his captors. If we conceptualize the coercive persuasion process in this fashion, it becomes evident that the process of identifying with another in the cell is in itself the solution to a problem, hence is an instance of internalization. The major consequence of this point is that it allows us to predict that changes which occur via identification will persist because the identification itself will persist even when the influencing agent is removed. The prisoner, having discovered some important personal solutions by identifying with cellmates, internalizes these cellmates as models and continues to use them as a reference group after release from prison. Such a process has been observed in some repatriates (continued admiration and adulation of the Chinese people as a generalization from the qualities allegedly observed in a given set of fellow prisoners). The degree to which this process will operate depends on the degree to which other competing models begin to create conflict requiring further influence to take place. Such competing models will gain salience (as we have stated in Chapter 7) as a function of the emotional relationships in which the repatriate finds himself after his return home (which in turn will partly, but only partly, be under his own control—see pp. 187–193).

In a complete description of coercive persuasion, then, it becomes necessary to consider the relevance of each of Kelman's processes of influence, and in particular to discover the interaction of identification and internalization. Kelman's model, as we have said, derives its virtue from the clear statement of the separate processes and their separate experimental validation, making possible a more precise fitting of a complex social phenomenon like coercive persuasion into social psychological theory.*

Studies of Group Pressure

A series of experiments carried out by Asch (1951, 1952), brings out the group-pressure aspect of the influence problem in bold relief. Asch had a group of "confederates" of the experimenter give unanimously incorrect responses to a simple perceptual problem preceding the public judgment of an experimental subject. When the subject arrived in the experimental situation he would find anywhere from 1 to 15 other Ss (all of whom were in collusion with the experimenter) and would be jockeyed into a position in the room in which he would have to give his oral answer following all the others. The problem was to match a given line with one of three others on an adjacent card (a task which control Ss did without error). On a series of 18 problems the confederates would then give unanimously incorrect answers to 12. The experimental question was, to what extent would the experimental subjects repeat their incorrect answer? Many groups were run using different types

* A further complicating problem is the fact that the experimental underpinnings of theories like Kelman's tend either to be weak or to involve situations of low applicability to real life situations. Only recently, for example, has there been a systematic attempt to study the influence process in a serial interaction situation to try to determine the terminal effects from several successive interactions which are experimentally controlled (e.g., Fisher & Lubin, 1958). Yet the possibility that the underlying mechanisms shift as the different phases of the influence process occur may be the most important feature for the understanding of interpersonal influence.

of Ss, and it was generally found that roughly one-third of the Ss tended to go along with the unanimous majority on most of the 12 "test" trials.

All Ss were interviewed following the experiment, and evidence was obtained that the yielding represented in different Ss a different psychological process. In some Ss it was a simple adaptation to the group involving a change in behavior (Kelman's compliance) with the subjective recognition by the S that he was giving the wrong answer in order not to "seem different" from the others. In other Ss there was an awareness of giving an answer that seemed wrong subjectively but accompanied by lack of confidence in own judgment resulting in the decision to trust the group's judgment. A third group of yielders denied that they had given wrong answers, leading to the conclusion by Asch that they had undergone genuine changes in perception (their need to be in tune with the group was so strong that they had to deny even to themselves that they had been influenced).

Additional findings by Asch were that the unanimous majority reached its potency when it reached 3 against 1; increasing it even to 15 against 1 led to no significant increase in amount of influence demonstrable. Even more significant, if a second experimental subject was inserted in the group to act as a "partner" to the lone "minority" subject, the yielding effect was almost completely wiped out. No matter how many members of the majority agreed, if the answer they gave was incorrect the test subject gave the correct one.

Asch's findings are obviously relevant to several aspects of the coercive persuasion problem even though they deal only with a single perceptual response rather than a series of beliefs and attitudes. Most relevant would appear to be the fact that a unanimous majority has tremendous influencing potential, but that a single supporter can break its strength. This is entirely consistent with our observation that only in those prisons where the target individual was placed in a cell with others who were unanimously arrayed against him was an influence process likely to be set in motion. If there were one or more cellmates who were resisting influence, this typically strengthened the target individual's own resistance.

The fact that yielding subjects showed different underlying psychological processes is consistent with our findings and supports a theory like Kelman's, but points in addition to the importance of individual predisposition for predicting the outcome of influence. A host of recent studies has attempted to define precisely those personality characteristics which correlate consistently with "independence of judgment" or with "tendency to yield to group influence." Unfortunately there has been relatively little agreement among such studies either in finding that yielding can be consistently demonstrated in a given individual across different kinds of tasks, or that specific personality measures relate to such yielding when it is found. Those studies which claim positive results have isolated factors like the following as being predictive of yielding: low intelligence, weak ego, high authoritarianism (Crutchfield, 1955); social inadequacy, inhibition of aggression, depressive tendencies, low self-esteem (Hovland *et al.*, 1953) submissiveness (Mouton *et al.*, 1956); high activity proneness (Schein *et al.*, 1957), etc. (See also: Adorno *et al.*, 1950; Linton, 1955; Schroder & Hunt, 1958; Berkowitz & Lundy, 1957; Fisher *et al.*, 1957; Hoffman, 1953, 1957; Hovland *et al.*, 1959; Singer & Schein, 1958). Until a higher degree of agreement is obtained on experimental studies there seems to be little value in speculating on the relevance of the specific kinds of findings that have been exemplified. (Our own tentative conclusions based on our subjects are summarized in Chapter 7, pp. 167–169.) The most that can be said is that there seems to be no simple pattern of personality which relates to the amount of influence evidenced either in laboratory studies of influence or in our own studies of coercive persuasion.

Communication Studies

A number of studies have concentrated on the systematic analysis of the determinants of opinion change when the medium of communication is an oral or written presentation to an audience (Hovland *et al.*, 1953, 1957, 1959). In these studies variables such as the nature of the communication source, the communication content, the audience predisposition, the nature of the response to be made by the audience, the order of presentation of positive and negative arguments, etc., have been investigated. A detailed analysis of the points at which these studies relate to the coercive persuasion process will not be undertaken here because the basic content of the attitudes under investigation in them is fundamentally different from the kind of attitude content which is central in coercive persuasion. Specifically, the Hovland studies deal with opinions and attitudes which do not centrally involve the self-concept or basic values the individual holds (e.g., they deal with attitudes toward broad social issues, product preferences, international affairs, etc.). If Communist methods of prison indoctrination were limited to the manipulation of verbal communication inputs, such studies would be highly relevant. Our exclusion of them hinges on our conviction that coercive persuasion involved much more intensive interpersonal influence processes, in the context of which the manipulation of mass media inputs, for example, played only a limited role. These studies have limited applicability to coercive persuasion in the same sense in which they have limited applicability to psychotherapy or resocialization in prisons, for example.

Extensive experimental work has also been carried out on the problem of opinion change in the small group deriving from Lewin's classical studies (e.g., Cartwright & Zander, 1953). To summarize and evaluate the relevance of these studies and other classics in the field (e.g., Sherif, 1936) would require far more space than is available here. Many of these studies deal with tasks of low importance to the subject hence are not relevant for the same reason that the Hovland studies are not relevant. Lewin's classical studies on the problem of overcoming resistance to change do deal with central issues for the subjects involved, and the model which emerges from them is, of course, the one we have found most useful and have made the basis of our influence model (Chapter 4).

CONCLUSIONS

In this and the preceding chapter we have attempted to assess the relevance of a number of psychological theories to the problem of explaining influence resulting from coercive persuasion. The kinds of theories or models reviewed may be classed in the following categories: psycho-physiological stress models, learning theories, psychoanalytic formulations, psychoanalytic formulations combined with sociological formulations, cognitive formulations, and social-influence models. One conclusion stands out above all others when one examines the relevance of these models to coercive persuasion —the models tend to supplement each other rather than to compete with each other. Taken singly, no one of the models gives an adequate account of the varied results of coercive persuasion; taken together, they provide a picture which makes the process and the outcome understandable without the need to resort to esoteric theories or demonology.

We can summarize best by attempting now to combine the model which we presented in Chapter 4 with the theoretical mechanisms spelled out in this and the previous chapter. We stated that no influence could occur in a prisoner unless the prison milieu tended to unfreeze him or unless he was already unfrozen (ready to change and motivated to do so). In Table 3 we indicated that unfreezing involved the undermining and weakening of the prisoner's initial attitude of resistance, physical stamina, social-emotional and cognitive supports, self-image, sense of identity, sense of integrity and inviolability, and basic personality integration.

Psycho-physiological stress theory contributes some degree of understanding of how this weakening occurs, particularly at the physical level, but requires extensive supplementation from the psychoanalytic and sociological formulations before it becomes clear why some of the environmental events observed in prison had the effects they did, in the sense of inducing or arousing motives in the prisoner which led him to change. Of particular importance are theories dealing with the role of self-image and identity, insofar as the loss of a viable identity seemed to be one of the key elements in the influence process. The extension of psycho-physiological concepts of sensory deprivation to under- and over-stimulation at the level of social cues (confirming or disconfirming interpersonal information) is also necessary, though here we enter a realm in which no good theory as yet exists. Notions of the breaking point also have to be conceived, in our opinion, in both physical and socio-psychological terms, insofar as the person's concept of himself is probably closely related to what he thinks he can stand physically, and is the psychological reality to him, regardless of what his body is capable of. Of course a key theoretical concept, coming both from psychoanalytic and socio-psychological contexts, is guilt in its various forms. The special role which guilt comes to play in unfreezing has been discussed in Chapter 5.

The process of changing was described in Chapter 4 as involving first of all a need to change, then the discovery of an information source which provides the direction of change, and a cognitive mechanism which describes or accounts for the altered psychological functioning at the level of belief, attitude, value, and behavior. The formulations which derive from learning theory and the cognitive analysis given in this chapter offer fruitful directions toward the discovery of a change mechanism at the cognitive level. The concept of identification coming both from psychoanalytic and sociological theory is a crucial supplement, however, in providing a dynamic and motivational element as well as an explanation of why the prisoner uses certain sources of information more readily than others. It also focuses on the interpersonal nature of influence or change and draws attention to the fact that such influence is not limited to the socialization process or childhood. It would, in fact, be interesting to test the hypothesis that identity change can only occur through identification, i.e., coming to see yourself through the eyes of some important others and accepting some of what he (they) sees (see). The chief competitor to the identification "theory" of influence would be the transfer of guilt-anxiety "theory" which argues that cognitive change occurs in order to avoid unconscious material, that is, as a defense against inner forces of destruction. We feel that both mechanisms probably operate, but that the transfer of guilt mechanism applies more to those cases who showed only temporary influence, while identification applies more to those whose influence was more or less stable.

The process of refreezing implies that any change will not remain stable unless there are forces continuing to operate to make it stable. Put in this form we have merely reiterated a well-known principle of learning, and what learning theory has to offer at the level of instrumental responses should certainly be applied and tested at the level of cognitive responses of the sort which coercive persuasion involves. Thus learning theory provides us with variables and causal relationships between them but does not specify the content of these variables. The psychoanalytic and socio-psychological formulations provide the content in the form of notions about self-image, identity, interpersonal cues of a confirming or disconfirming (reinforcing or not reinforcing) sort. It should at some point in the development of the field be possible to put the two formulations closer together and determine whether the traditional learning laws can provide useful insights into the processes occurring between people. Some of the immediate complications which one can imagine would be our hypothesis that confirmation need come from only one significant other; that the same interpersonal cue will have very different meanings depending on whom it came from (i.e., how the recipient perceives and defines the sender); that the relationship between the target of influence and the model through whom the influence occurred can sustain itself symbolically or through surrogates; and that the person can to a degree control the amount of confirmatory (reinforcing) cues he will get by seeking out others who will or will not provide it. Clearly, refreezing can occur intrapsychically through cognitive and affective internal processes producing a reintegration which may have considerable internal stability.

If one could engage in coercive persuasion in an experimental situation, it would be tempting to derive and test a more parsimonious model than that which is suggested by the complex combination of all the theories mentioned above. Without having access to such experimental verification, however, it would seem the more appropriate course to put into the theoretical model a sufficient richness to encompass the extremely rich data. We do not have sympathy for the attempt to squeeze the many types of experiences which the victims of coercive persuasion report into simple, one-factor, theoretical models. Such squeezing serves neither to increase our understanding of the process nor to advance our knowledge of theory. We feel that the change or influence model presented in Chapter 4, supplemented by the specific mechanisms mentioned in this chapter, is as close as we can come at this stage to giving a theoretical model of the coercive persuasion process.

PART FOUR *Implications for a Theory of Influence*

ONE OF THE most significant trends in current social psychology is the gradual broadening of theory to encompass seemingly widely divergent kinds of phenomena. Particularly with respect to the study of social influence one finds increasing attempts to bridge the gaps which have traditionally separated studies of socialization and initiation in anthropology, of the learning process in the field of education, of the process of psychotherapy in psychiatry and clinical psychology, of reform and rehabilitation in penology and criminology, and of confession extraction and indoctrination in studies of Communist practices as well as in police practices in other societies. The search for common practices in the art of influence and for common theoretical mechanisms promises not only to improve our understanding of the influence process in general but also to shed light on the many separate kinds of activities which thus far have produced only separate bodies of "wisdom" that get passed from one generation of practitioners to another.

The next two chapters are a deliberate attempt to contribute to this trend by examining those elements which coercive persuasion has in common with other kinds of influence situations. We have deliberately focused on common themes and have ignored some glaring differences between situations or processes. We have at times taken great liberties in making assumptions about influence processes with which the practitioner or specialist in that area might rightfully wish to quarrel. Our only justification for such stretching of the limits of the areas discussed is to stretch all of our imagination a little in the hope that this stretching will lead to some new approaches to the analysis of situations in which influence occurs.

10

The Ritualization of Belief

OUR THEORETICAL discussion thus far has only peripherally dealt with the problem of how beliefs, attitudes, and values are integrated into the total personality and what functions, if any, they perform for their holder. The question not only is important for any theory of influence but also, as will be seen, brings us back full circle to the problem of the impact of coercive persuasion on those who continue to live within totalitarian society. There has been a good deal of speculation concerning the relationship between publicly expressed and privately held beliefs, attitudes, and values in the citizen of such society. In Chapter 3 we examined some of the assumptions which can be held concerning this relationship and tried to indicate that the simple dichotomy of overt public behavior versus covert private behavior is insufficient for an understanding of what can happen to cognitive-affective responses under the impact of coercive persuasion. It is from this starting point that we should like to resume our analysis.

Smith *et al.* (1956) have distinguished three functions which opinions * can serve for the person. They can serve to *appraise reality*—through his opinions the individual can test reality, categorize incoming information, and reach rational conclusions about his environment. They can serve to facilitate and reinforce *social adjustment*—through his opinions the individual can relate him-

* The term "opinion" is used by Smith *et al.* to represent in general what we have been referring to as beliefs, attitudes, and values.

259

self to others, express his membership in certain groups, and his sense of identity. And they can serve to *externalize* inner problems —through his opinions the individual can express his personal conflicts, his conscious and unconscious feelings and motives.

If opinions are to be changed, the strategy of change will have to depend upon the function they serve: opinions which serve object appraisal functions will be most responsive to facts; opinions which serve social adjustment functions will be most responsive to information concerning what significant others think; opinions which serve to externalize inner conflict probably become more rigid with increased external pressure and can only be changed in a permissive and reassuring environment by some kind of personal reorganization.

If a change strategy is employed which is incongruent with the basis on which the opinion is held, it may lead to less expression of the opinion (making it less public) but not necessarily to opinion change. If the environment, however, has the means of checking private opinions (as the group cell did), the individual will find himself in difficulty if his opinions are either expressive of personal conflicts or serve to appraise reality.* He can then change in some deep personality sense so that expressed opinions are now congruent with what the environment demands, or redefine the criteria by which reality is to be judged, or suppress the use of opinions to fulfill the expressive or object appraisal functions and try to fulfill these functions through some other means.

We have seen that some prisoners found it possible to redefine the criteria of reality by adopting the "people's standpoint," and that some prisoners underwent significant personal reorganizations. The category of individual whom we have not treated in detail is the one who did not change in either of these ways, but who found it possible to separate the realm of opinion expression from the realms of object appraisal and personality expression, i.e., who initially or terminally used opinions solely to facilitate social adjustment. This kind of response, which we have labeled *ritualization of belief,*

---

* If his opinions serve primarily social adjustment functions he will readily change them to adjust to the demands of the cellmate, as will be indicated below.

is to be found not only in the kind of climate which is created by a totalitarian regime, but also in the climate of any "total institution," i.e., an institution which has the responsibility of caring for all aspects of its inmates' lives (Goffman, 1957b).

The ritualization of belief is the psychological process which results when a group's formal doctrine and its manner of expression is completely controlled by the leaders of that group. Such control is present in totalitarian societies and in total institutions such as monasteries, nunneries, fraternal orders, certain kinds of academies and schools, certain kinds of reformatories, mental hospitals, prisons, etc. The degree to which the ideology of the organization or society is explicit may vary independently of the degree of control which is exerted by the authorities over the inmates' expression of ideology. However, the more committed the organization is to an explicit ideology, the tighter the controls on the inmates with regard to learning it, assimilating it, and expressing it appropriately. By contrast, the individual who is not controlled by a group in this sense can maintain belief systems which grow and change, which are responsive to external information and internal forces in the individual, which he may use to fulfill object appraisal and expressive functions, which he may test against the beliefs of others, and the expression of which is curtailed only by the patterns of social forces to which he exposes himself.

From the point of view of the individual, the psychological essence of the ritualization of belief is his ability to gain control over both his overt expression of belief and his private expression (even his expression of it to himself in his own thoughts), which means that beliefs serve only the social adjustment function for him). Learning to control overt expression is, of course, not difficult, but learning not to have thoughts other than the ideologically correct ones is difficult indeed and is probably only attempted by individuals who are highly motivated to do so.

In the training of a nun, for example, this goal is sought by two methods—the novices attempt to learn to maintain an "interior silence," i.e., to think of *nothing* if they are not thinking about their faith, or to fill mentally unoccupied periods with prayer and other routine activities (Hulme, 1956). The function of both of these methods would appear to be to gain control over the fantasy life so that mental activity can be restricted to religious thoughts. As an aid in this process other mental activities are prescribed, such as "self-examination." It is possible that the strong emphasis on self-examination in coercive persuasion serves the dual function (as it does for the novice nun) of rooting out incorrect thoughts and providing a routine mental occupation which can be engaged in whenever the individual feels himself threatened by uncontrolled fantasies. The threat in these fantasies lies, of course, in that they could readily lead the individual to engage in impulsive actions or belief expression which would bring strong sanctions from the group, or the authorities.*

As the individual learns to control his overt and covert belief expression he comes, in a sense, to be emptied of belief and filled with ritual. That is, he gives up that which the word belief implies in common usage—a dynamic, changing, viable and useful kind of cognitive response. The more the individual adapts to the group's ideology, the less able he will be to think productively and creatively because he will have lost some of the cognitive tools with which to do such thinking. We have informally observed that an individual who has accepted ideology in this sense is quite unable to discuss it in terms other than clichés; he is likely to repeat compulsively certain stock arguments and premises, or else to refuse to discuss the ideology altogether. In any case he is likely to give the impression either of being quite devoid of fantasy and creative thought or filled with certain kinds of routine and stock thoughts which he is unwilling to examine critically.†

At the same time, his beliefs and their overt expression will be-

---

* Whether such fantasies also produce anxiety or guilt in the clinical sense is unclear. Since they are in conflict with *external* authority rather than internal values, one may expect more fear and less anxiety and/or guilt.

† The frequent allegation that defectors from Communist secret police operations appear, upon being interviewed, to be "inhuman" is apparently in part due to the defectors' appearing to be cognitively "empty" of anything other than the ideology. They cannot respond to interviewing except in stock ideological clichés. Interestingly enough one of the subjects in the Smith *et al.* study for whom beliefs served primarily to facilitate social adjustment had similar difficulties in being interviewed. He either answered in a cliché or went blank.

come more labile in that they lose their anchorage in the total personality. Their prime source of stability is the authority of the group which has defined them and their prime function is to facilitate the individual's adjustment. When the group no longer provides authority, i.e., no longer tells the individual how to adjust, the individual is lost and has only the alternative of finding another group which will provide an ideology comparably well organized (possibly this accounts for some of the conversions from Communism to Catholicism); on the other hand, if the group or its leaders change aspects of the formal ideology, the individual can readily accept the new formulation even if it disagrees with the one held previously.

A number of observers of the citizen in totalitarian society have described a process which we feel is essentially what we have called the ritualization of belief. For example, Guillain describes the situation in Communist China as follows:

The socialization of heads proceeds therefore from a sort of abandonment on the part of the individual of the faculty of thought. He delegates it to a group, he externalizes it. He yields it to the party, the representative and guide of the people, and to the leaders, considered as the wise men of the regime, who cannot err. One could truly speak of "mental alienation," in its medical sense, meaning "insanity," a renunciation of the mind. One is ever tempted to use the word "alienation" here in its Marxist sense. Man finds himself deprived of that little superfluous product, of that surplus—thought. [Guillain, 1957, p. 134]

Hoffer sees the ritualizing aspects in noting about mass movements that:

Where unity and self-sacrifice are indispensable for the normal functioning of a society, everyday life is likely to be either religiofied (common tasks turned into holy causes) or militarized. [Hoffer, 1951, p. 156]

The best statement of the functions of beliefs and the lability which results from ritualization is found in the excellent analysis by Katkov:

People refrain from spitting on the floor and bother to put on ties, not because they believe that spittle spreads infection or that ties add to their personal beauty, but because otherwise they would not get on with their fellow creatures. And the Soviet citizen who does not want to be considered a leper professes the official ideology for a similar reason . . .

It stands to reason that beliefs which are held and professed for these pragmatic reasons will persist and function in quite a different way from beliefs which are held because of their recognized or alleged truth value. To begin with they cannot easily be modified by argument. At the same time they will be relatively easily discarded as soon as those who hold them discover that in changed circumstances they become useless for pragmatic purposes and indeed might be dangerous. This explains the astonishing number of "conversions" or "changes of heart" which Soviet citizens undergo as soon as they are withdrawn by force of circumstances from the control of Soviet State authority. In fact, in the majority of cases, these are by no means "conversions" . . . The beliefs were not held because their truth was demonstrated, but were instilled by those means of persuasion against the background of coercion . . . [Katkov, p. 8]

It is futile to treat political opinions instilled by the persuasion-cum-coercion method by mere argument, as if they were held for their truth value and not for their pragmatic and life preserving reasons. But they also should not be approached as if they were merely insincere, make-believe attitudes, concealing elaborate alternative views on the same subjects. [Katkov, p. 12]

The fact that belief systems can and do become ritualized seems amply demonstrated in analyses like the above and in more detailed clinical studies of individuals who adapt to a coercive organizational context. We do not know, however, to what extent such ritualization actually leads to an atrophy of a private cognitive world. Does the individual preserve a sense of self which is independent of the self which the organization defines for him, or is it impossible to preserve such a sense of self without interaction with others? If it is true that a viable private cognitive world depends on some interaction with others, or at least one significant other, it becomes crucial to analyze in detail the extent to which a totalitarian society or any group actually manages to sever all emotional links which are not politically or ideologically defined. In Chapter 3 we have indicated that there are forces in totalitarian society which operate to destroy any vestiges of private relationships. One wonders whether in the process they also destroy the capacity of the citizen for creative effort or whether the citizen always manages to find outlets in non-political areas for functions which beliefs and their expression can no longer fulfill.

In order to indicate the relevance of the ritualization of belief for our study we have to distinguish certain features of the experiences of our American subjects from the experiences of Chinese or others whom thought reform was intended to make useful members of Communist society. The most important difference is that our subjects were expelled from Communist China following their imprisonment, whereas the others went to work within Chinese society.

The long-run changes in our American subjects have to be assessed in terms of the impact which the return to Western society would have on someone who had been "reformed" in prison. If he had accepted new criteria for appraising reality, such criteria would either be dropped upon his return or integrated with Western criteria (thus producing someone who might appear more liberal, more to the left, possibly more confused and labile in his thinking, or someone who seemed to have a number of "logic-tight" compartments). If he had undergone some personality reorganization and adopted some of the broad ethical principles of Communism he could no doubt make a very successful and happy adjustment in Western society inasmuch as such principles would not conflict with our own. If he had learned to use beliefs (and their expression) solely to adjust to a social environment, i.e., had begun to ritualize them, he would have found responses in his friends and relatives which encouraged the abandonment of such ritual and the readoption of the object appraisal and expressive functions. The individual would likely find a supportive and encouraging kind of response in which the compulsive clinging to clichés and stock arguments would fail completely to be reinforced. There would be little support in Western society or ideology generally for a continued ritualization of belief unless the individual entered a total institution which supported those same beliefs.

The situation is entirely different for the native prisoner. All the institutions in Communist society support the continued use of expressed beliefs and opinions purely in terms of their social adjustment functions. Even private expression becomes subject to government scrutiny and the entire social control apparatus operates to insure a continued expression of only those beliefs, opinions, and attitudes which are currently sanctioned by the party. The consequences of this for the reformed native prisoner are probably the following.

If his thought reform has led primarily to the adoption of new criteria for appraising reality (if he has internalized the Communist point of view thoroughly, understands it, and can reason from it), he can enter society with some hope of acceptance as a dedicated and useful member (useful in that he could, through his own understanding of the theory, help others to understand it). He would probably be perceived as the type of Communist who has been described as the idealist or the true convert and would adjust successfully until such time as party policy and actual operations would lead to disillusionment and disaffection. Once disaffected he would, like others, find himself in the position of having to ritualize his beliefs in order to survive physically in the system.

If his thought reform had led to personality reorganization, the adoption of the broad Communist ethic, and the intention to lead a "good" life, he would quickly discover that such a life was impossible and that the ethic was not in evidence in the daily operation of the Communist state. He too would then become disillusioned and either commit acts leading to rearrest, attempt to defect, commit suicide, or undergo a further influence process leading to the ritualization of his beliefs.*

---

* One of the chief points of conflict between the actual operation of the system and the personality reorganization encouraged by reform lies in the concept of individual responsibility. The method of reform and much of its theoretical emphasis places the individual in a situation of taking personal responsibility for meeting the organizational goals of the system; the more he learns to take responsibility, however, the more likely he will find it impossible to adjust to the

If his thought reform has led to a ritualization of his beliefs and a corresponding submersion of other functions for belief expression, the system would support a continued reliance on this type of psychological adjustment, in fact would reinforce and further the process of ritualization.

The observations of our subjects concerning the type of adjustment which their Chinese cellmates were making to thought reform suggest that most of the Chinese were sufficiently aware of the realities of Communist operations not to allow themselvess to be too deeply touched by the reform process (in the sense of opening themselves up to personality reorganization). Rather, one gets the impression that they were attempting to ritualize their beliefs and to learn the role of the reformed person without completely giving themselves to it. Whether this would be equally true of the young people being reformed in Revolutionary Colleges we do not know. Our statement applies only to those Chinese cellmates who were observed by our American subjects.

In conclusion, it can be seen that the loose distinction between overt behavior and private belief does not provide enough refinement to make possible an understanding of what happens to beliefs under the impact of coercive persuasion and totalitarian or total institutional social control. Only if we combine the public-private concept with hypotheses about the functions of beliefs in the personality is it possible to spell out some of the results. What we have argued here is that the main result of totalitarian control is that the sphere of private activity becomes restricted or eliminated, that the belief systems become ritualized and come to serve solely an adjustment function, and that such ritualization may leave the individual without the cognitive tools to lead a creative private life; i.e., in the end both his public and private spheres may become dominated by ritual. The concept of beliefs playing only a social adjustment function explains two important facts about citizens in totalitarian states: their cognitive "emptiness" and inability or un-

---

operating realities of the regime since he will most likely find himself repeatedly in situations where he must be totally obedient to arbitrary authority. He can resolve the conflict only by leaving the system or else abandoning the psychological gains of thought reform.

willingness to examine their own cognitions or fantasies; and their ability to change their belief systems frequently as the regime's official dicta change the ideology.

The importance of the concept of ritualization for a theory of influence lies in the fact that some of the most important influence processes within our own society occur in institutions which may quite properly be called total institutions. If ritualization is one kind of outcome of a certain strategy of influence (quite apart from the content of the material involved), it is important to ask whether such an outcome was intended or not, and what side effects, wanted or unwanted, accompany ritualization. This question is especially relevant to those institutions which we sanction morally—our mental hospitals, reformatories, academies, etc. Most theories of influence limit themselves to a consideration of the conditions under which opinion change will or will not occur. Our argument is that if we are going to consider influence processes which go deeper than advertising or the mass media, processes which might properly be called resocialization, acculturation, or re-education, we must consider not only the conditions of change but also the nature of the new integration which the change produces in the target individual.

11

Coercive Persuasion in Non-Communist Settings: Some Parallels

THE MODEL of coercive persuasion we have proposed is not limited in its applicability to what the Chinese Communists did to their Western political prisoners. Rather, it is applicable to all instances of persuasion or influence in which the person is constrained by physical, social, or psychological forces from leaving the influencing situation. The model is also morally neutral in that it explicitly ignores the content of the beliefs, attitudes, values, or behavior patterns which are involved in the influence process. If we preserve this moral neutrality we can raise the question whether the events in Chinese Communist prisons provide any clues to the understanding of other influence processes, even those which we condone and consider to be valuable, e.g., psychotherapy, reform in prison, etc. It is important in considering such parallel phenomena not to fall into the trap of thinking that because we use methods similar to the Communists our methods are bad and should therefore be abandoned on moral grounds. It could just as well be argued that the Communists are using some of our own best methods of influence, and therefore coercive persuasion really has some good features to it. We feel that neither approach helps us to understand the nature of the influence process, hence prejudgment must be avoided in so far as is possible.

In spelling out the parallel phenomena it will be useful to consider them in terms of the basic categories of unfreezing, changing, and refreezing. Particular attention must go to unfreezing because too often this process is overlooked as an integral part of the influencing situation.* Yet it seems clear that the unfreezing of a belief or attitude is a necessary condition for any influence to occur.

UNFREEZING

If we look at institutional influence of the kind which goes on in prisons, reformatories, hospitals, educational institutions, religious orders, etc., we find a great concern with unfreezing which may, in fact, be the reason for the success of such institutions in producing influence. Possibly the most interesting aspect of such unfreezing is that its basic components are similar regardless of the content which is to be taught in the influence process, ranging all the way from Communist ideology to a specific set of religious doctrines. The similarity in unfreezing procedures is probably most closely related to the fact that total institutions of the kind we have mentioned all are in the business of influencing the person's self-image or identity and that a certain amount of folk wisdom has accumulated concerning the best way of doing this.

For example, most influencing institutions separate the target individual from his normal social contacts and daily living routines, thus reducing sharply the amount of interpersonal confirmation he can obtain. In prisons, mental hospitals, convents, and monasteries this is obvious; in educational institutions it is somewhat less so. In the latter the reduced contact results from a combination of

---

* The experimental study of social influence has failed to draw attention to unfreezing because it generally lies outside of the experimental design itself. Subjects are usually allowed to volunteer; if they do not pay attention to the experiment they are either thrown out of the analysis or treated as part of the uncontrolled error variance; if they or others object too strenuously to parts of the experiment on moral grounds it often has to be discontinued, etc. Most experiments on influence do not directly concern themselves with unfreezing at all, except at the cognitive level, by presenting material which it is presumed or hoped will create readiness for accepting the influencing message.

factors: a very heavy work routine; social norms that too much attachment to home is somehow bad or unmanly; and the physical isolation of the academies, schools, and workshops that makes contact with significant others from home difficult. Christie (1954) reports the interesting finding that Army basic trainee adjustment tends to be better the farther away the trainee is from home and the less frequent his contact is with home folks.

Most total institutions have as part of their routine of inducting a new member what may best be described as "mortifications of the self," which serve symbolically to destroy the old self by destroying its external trappings. Thus entry into religious orders involves giving up one's usual clothes, one's usual physical comforts, one's normal physical routine, even certain basic physical characteristics as in the case of the shaving of the novice's head. There is usually a deliberate degradation of the individual when he enters the institution. His clothes are taken away, his possessions are logged in, nondescript institutional garb is issued to him, and the expectation is stated that he is to assume a routine of life which is indistinguishable from the routine of countless others. He becomes a number, a nonentity; his former self ceases officially to exist.

Again, the process is perhaps most obvious in religious orders, hospitals, reformatories, or prisons, but it has its counterpart in such educational practices as issuing uniforms to students and in the sanctioning of severe and degrading hazing for new members, thereby ratifying the perception that the newcomer is "nothing" until he becomes a full-fledged member. In religious revival meetings a similar process occurs in the practice of making all members of the congregation feel as if their old self was so corrupt and sinful that only a conversion could reinstate a feeling of selfhood and self-esteem. In initiation rites, whether in relation to puberty or upon entrance into an organization like a fraternity, there are usually long periods of degrading the incumbent, even physically as in the practice of scarification in non-literate societies (or tattooing in our own adolescent culture), which seem to have a similar function of destroying the old self and at the same time testing the motivation and worth of the incumbent for the new status which is about to be officially bestowed upon him. In the initiation rites of the Mau Mau or of cults of witchcraft (Carothers, 1954) the destruction of the old self is accomplished in part by forcing the individual as part of his oath or as a test of his worth deliberately to desecrate or profane important symbols or relationships (e.g., spitting on the crucifix, swearing to kill father or brother if ordered to do so, committing sexual acts which are revolting to the initiate, etc.). Even the relatively non-coercive sales relationship involves a measure of unfreezing in this sense in that the good salesman will prepare his customer either by showing him that his old self-concept needs revision or that by buying the product he can better achieve some idealized self-concept he may have.

Certain organizations like Alcoholics Anonymous (AA) do not deliberately unfreeze an individual but refuse to take anyone under their care who is not already unfrozen. Thus a person does not become eligible for care by AA unless he has really become desperate, is dissatisfied with himself, and is prepared to turn his fate over to some greater power. A comparable criterion exists to a degree in private psychoanalytic practice, in that an individual who claims to have a problem will generally not be accepted for treatment by the psychoanalyst unless he demonstrates real motivation to get well (i.e., unless he is already to a degree unfrozen and prepared to change). Of course, the person may have motivation to enter analysis for reasons other than a dissatisfaction with his present sense of self. In fact one suspects that those patients who get turned down by analysts are precisely the ones who say they want analysis but who are in fact not unfrozen and are not willing to allow themselves to enter a situation in which they may be unfrozen (e.g., by accepting the basic rule of psychoanalysis and genuinely attempting to cooperate with the analyst in an exploration of their unconscious). A similar point applies to the voluntariness of entry into religious orders. While it may be true that the individual initially is strongly motivated to become a nun or priest, this is not equivalent to being psychologically prepared for giving up one's old self. The degree of effort which religious orders put into the training of their incumbents suggests that a good deal of unfreezing has to occur *after* the incumbent has entered the institution and exposed himself to the full force of the new environment. Of course, where the new self is particularly different from the old self, an additional strain on the subject is imposed and greater institutional support has to be given him to make the transition possible.

Beside the physical and social isolation, and the mortification of self, other parallels can be found between the unfreezing in coercive persuasion and that in other influencing institutions. For example the monopolization of the attention of the individual by controlling the communication flowing into and out of the institution is an obvious parallel. In some institutions like academies, limitations are placed on the number of letters which can be received or sent; in prisons or mental hospitals the inmate may actually be exposed to censorship of his mail and certainly is limited in terms of the mass media to which he is permitted to expose himself. A retreat or period of total isolation from all communication often precedes important initiation rites or is co-ordinated with those times when a reaffirmation of faith is officially sanctioned or demanded.

A closely connected parallel is the emphasis which is put on self-examination in many influencing institutions, often co-ordinated with a deliberate attempt to destroy the internal cohesion of inmate or student groups. In prison there is the injunction, backed by institutional rewards and punishments, to "serve your own time" (Cressey & Krassowski, 1957); in mental hospitals there is some tendency to move patients who form a clique with other patients if that clique, in the opinion of the staff, works toward other than therapeutic goals; in religious orders there is the emphasis on self-examination and contemplation combined with a carefully circumscribed and supervised social life and the giving of individual cells as sleeping quarters. In prisons solitary confinement is generally used as a punishment for behavior counter to institutional norms; in school the pupil is punished by being made to stand in the corner; in the mental hospital getting sicker usually results in being isolated; in British labor unions the deviant is punished by being "sent to Coventry," which means complete ostracism by fellow group members; etc.

An interesting sidelight which should be mentioned here is that the small informal group can, as we have seen, be the greatest aid as well as the greatest hindrance to successful influence. The small group can usually generate a powerful field of forces for the individual and, in effect, induce conformity to its norms whatever they be. If those norms support the institutional norms and goals, as in the case of group cells in thought reform, they are not only tolerated by the institution but encouraged and organized for that purpose. If the group norms run counter to the institutional norms or goals, as was the case in POW camp (Schein, 1956), they have to be undermined and destroyed so that the commitment to the group as a source of resistance to influence can be made inoperative.

The interesting question arises, then, in what way are groups in fact used in the unfreezing of individuals in the parallel types of institutions which we have discussed? We have already mentioned several instances of the breakup of groups by institutional authorities; are there examples of the use of groups? In AA the small discussion group plays a key therapeutic role; in mental hospitals there has been an increasing reliance on therapy groups, work groups of various sorts, and/or patient self-government groups, where in each case the assumption is made explicitly or implicitly that for the new group member the membership experience will produce influence of a kind desired by the institution; in educational workshops, like those concentrating on human relations training, the group experience is considered the key educational experience; in the "hell week" hazing engaged in by fraternities one of the key experiences is "the ride" in which a small group of pledges without money is taken somewhere far away from the chapter house to return by its wits; and so on. One of the more interesting strategic problems for the influence agent would seem to be how to make the small groups in his target population work toward his own goals rather than at cross purposes with him. Once he has allowed or encouraged the formation of small groups, he must be prepared for the severe resistance which may be generated if such groups turn against him.

As a final parallel concerned with unfreezing, we shall examine the coercive element of the coercive persuasion process. Have we been engaging, in the above paragraphs, in a flight of fancy in so far as there is a fundamental difference between our own institutional persuasion and that which occurs in Communist prisons because the target individual in our institutions can generally escape before he is too severely unfrozen?

Clearly the parallel is applicable to those institutions which are entered involuntarily and/or which confine their inmates by force for varying lengths of time. Prisoners and mental patients can be forced to attend meetings, lectures, and therapy groups; they can be forced to visit psychiatrists, social workers, teachers, and others who are concerned with resocializing them; they can even be forced to share cells with others more "reformed" than they or put into solitary confinement; they are subject to the institutional system of rewards and punishments in the same final way as the political prisoner in that any degree of privilege can be withdrawn and any degree of punishment exacted by the authorities without anyone needing to be any wiser (at least it may be perceived in this fashion by the inmate).

But what of those institutions which are entered voluntarily and from which the individual may withdraw voluntarily—educational institutions, religious orders, AA, psychoanalysis, revival meetings, fraternities, and so on? We believe that in such institutions the social pressures which can be generated can be as coercive as the physical constraints previously described.* Not only is voluntary withdrawal generally defined as failure, but the act of entry into the institution may constitute a more or less irrevocable commitment in that the individual often cuts himself off from alternate paths when he makes his decision. In addition to these two forces there is acting perhaps an even more powerful one, the confirmation by fellow group members and by "back home" significant others of the emerging institutional identity. The young man who has entered a religious order and wishes after half a year to leave it will have a difficult time psychologically if he is considered by his peers and teachers to be a good student, if his parents have their hearts set on his becoming a priest, if his friends have already abandoned his old identity in their own eyes and treat him only in terms of his new one, and if his

---

* An excellent analysis of socio-psychological constraints which exist in military interrogations has recently been made by Biderman (1960). He shows that the socio-psychological forces in the situation are as crucial as or more so than physical forces in accounting for the compliance of the prisoner.

termination is defined by all concerned as an act of moral weakness. Obviously these pressures are not always as strong as we have implied, and obviously people do leave institutions like religious orders, but equally obviously it generally requires an act of great courage to do so. Such courage is not too dissimilar to the courage required to resist the pressures of thought reform.

In the case of therapeutic institutions the pressures to remain until the therapist terminates the relationship or until the patient feels well enough to do so himself, i.e., when he has been successfully influenced, are somewhat different but equally potent. First of all, the situation is defined as one where cure will not come quickly or painlessly, thus predisposing the patient to tolerate some of the painful aspects of unfreezing. Second, the patient is put into a position of being less expert about his condition than the therapist and therefore less able to judge when termination is appropriate. Third, the patient feels the tremendous threat that if he does anything to displease the therapist he may lose the help which is being offered as well as incur the displeasure or wrath of a person whom he has invested with considerable authority.

In the face-to-face kind of influence situation such as in a buyer-seller relationship there are also strong forces operating to keep the buyer in the situation once it has been established (hence the well-known "principle" that the important thing for the salesman is to "get his foot in the door"). These forces are primarily the moral norms which govern face-to-face relationships (Goffman, 1955; Biderman, 1960). It is generally not possible in terms of these norms openly to ignore another with whom one is talking, or to cut him off abruptly, or to allow him to embarrass himself too severely, because each of these offenses would produce considerable guilt in their perpetrator. When we allow someone else to lose face or to embarrass himself, we are thereby threatening our own status in the situation because of having failed to exercise the necessary counter-measures to prevent the incident from occurring in the first place.

In the case of situations like revival meetings, lectures, etc., the group forces generated in the situation can have similar coercive components. How many of us would find it easy to leave in the middle of a church service even if the minister's words were beginning to generate acute discomfort, anxiety, and guilt in us? Pluralistic ignorance is of obvious importance in these kinds of situations insofar as everyone may be equally uncomfortable and equally desirous of leaving, yet be ignorant of the fact that anyone else feels this way, a situation strikingly reminiscent of the plight of the deviant in a totalitarian society. For the agent to maintain this coercive atmosphere obviously requires careful management; if he permits open communication to occur between members of his audience they may discover their shared discomfort and thereby break the coercive tie holding them.

We do not need to belabor the point, but it should be clear that the term coercion is applicable to the entire continuum of forces ranging from small constraints imposed by the very nature of the moral order governing interpersonal relationships to very sizable constraints which derive from a combination of physical and social forces such as those found in Chinese Communist group cells. In other words, many more influence situations are really instances of coercive persuasion than might at first blush seem to be the case.

In highlighting the unfreezing pressures which can be found in such varied institutions as education, therapy, religious training, salesmanship, and thought reform we are suggesting that they can be understood better if analyzed from the standpoint of their engaging in coercive persuasion. We are not suggesting that coercive persuasion is the only important activity which occurs in such institutions; on the other hand, little is to be gained by denying the relevance of a process the occurrence of which is clearly demonstrable. Ultimately what distinguishes processes like education, therapy, etc., from each other is their goals and the content of the material which defines the outcome (knowledge, better self-understanding, etc.). But at the level of means these institutions have borrowed heavily from cultural traditions of how to influence and persuade and have incorporated similar techniques for different ends.

CHANGING

The most potent source of influence in coercive persuasion was the identification which arose between a prisoner and his more reformed cellmate. The cellmate often became a model of how to behave, think, and feel in an acceptable manner. In terms of a status or rank hierarchy the cellmate occupied a peculiar position relative to the subject; he was a person in transition from the status of guilty criminal to the status of redeemed citizen, but he still possessed elements of both statuses. The hypothesis suggests itself that where the degree of change expected of the person is very drastic the change agent most likely to be successful as a model will be the person in transition who still has a foot in each camp. He is sufficiently like the target person to make possible an identification, but his loyalties have shifted partially or totally toward the institution desiring the change. He is still in a category similar to the target and hence is more likely to be trusted than the authorities, yet he is willing to use the target's trust to exert pressure on him to change. He is in closest touch with the target, hence is often in the best position to know the target's state of readiness for influence, the points of strategic leverage for inducing change in terms of the target's strengths and weaknesses, and the kind of idiom in which best to communicate with the target.

On the other hand, this change agent must not be perceived as being merely a conscious agent of the authorities, a plant or a stooge, or one who has "sold out" or become a "company man." His shift in loyalty must be perceived as spontaneous and sincere if he is to continue to have the power to influence others. All the conditions listed above are essentially true of the cellmates as described by our repatriates. But does a model like this apply to any of our own institutions?

We cannot provide extensive evidence, but some dramatic parallels can be cited. In the treatment of juvenile delinquents it has been frequently observed that the psychiatrist or social worker cannot get anywhere with an individual if that individual is still loyal to (is "sewn up by") a gang which itself mistrusts treatment. In this kind of an impasse the only chance the therapist has is to get through to one of the influential members of the gang, win his confidence, and use him to get the co-operation of the others. The crucial change agent is not the therapist, but the gang member in transition from loyalty to the gang's mores to loyalty to the therapist's mores, whatever they may be.

A similar situation apparently exists in prisons if the informal groups are powerful in resisting rehabilitation. Only if the leaders or influential group members can be won over is there a chance to influence others. On the other hand, the prison situation shows up clearly how delicate the timing must be for the process to be effective, because if the prisoner in transition moves too far toward the authorities before influencing others he may come to be seen as a "stool pigeon" or defector and be repudiated by the other prisoners. The trusty may have a more comfortable life in prison by co-operating with the authorities, but he does not have much power to influence others once his role as trusty has become clearly defined.

In the mental hospital a comparable phenomenon appears to exist in that the people most capable of influencing patients are often the attendants and ward personnel who are most similar in status to the patient. In fact it is commonly stated among hospital personnel that attendants have frequently been patients themselves. Whether in fact the power to influence is used by the attendant to achieve therapeutic goals or not probably depends on the particular circumstances in any given hospital. Our point is that if the attendant is trained to further the hospital's goals and is motivated to do so, he is probably more effective as an agent of change than the doctor or nurse.

It is often stated that patients can influence each other more than the doctors and nurses can influence them. In support of this hypothesis one finds some hospitals using leaderless group psychotherapy (letting groups of patients meet without a therapist). Again, if the group works toward institutional goals it may be highly successful in achieving them, but if it works against them it will serve as a basis for more powerful resistance and will make it necessary for the institution to destroy the group's structure before further influence can be achieved.

The use of a "big brother" or "buddy" system is, of course, widespread as a way of influencing new members of groups. In AA the key change agent is the person who becomes responsible for and closest to the new member. In colleges the faculty advisory system is frequently supplemented by a big-brother system in which the expectation is that an upper-classman will properly orient the freshman to the campus norms. Upon entering a job the newcomer is often paired with someone who is of the same rank but greater seniority than he, or of only slightly higher rank. One industrial concern has reported that it has abandoned the apprenticing of newly hired college students to high-ranking members of the company in favor of low-ranking ones. Because of lack of time and inability to communicate, the higher-ranking manager fails to imbue the young man with enough of the company ideology to get him to remain with the company. The person of equal rank or only slightly higher rank can, in the process of teaching "the ropes" to the newcomer, teach him the company ideology. However, as in the case of the prison or mental hospital, the influencing agent can, if he wishes, also create pockets of resistance by poisoning the attitudes of the new employee.

The person in transition or the person close in rank to the target of influence may be in the best position strategically to exert influence, but obviously is only one link in a chain. He himself must be influenced by someone in authority to be loyal to the institution and to want to achieve its goals. The person in authority (the officially defined teacher, doctor, interrogator, judge, coach, or parent) may be directly influential, but often his very position of authority leads the target to mistrust his motives. Also the gulf between him and the target may make it difficult for the target to identify with or understand the authority figure.

We indicated earlier that there may be two basic types of influence process involved, depending on whether the target individual identifies with a person in authority or with someone who is essentially a peer-group member. One task for future research would be the determination of the conditions under which each of these is most likely to be effective and an assessment of whether "authority influence" produces different results from "peer influence" in terms of type and degree of influence accomplished.

REFREEZING

The importance of refreezing is implicitly or explicitly acknowledged by all institutions of influence. In the case of prison rehabilitation or resocialization in the mental hospital, elaborate systems of transition and follow-up are usually considered to be an integral part of the total therapy program. Of course, where the person is being influenced in the direction of the acceptable norms of society, he will normally obtain support and reinforcement for attitude changes from a wide variety of others. One of the difficulties with ex-prisoners is that they return to a subculture in which norms of lawfulness, etc., are in fact not supported and reinforced, thus leading to recidivism. A comparable problem exists for the mental patient who is returning to a family situation which stimulated his breakdown in the first place. His more "normal" behavior might not be supported, forcing him either to seek support elsewhere or to break down all over again.

In religious orders the support and reinforcement for a new self-conception comes from a whole series of role prescriptions, rituals, and general social expectations. Within the monastery or convent the joint performance by all members of the group of behaviors which confirm the new self operates as immediate and constant support. But beyond this, society is well oriented to the kind of person the member of a religious order is, and hence everyone with whom the nun or priest comes into contact supports the new self by expecting behavior consistent with it. The role of social expectation as a re-freezing force is perhaps even more clearly seen in society's treatment of the doctor. In order for him to perform capably he must have a self-conception which justifies major interventions in other people's private spheres. Much of this self-conception he learns in medical school through a variety of means, but his most significant support comes from the fact that his patients freely grant him the right to intervene in their lives and expect him to exercise it. The doctor's authority lies not only in his knowledge but also in the faith which others have in him.

In the field of education it is generally acknowledged that unless the person begins to use what he has learned he will soon forget it. Where education is concerned with beliefs and attitudes, particularly about people, self, and interpersonal relations, as in human relations training, it has been found that giving training to isolated members of an organization is not very effective in producing lasting changes in them. Consequently the workshops encourage teams of people to come on the assumption that they will support each other once they are away from the workshop. The importance of such support in sustaining new attitudes has been widely documented. In those cases where entire organizations have gone through a training program, it has been possible to initiate far-reaching organizational changes.

The importance of specifically *social* support was illustrated in the recent Billy Graham crusade in New York City. An informal survey of individuals who came forward and converted when Graham called for converts indicated that only those individuals who were subsequently integrated into local churches maintained their faith. For the others the conversion was merely a temporary response which was neither integrated into the rest of their personality nor received support from significant others.

The purpose of presenting these parallels was to show that one could view a whole variety of influence phenomena within the general model of unfreezing, changing, and refreezing; and that, from the standpoint of such a model, Chinese Communist coercive persuasion is not too different a process in its basic structure from coercive persuasion in institutions in our own society which are in the business of changing fundamental beliefs and values. By showing the parallels, we hope to illuminate both our version and the Communist version of coercive persuasion, and lay the groundwork for a more general theory of influence.

The virtue of the particular model we have chosen derives from the fact that it draws our attention to the time dimension in influence and reminds us that successful influence must start long before the actual change is brought about and must be followed up by supporting and reinforcing kinds of experiences. Too often we forget this point, particularly in the field of social psychology, when we institute training programs in human relations or offer advice on how to change attitudes in various areas of life.

CONCLUSIONS

We stated at the outset that our aim was to analyze the process of coercive persuasion from a socio-psychological point of view. Our major conclusions therefore are not about China or about Communism, but about coercive persuasion as a social process. Perhaps our most important conclusion is that coercive persuasion can be understood within the framework of existing knowledge about man and groups. There is in the Chinese Communist approach to prisoners little that is theoretically new or difficult to understand. What novelty there is lies in the willingness of the Chinese to use all of their experience and interpersonal sensitivity to create an environment conducive to influencing the political attitudes of even initially hostile individuals, and to put untold quantities of effort into this enterprise.

A second broad conclusion is that the Chinese efforts have been successful in a very small number of cases of American civilian prisoners. This conclusion must be qualified somewhat, however, because the effects produced by coercive persuasion were not completely in line with Communist aims. Some subjects benefited personally from the experience in that they feel they have become better people, but their dedication or loyalty to Communism has not risen sharply and their willingness to subordinate themselves to an absolute authority has apparently decreased.

A third conclusion is that the total program of Chinese Communist thought reform is extremely difficult to evaluate in that the program itself operated so unevenly and the initial experiences of the target individuals varied so widely even prior to exposure to thought reform. We can evaluate the outcome and understand the coercive persuasion process in those few cases who were influenced and whose influence made headlines. We cannot say much about all the many individuals who remain in China or who came through coercive persuasion without ever getting to the attention of anyone. However, these many cases were not our interest in the first place. Our interest throughout has been to increase our understanding of those

284 Coercive Persuasion

cases where influence was demonstrable.

A fourth conclusion is that the influence process as exemplified in coercive persuasion is best thought of as a complex series of events occurring over a considerable period of time. These events can best be understood in terms of a model of change which includes three phases—unfreezing, changing, and refreezing. For influence to occur there must be induced a motive to change, there must be available some model or other information source which provides a direction of change, and there must be reward for and support of whatever change occurs. Furthermore, the changes associated with coercive persuasion are basically changes in perceptions of, beliefs about, and attitudes toward the self and interpersonal relations, and the political changes observed derive from the connection in Communism between political ideology and the class attitudes toward self and others.

In other words, the basic political premises promulgated in prison were essentially moral doctrines about interpersonal attitudes from which could be derived the concept of crime which established the guilt of the prisoner. Because of the close connection between political and interpersonal values in the coercive persuasion process, those theories of influence which deal with ego, self, or identity change appear to be most applicable to an understanding of the changes observed in the prisoners. However, it was found that most of the theories which have been offered to explain brainwashing tend to be relevant and to supplement each other. This supplementation becomes clear if one sees influence as consisting of different phases in that the different theories tend to account for different phases of the total process.

A fifth conclusion is that it is exceedingly difficult to predict whether a given prisoner will be successfully influenced or not because of the large number of variables which appear to be involved as determinants of influence or resistance. In terms of predicting influence, the only feature which stands out consistently is that the influenced prisoner underwent intensive "struggle" at the hands of a number of more reformed cellmates; the crucial influence step was then the growth of an identification with one or more of these cellmates. In terms of predicting resistance, a number of variables can be stated but no clear-cut evidence supports one over any other. Because each requires explanation we shall not repeat them here (they can be found at the end of Chapter 7), except to mention that experiential factors seem to be just as important as personal attributes. That is, a man who happened to be a witness to some Communist brutality was possibly more likely to resist, regardless of his personality, than one with a very strong sense of integrity, etc., who did not see Communist operations at first hand.

A sixth conclusion is that the process of coercive persuasion used as a way of influencing beliefs and attitudes may have unanticipated and undesirable consequences for the influencing institution, in that it may lead to a ritualization of belief and a gradual atrophy of creative abilities which presumably the institution wishes to preserve and harness toward its own goals.

A seventh and final conclusion is that the process of coercive persuasion as observed in Chinese Communist prisons has its counterpart in various kinds of total institutions in our own society and elements of it exist in any influence relationship in which there are physical, social, or psychological constraints which tend to force the person to expose himself to the pressures of the influence agent. In putting our emphasis on the content of the influence we have often tended to overlook similarities in the nature of the influence process. There is a world of difference in the content of what is transmitted in religious orders, prisons, educational institutions, mental hospitals, and thought reform centers. But there are striking similarities in the manner in which the influence occurs, a fact which should warn us strenuously against letting our moral and political sentiments color our scientific understanding of the Chinese Communist approach to influence.

APPENDIX 1

The Lenient Policy *

THE KEYNOTE of the Chinese Communists' attitude to their pris-oners-of-war is the celebrated "Lenient Policy." On several occasions Commander Ding gave long lectures on this theme. We were some-times faced with questionnaires about it. The subject was always cropping up.

It was a freezing afternoon in January, 1952, when for several hours "Snake-eyes" first expounded it in my hearing. We squatted before him on the floor, chilled and hungry, to learn once again the lesson of Chinese leniency. Big Wong interpreted. This is the gist of his discourse, many phrases of which ring as clearly in my ears today as when I first heard them.

From the very first days of our People's Liberation Army we have car-ried out the Lenient Policy towards war prisoners. It is not something first invented in the Korean War, but a policy rooted in our People's Army from the beginning.

We know you believe in the Geneva Convention and the Red Cross. These are instruments of bourgeois idealism which it is impracticable to carry out, as we believe you will eventually realize. Moreover, they are used by the imperialists and capitalists to cover their evil plans. Our Lenient Policy is perfectly sufficient for all your reasonable needs. It is a sincere policy, based on principles of humanitarianism, equality and in-ternational law. When you really understand it, you will no longer be critical of it.

You have come here as dupes of the imperialists, the warmongers, and

* This entire Appendix is a quotation from a British chaplain's account of his imprisonment in Korea (Davies, 1954).

286

the Wall Street big-shots, who have forced you to come from your homes, and your loved ones to fight their dirty war for blood-soaked profits against the Korean people. We could justly kill you as war criminals, and enemies of the peace-loving people of the world. But we know you are only dupes and tools of the warmongers. You have been liberated now. We shall not harm you. No, true to our Lenient Policy we shall deliberately preserve your lives and help you to learn the truth. Later on you will self-consciously realize this and thank us. We extend leniency towards you and help you.

Some of you accuse us of not taking care of you, and of letting our prisoners die. We tell you many of your men fell sick and died because they could not eat our type of food. Also, they had many bad diseases, brought on by vice, which are hard to cure. The American 'planes, too, caused great damage, and food supplies could not get through. Some of you think you should be living in luxurious conditions like an hotel in the Pentagon. We did not invite you to come to Korea to slaughter and rape the innocent, peaceful Korean people.

Now you are here we do our best for you, and we give you this opportunity to open your eyes and see the truth. You should be grateful. This is our Lenient Policy. But many of you care only for dollars and girls' legs, and do not wish to study hard and learn the truth. We think there are four types of men among you:

First, there are the righteous, progressive men who are self-consciously learning the truth. These men are our friends, international friends, who are struggling free from the toils of the warmongers, and gaining solidarity with the peace-loving people of the world. We shake their hands.

Secondly, there are the semi-righteous men who are uncertain. They are swayed by every wind that blows. They incline this way and that way. They listen to both sides, but cannot make a self-conscious decision. They are basically good men, but too weak. We want to be friends with them, but they cannot make up their minds to accept the truth.

Thirdly, there are the men who are easily influenced by the bad men. These are they who believe all the slanderous things, and who are afraid of the bad men and easily intimidated by them into closing their minds against the truth.

And fourthly, there are the bad men who are basically hostile to us, and who do their best to influence all the other prisoners against us. These are the real enemies of the people, the hired tools of the Wall Street war-mongers, the absolute reactionaries, members of the capitalist, ruling clique.

Most of you are basically righteous men, and we hope you will learn the truth, but there are a few of you who are the real enemies of the peace-loving people, and who wish to organize subversive activities against the camp authority, and disrupt the study programme. These men think they are clever—little Carnes,* little Brownes *—but they will find they cannot outwit the powerful and intelligent C.P.V. Our Lenient Policy is not limitless. It cannot be extended forever to those who are deliberate reactionaries with a hostile attitude towards us.

So we remind you again of the Lenient Policy of the Chinese People's Volunteers. We give you warm clothes for the Korean winter; we feed you; we give medical attention and regular inoculations; we look after you; we have even been known to return sick prisoners to your lines; we give you full religious freedom. If you have a conscience at all you must see how lenient we are to you.

I am not a Christian, and I do not know all your religious beliefs, but I *do* know it says in the Bible you should have a good conscience. Ask your chaplain, he will tell you. So if you really are Christians, you should have a good conscience towards us, and honestly and conscientiously appreciate our Lenient Policy. Your religion says men with a bad conscience go to Hell. You should self-consciously examine yourselves and consider our leniency to you, and adopt a good attitude to us and drop a hostile attitude.

At Panmunjon the American imperialists and their running dogs and lackeys, the British capitalist ruling clique, are holding up the peace talks. In the imperialists' prison camps they are torturing, starving and killing the Korean and Chinese prisoners, but we will remain calm and will never torture or kill you. You are safe with us. We shall always self-consciously carry out the Lenient Policy and thus shall continue to give you the chance to study and learn the truth, and see how your leaders are catching the people in a web of lies and preparing to extend the Korean conflict, and unleash a third world war.

* Carne and Browne were the senior POW officers from the Gloucester Regiment.

The basis of it all was the preservation of the prisoner's life so that he might "learn the truth," as his captors saw it, be converted, and join the ranks of "the people." It seemed to me a kind of political system of salvation, parallel with the Christian one. [Davies, 1954, pp. 71–75]

APPENDIX 2

The Group Discussion in Thought Reform

CURTIS H. BARKER

THE FOLLOWING is an attempt to describe the role of the group discussion as a technique in the Chinese Communists' efforts to establish a common frame of reference in Chinese society, ideologically and behaviorally.

These group discussions take many forms, but they are here described in terms of basic function and content, with examples of the situations and the conditions in which they are held. The four basic types are as follows:

1. ACCUSATION MEETINGS. Often called "grievance-telling" meetings, they are referred to as "self-education in class-consciousness." The number attending these meetings may vary from fifteen to fifty or more, and they are organized in every neighborhood, village, and farm co-operative throughout China. Everyone is asked to tell about his life, family, and work. Meanwhile the propagandist carefully notes the highlights of each one's grudges or grievances. At the accusation or complaint meeting, carefully briefed "activists" start to "pour out their bitterness." The propagandist begins to "dig out the root of bitterness" of the people in his group. Their suffering is not because of fate, but because of Kuomintang reactionaries, landlords, feudalism, and most of all, American imperialism.

When given an outlet, suppressed feelings resulting from social injustice, economic misery, and outworn tradition can generate tremendous power. Even if there were a normal distribution of attitudes toward these "enemy" classes ranging from "for" to "against," the propagandist would skillfully stifle any positive comments so that any succeeding comment about these classes would be more negative than the preceding one. The trend can only move in one direction— against. The fervor and emotional pitch of these meetings is frequently such that it leads directly to the open trial of landlords, the punishment of undesirable officials, or demonstrations and parades.

2. STUDY (*Hsueh Hsi* *) MEETINGS. To study is to "correspond one's subjective thoughts to objective facts." Objective facts in this case are: (a) Marxist-Leninist theory of social development; (b) the study of history; (c) party policies and directives; and (d) study of work or one's occupation. These "facts" are presented to groups of ten to fifteen people orally and through such reference materials as pamphlets, posters, cartoons, wall newspapers, magic lantern shows, etc.

The next step is "thought revealing." The Chinese characters for this term actually mean to draw out, with a sense of enticement or seduction. Everyone must talk. This exposes the mental processes, and aids self-indoctrination, psychologically speaking. It then remains for the leader or propagandist to provide the "correct" interpretation.

Be it a large city or a remote village, no one escapes. With the illiterate groups, the emphasis shifts to what is called "cultural study," the Communist term for literacy campaign. The number of characters required for minimum literacy has been reduced drastically as a result of extensive simplification of the written language. The success of this campaign would surprise the most sophisticated of educators. Needless to say, the phrases used in learning to read and write do *not* say, "The pen of my aunt is on the table," but emphasize propaganda slogans, and so on.

3. CRITICISM AND SELF-CRITICISM MEETINGS. As with all other types of meetings, no one escapes these either. They usually involve about six to fifteen people. One's initial act as a member of this group is concerned with the writing of a detailed autobiography beginning

---

* For an excellent description and analysis of the methods of *hsueh hsi*, see Barnett, 1954.

at the age of seven. The illiterate can always find a scribe in designated places in rural areas, or in a booth in the city streets, where they may go to dictate their life story. This serves as a basis for pinpointing sources of "backward elements" in one's past, and it also helps to prepare one psychologically for the revealing of his "innermost thoughts."

An interesting technique is evident in these groups. On the surface, to the researcher, there seem to be two main areas of content: (a) political ideology, regarding feudal, reactionary, imperialist thinking, etc.; and (b) moralistic principles, regarding selfishness, arrogance, one-sidedness, responsibility-shirking, thoughtlessness, etc. But, in practice, the cadre or activist who leads these groups very cleverly blends these two areas together, so that they become indistinguishable. This facilitates identifying the ideology with everyday life and with moral values that anyone would accept.

The most outstanding characteristic of these meetings is that it is virtually impossible to hide your true feelings under the efforts of all the group members to see through your rationalizations or other defenses. Intimacy must result where this experience, which does not allow withdrawn behavior, is repeated daily. One must also remember that hostility does not motivate this relentless effort to break down a fellow's defenses—it is a sincere desire to "help" him in his "struggle" to be honest with himself. It is this, more than anything else, that inspires gratitude for this experience.

4. Discussion Meetings in Support of Nationwide Campaigns or Movements. A substantial portion of discussion groups operate in direct support of the current campaign or movement. When one of these is launched, every effort of the regime is geared to its content. This is tantamount to saying that the thought of virtually everyone in Chinese society is concerned with the current movement at least once a day. The implications of this fact alone could not be exaggerated.

Immediately after the Communist take-over came the "Study" movement, where the importance and function of study, per se, was developed. Next came the "Land Reform" campaign, followed by "Resist America—Aid Korea," "World Peace," "Suppression of Counter-revolutionaries," "Increase Production and Austerity," "Donation

for Buying Airplanes and Artillery," etc. The principle of involving
the masses in one central task at a time seems worthy of note.

The content of these discussion meetings involves a very rational
analysis of the merits of the movement. Participants are encouraged
to be skeptical and even to bring up negative aspects, whereupon
the fallacies of this type of thinking are clearly demonstrated by a
skillful cadre, largely on moralistic grounds.

One of these campaigns may last from three to six months. One
month may be devoted to the development of slogans. Not only does
every slogan presented have to be learned and recited from memory,
but every single participant has to invent or compose a slogan of his
own. It should be noted that the use of slogans is a major device of
Chinese mass media, and when coupled with meetings such as these,
the slogans, plastered on almost every available vertical surface
throughout China, are anything but "empty." It has been observed
(Millin, 1955) that this emphasis has much to do with producing the
type of mentality one finds in the new China. It is compared with
the memorization of Bible verses by an earlier generation of Christians—by the possession of these slogans, the Communist is provided with a ready answer for all questions which might be asked,
by others or himself.

Another effective device in these meetings is the narration of an
endless number of stories, or parables, by the group leader, which
cite myriads of everyday situations and relate these situations to the
movement under discussion. Soon the participants themselves volunteer illustrations from their own experience—vocal testimony for the
effectiveness of this device.

We have now discussed four basic types of meetings by content
and function. It would be appropriate to raise the questions: How
does the CCP manage to get 650 million people to attend these meetings? Under what conditions does this occur? The answers might be
better understood if one realizes that the average number of propagandists (group leaders and organizers) in every factory, farm, or
production unit is about 10 per cent of the total people in the unit.
This may range from 6 to 13 per cent. It is also important to realize
that, while in the United States one's working hours are the only
rigidly scheduled segment of everyday life, in China the time one

spends in these group meetings is just as rigidly prescribed. This may vary from one to four hours daily, including Sunday.

In answer to the question, why do people show up at these meetings, it should be pointed out that while all party cadres, agitators, propagandists, etc., are commanded to use persuasion rather than coercion, a subtle form of terrorism is always at work. The vast number of persons in thought-reform prisons, and the unknown number of those executed, provide mute testimony of the price one pays for not trying, sincerely and enthusiastically, to rehabilitate oneself into the new China. The intrinsic value of being sincere and enthusiastic is also an important appeal to many.

It happens every day at 11:00 A.M.; in the hotel all seven of the porters on the third floor meet on a stair landing around a low table. From his breast pocket each one pulls a small pad of paper and a pen—the badge of the new citizen. One says, "Comrades, Room 312 had to ring three times before I answered." This is discussed at length until someone else mentions a petty failure in hopes of impressing others with his willingness to admit his shortcomings. There is always *someone* in the group who quickly perceives it as just that, and the motive for such an act becomes the subject for discussion.

A train pulls into the station for a fifteen-minute layover, and the entire crew meets on the station platform to help the brakeman arrive at the conclusion that "I have freedom. I am free to play basketball. I used to play before, but when I tore my shoes, I was too poor to buy more—I could no longer play. Today, I have two pairs of shoes. I am now free to play basketball." This could be a group of bank employees, peddlers, sales clerks, teachers, or village co-operative members.

One factory schedules a "Criticism and Self-Criticism" meeting from 4:00 to 4:30 P.M. Following supper at the factory cafeteria (the wife joins him; the children are fed at the nursery) they meet again at 6:00 P.M. for the group reading of the *People's Journal,* where the "correct" interpretation of the government's policies and directives is arrived at through an "open-minded" discussion of the issues, during which *everyone* speaks. At 7:00 P.M. begins ninety minutes of "study" which consists of a political instruction lecture followed by an educational discussion. This might be replaced with a scheduled ninety minutes at home listening to a broadcast of a speech explaining a new directive or describing the latest nationwide movement. (These examples are drawn from an article entitled "China Behind the Red Mask," in *Réalités*, August 1956, No. 69.)

According to one official report for a two-week period in the city of Peng Chi, in the Northwest, high-ranking cadres in factories and mines made 625 reports to a total audience of 70,000; there were 270 group discussions in which 25,000 people participated; 30 accusation meetings and 15 oral contests were held. In addition there were storytelling evening meetings, memory meetings, and farewell meetings for those joining the armed forces. Then cadres were organized to conduct interviews in every family in the city (Yu, 1955a).

One of the most significant factors is the mere *knowledge that one's experiences in these groups are being shared by virtually everyone else in China.* One obvious implication here is that the energy required to put yourself in someone else's place is greatly reduced. And this someone else can be *anyone* in the society—even Mao himself practices daily self-criticism! This population of others becomes a very dominant reference group for any individual who is seeking to evaluate not only the content, but the legitimacy of the program, per se.

There also seems to be a familiar principle of salesmanship operating. A good salesman will tell you he has a better chance of selling someone who really thinks he doesn't want the product than someone who doesn't care whether he has it or not. In other words, a man isn't vulnerable to as many techniques until he is involved in the issue. The two-way, face-to-face nature of this medium facilitates *planned involvement,* allowing for the operation of two pertinent factors: (1) involvement implies selective perception—one's receptors are tuned to relevant data, be it pro or con; and (2) as involvement increases, emotional factors tend to dominate the rational aspects of evaluating the data.

The accusation meetings actually succeed in locating the source of condemnation of enemy classes (landlords, moneylenders, etc.) in the hands of the people. Fu Cheng-sheng, the party's Propaganda Chief in the Northeast, writes:

The reason the accusation meeting is an effective method of educating the masses is because it educates and mobilizes the masses by their own experiences, sufferings and interests. . . . Through the accusation meeting, the masses are able to concentrate their old and new hatreds, to unite their today with tomorrow, to connect their individual interests with the interests of their country, and to understand the greatness of people's China, and the preciousness of the new life. [*How to Be A Propagandist,* 1951, pp. 69–70]

In the study meetings, while social theory and ideology are skillfully brought to the people's level, and related to daily life, it must be remembered that not only are these issues new to the participant, but so is the intellectual exercise of debate. And while the citizen is encouraged to indulge in this new-found exercise, he is no match for the propagandist. Again, through the leader's skillful manipulation, the participant's experience usually results in a very reverent respect for the knowledge, skill, and sincerity of the leader, who himself becomes an image for potential identification.

The activities of criticism and self-criticism have several implications: (1) Individualism, a characteristic of Chinese people, is minimized first by the content—self-centeredness is condemned, etc.—and second by the technique—the very process of exposing one's mistakes or defects in public implies submission to the social group as well as subjection to the group norms. (2) In a society where being "two-faced" was included in socially accepted behavior, it might be difficult to obtain an accurate picture of the sentiments of the people. These meetings make an issue of sincerity, which is semantically equated with truth, regardless of content. (3) The cathartic effects of such a meeting cannot be overemphasized. Very few of us live up to the ideals that have been set for us, either by others or by ourselves. It is not difficult to exploit the resulting guilt toward the end of justifying the use of this technique. (4) It becomes a simple matter to shift the blame for shortcomings in the regime's programs from the party or government to "reactionary thinking" or "backward elements" who must reform their thoughts, or to "enemies" who will ultimately be eliminated.

When an individual suddenly "realizes" that the underlying motivation for his "reactionary" behavior of the past has been concern for himself, it is a blow to his ego. But lo and behold, right before him is a way of life that not only thrives on unselfishness, but can provide an infinite source of referents to support its ideology.

This latter feature is dramatically communicated through the nationwide movements. To know that the little bit you are doing to "increase production and austerity" is being multiplied by hundreds of millions gives not only legitimacy but importance to your decision to do so.

How do all these stimuli figure in the development of a new identity for the Chinese citizen? Through the techniques described above, each citizen gets a clear image, in his own terms, of the kind of thinking and behavior encouraged by the regime, as well as an even more clearly defined image of that which is not tolerated by the regime. The individual then, through interpretation and evaluation of the external world—past, present, and future—comes to accept these images as valid, even if inappropriate for his own case. And finally, through reinterpretation of his own past, these images become integrated into the role he now sees himself playing in the new society. Obviously the degree of success of such a plan is highly dependent upon the clarity with which these images are communicated.

In evaluating the success of this medium, several factors must be noted: (1) The nature of the described identity shift does not necessarily involve the individual identity crisis found as a stage in personality development; rather it is the identity given to the role one plays in finding his niche in society. (2) Since the revolution had rejected so much of the old society, new roles had to be found anyway. (3) This new image or identity can sustain itself only if the environment continues its supportive function utilizing both persuasion and coercion. (4) The question of permanence of effect is almost academic, if not unanswerable, in that its success is most crucial in the early post-revolutionary period. Regardless of what happens in the next ten years, the accomplishments of the first ten years of "rebuilding" China will still be recognizable.

It may be safely stated that: (1) Communist China has reached her entire population; (2) she has communicated a clear image of what she stands for; and (3) she has succeeded in involving her population in the problems of perpetuating that image. These accomplishments are clearly due to this newcomer to the field of mass media—the group discussion.

APPENDIX 3

The Agents Involved in Coercive Persuasion

CURTIS H. BARKER

ONE OF THE questions raised in our basic outline concerns the problem of who is actually instrumental in producing influence in the prisoner (target). During his imprisonment experience the target deals with many representatives of the government and with many fellow prisoners. In what way is each of these types related to coercive persuasion, or, to put it another way, what function does each seem to play in the process, particularly with respect to the production of a confession and attitude change? It is also of interest to determine who these agents are in terms of their social origin, education, occupation, specific experience, etc. On this latter question we have not found much of significance which has not already been reported, though we have confirmed most of the conclusions of other studies (Hinkle & Wolff, 1956; Lifton, 1956).

Types of Agents

1. Arrestor	5. Administrator
2. Guard	6. Interpreter
3. Interrogator	7. Cellmate
4. Indoctrinator	8. Judge

1. ARRESTOR. Function is to set the tone of treatment and communicate to the target the attitude of the captors through the initial

contact with the target. The atmosphere, thus set, can range from leniency to terror, as desired. In this context the interaction usually takes the form of an official act between the target and the regime, and it has the effect of creating an image of the regime in the eyes of the target, as well as his psychological set. These agents are usually attached to the military and are accompanied by militia.

2. GUARD. Primary function is to see that the prescribed prison regimen is carried out to the letter. Since the context is institutional, with complete isolation from the outside world, it is important that this enforcement be carried out in a most impersonal manner, leaving only the prescribed agents to develop social relationships with the inmates. (In some cases, targets withstood the social isolation *only* because a guard, with as little as a gesture, indicated that a relationship might exist.) This impersonality also has the function of preventing the target from feeling that "these efforts are personally directed at me" and, rather, encouraging the feeling that he (target) is in the hands of an impersonal institution. The guards are almost always identified with the military.

3. INTERROGATOR. It is his job, primarily, to do the tearing down of the old ways of thinking. In the atmosphere of omnipotence, and with the accompanying unlimited array of techniques, he tries to show how target's thinking was faulty, how his behavior was criminal, and how he can repent. In this authoritarian context, the interaction is highly personal, permitting an intensive relationship to develop. Ensuing emotions in the interrogator may range from paternal friendliness to contemptuous hate—the only sure thing being its fluctuation. If things take a turn for the worse, or for other reasons, this relationship may be abruptly terminated or interrupted for as much as six months. It is hard to pinpoint the institution from which this agent comes, but I would guess he has had experience as an intelligence interrogator since his techniques are so similar. The extension of these techniques is made possible by the fact that the target's perceptions and interpretations are the content of discussion as opposed to objective data. This agent is usually perceived as distinct and separate from the military and has been described as being from the "intellectual" class, many of them having been students in the United States. This agent is also perceived by the

target as the one who can "clear up his case" or the power figure.

4. INDOCTRINATOR. This man partially fills the vacuum which is created by the weakening of social and perceptual supports, ego, self image, etc., by giving lectures or in some other way communicating the Communist point of view. He also provides for the target the referents by which vague generalities can be tied down to real personal meanings. This is done in a non-hostile atmosphere or not at all. In other words, the target must be "ready" for this phase before it begins. It is not too important that an intense social relationship develops between target and this agent (I don't remember it ever happening), since it is more important that the target's confused thoughts can anchor themselves semantically and "logically." This agent "makes sense" out of the content. This man usually is in the role of the political commissar and is identified with the political organs of the Communist Party, as opposed to the local institution (prison). For many of our cases this role was fulfilled by an interrogator or cellmate.

5. ADMINISTRATOR. With the exception of the Korean War where some prison camps were set up and run by the political commissars, the institution administration is concerned solely with administrative duties including disciplinary action for infraction of regulations. They are also concerned with the effective execution of institution-wide campaigns, (i.e., for six months *everybody* thinks of all the bad things they have done; the next six months, all think of the good things they've done, etc.). The face-to-face contact with this agent is usually restricted to the floor or corridor warden as the above-mentioned duties are carried out, or when the target is moved from cell to cell for whatever reason. The context is usually impersonal and in an official atmosphere, and like that of the guard, is accepted and identified with the institutional regimen.

6. INTERPRETER. This agent sometimes has an identity of his own and sometimes may be defined as just another interrogator. To my knowledge, the intrepreter was utilized mainly in the POW situation, and at that only some of the time, because many interrogators could speak English. However, there is evidence that these agents were sometimes used even when the "apparent" interrogator could speak English, indicating that the interpreter was probably planted there

as a device. This is substantiated by the fact that some interpreters played various roles, usually in contrast to that of the interrogator, e.g., sometimes feigning direct solicitude toward the target offering to help him to settle his case. While his efforts are usually in support of the interrogator's function, some sources have identified the interpreter with the political corps. He also played an important role in the courtroom interrogation.

7. CELLMATE. While no single change agent could accomplish the phenomenon of coercive persuasion by himself, the cellmate is the primary agent who gives this phenomenon its identity. His primary function involves the destruction of the target's ego and the rebuilding of his self-image. To begin with, the cellmate is identified with the target population by virtue of his own incarceration. Simultaneously, however, the cellmate identifies behaviorally with the other change agents (e.g., interrogators) in his relations with the target. If he has accepted the Communist interpretation of his past behavior, he sincerely (if not vindictively) tries to help the target to do the same. The context in which this agent operates is that of strict physical and social confinement. The cell, which is always too small, becomes the target's universe and is shared by from 1 to 18 cellmates—the majority of known cases having from 5 to 8. One of these cellmates is selected by the authorities as the cell leader, but there always seems to be at least one or two others bucking for the job. The characteristics of this agent seem to be: (1) a fairly advanced state of reform (but far from the security of knowing how advanced he is!); (2) leadership qualities of an interpersonal nature; (3) extreme enthusiasm, vehemence, sincerity, aggression, etc., in carrying out his perceived task. He is aware that his position as cell leader, as well as his state of advancement, is dependent on his performance in this role.

The interaction involved is highly complex, mainly because of a conflict of emotions: the intense social relationships resulting from the enforced and prolonged intimacy versus the hostility and aggression which characterize these relationships; confusion of cellmate's dual role as member of target group as well as a change agent. The effect usually is for the target to identify with these cellmates regardless of the role they play, even to the adoption of their behavior.

8. JUDGE. This agent usually supported the functions of the interrogator. However, the context was connected to the legal issue with the courtroom being the stage. The techniques and interaction are similar to those of the interrogator, but the effects on the target have an added dimension—the underlying hope or fear that a decision regarding his fate may be forthcoming before he leaves the room. Some sources reported having as many as thirty interrogations in this courtroom setting. The judge was usually identified with the political commissars.

CONCLUDING COMMENTS

It should be noted that while the above descriptions are typical, they are neither rigid nor exhaustive. There may be overlapping or combining of roles. (There is one known case of an indoctrinator-type living along with the target in a small cell for two years!) Nor is the line always clear where one role ends and another begins. Aside from their relationship to the basic phases of the total process, the main differences between these agent types lie in the context in which they operate and the techniques they utilize. The degree of importance of any particular agent, in a given case, is modified by the necessity for, and the effectiveness of that particular agent.

There do not seem to be enough data even to speculate about such points as the class background of these agents, their motivation, cynicism, training, or even personality syndromes. On the crucial matter of whether or not they believe in the target's guilt, this would seem to be a function of their actual position in the hierarchy. Those persons who were the most crucial change agents, the cellmates, appeared to believe in each other's guilt (if they had already made a confession and to some extent adopted the new point of view), and were therefore quite sincere in their attempts to "help" their backward mates. The point is important because it was apparently their sincerity in reforming themselves and in wanting to reform others which facilitated for the target an identification and growing emotional relationship with them. Administrators and guards who were in a position to witness the entire cycle from imprisonment to release were probably cynical or not, depending on whether they were witnesses to successful reform or not. Interrogators were sincere, one may guess, in so far as a belief in the guilt of the target facilitated the comfortable performance of their own job, and, in so far as they often managed to produce the confession they sought, they reinforced their own beliefs. With increasing rank and administrative responsibility in the party, one may expect the broadening of their perspective and an increasing tendency to operate according to political expediency rather than abstract reform ideals. The same trend would undoubtedly be true of the indoctrinator. The arrestor was probably sincere to the extent that he himself had been through thought reform and had thoroughly assimilated its philosophy. One of the reasons why the CCP has won so much sympathy, it may be recalled, is precisely its ability to make its soldiers and policemen somewhat zealous converts. The target individual often sensed from the moment of arrest that he was dealing with something more than a routine police or military operation. On the other hand, we have cited above how damaging it could be from the CPP point of view to have inexperienced, crude arrestors who firmly fixed the target's disgust and hostility for the CCP and its operations.

BIBLIOGRAPHY

ADORNO, T. W., FRENKEL-BRUNSWIK, ELSE, LEVINSON, D. J., & SANFORD, R. N. (1950) *The authoritarian personality*. New York: Harper & Brothers.

ASCH, S. E. (1948) The Doctrine of suggestion, prestige, and imitation in social psychology. *Psychol. Rev. 55*, 250–76.

——————. (1951) Effects of group pressure upon the modification and distortion of judgments. In Harold Guetzkow (Ed.), *Groups, leadership, and men*. Pittsburgh: Carnegie Press.

——————. (1952) *Social psychology*. New York: Prentice-Hall.

BARNETT, A. D. (1953) Social controls in Communist China. *Far Eastern Survey, 22*, 45–48.

——————. (1954) *Hsueh Hsi*—weapon of ideological revolution in China. *American Universities Field Staff Letter*, ADB-3-1954.

——————. (Ed.) (1956) *The United States and the Far East*. New York: Columbia University Press.

BAUER, T. J. (1954) *The systematic destruction of the Catholic Church in China*. New York: World Horizons Press.

BECK, F. & GODIN, W. (1951) *Russian purge and the extraction of confession*. New York: Hurst & Blackett.

BECKER, K. (1958) *I met a traveller: the triumph of Father Phillips*. New York: Farrar, Strauss, & Cudahy.

BERKOWITZ, L. & LUNDY, R. M. (1957) Personality characteristics related to susceptibility to influence by peers and authority figures. *J. Person., 25*, 306–16.

BERLE, A. A. (1957) Legal background of Communist methods of interrogation and indoctrination. *Bull. N.Y. Acad. of Med., 33*, 645–53.

BETTELHEIM, B. (1943) Individual and mass behavior in extreme situations. *J. abnorm. soc. Psychol., 38*, 417–52.

BEXTON, W. H., HERON, W., & SCOTT, T. H. (1954) Effects of decreased variation in the sensory environment. *Canadian Journal of Psychology, 8*, 70–76.

BIDERMAN, A. D. (1957) Communist attempts to elicit false confessions from Air Force prisoners of war. *Bull. N.Y. Acad. of Med., 33*, 616–25.

305

BIDERMAN, A. D. (1960) Social-psychological needs and "involuntary" behavior as illustrated by compliance in interrogation. *Sociometry, 23,* 120–47.

BIDERMAN, A. D., & SANDER, H. (1956) Hearings of the Committee on Government Operations. *U.S. Senate,* June 19, 20, 26, 27, 140–54.

BONNICHON, A. (1955) Cell 23—Shanghai. *The Month,* 1–32.

——————. (undated) *Law in Communist China.* The Hague: International Commission of Jurists.

BRANDT, C., SCHWARTZ, B. I., & FAIRBANK, J. K. (1952) *A documentary history of Chinese Communism.* Cambridge: Harvard University Press.

BRINTON, C. (1952) *The anatomy of revolution.* New York: Prentice-Hall.

BULL, G. T. (1955) *When iron gates yield.* Chicago: Moody Press.

CAROTHERS, J. C. (1954) *The psychology of Mau-Mau.* Nairobi, Kenya: The Government Printer.

CARTWRIGHT, D. P. & ZANDER, A. (Eds.) (1953) *Group dynamics.* Evanston, Illinois: Row, Peterson.

CHEN, T. H. & CHIU, S. M. (1955) Thought reform in Communist China. *Far Eastern Survey, 24,* 177–84.

CHEN, W. H. C. (1955) *Wartime "mass" campaigns in Communist China.* HRRI Research Memorandum No. 43, AFP & TRC, Lackland AFB, Texas.

CHRISTIE, R. (1954) *Transition from civilian to army life.* Washington, D.C.: George Washington University Human Resources Research Office.

CRESSEY, D. L. & KRASSOWSKI, W. (1957–58) Inmate organization and anomie in American prisons and Soviet labor camps. *Social Problems, 5,* 217–30.

CRUTCHFIELD, R. S. (1955) Conformity and character. *Amer. Psychologist, 10,* 191–98.

DAVIES, S. J. (1954) *In spite of dungeons.* London: Hodder and Stoughton.

DEJAEGHER, R. J. & KUHN, IRENE C. (1952) *The enemy within.* New York: Doubleday.

ERIKSON, E. H. (1956) The problem of ego identity. *J. Amer. psychoanal. Ass., 4,* 56–121.

——————.(1958) *Young man Luther.* New York: Norton.

FAINSOD, M. (1953) *How Russia is ruled.* Cambridge: Harvard University Press.

FARBER, I. E., HARLOW, H. F., & WEST, L. J. (1957) Brainwashing, conditioning, and DDD. *Sociometry, 20,* 271–85.

FERREUS. (1957) The menace of Communist psychological warfare. *Orbis, I,* 97–121.

FESTINGER, L. (1957) *A theory of cognitive dissonance.* Evanston, Ill.: Row, Peterson Co.

FESTINGER, L., RIECKEN, H. W., & SCHACHTER, S. (1956) *When prophecy fails.* Minneapolis: University of Minnesota Press.

FISHER, S. & LUBIN, A. (1958) Distance as a determinant of influence in a two-person serial interaction situation. *J. abnorm. soc. Psychol., 56,* 230–38.

FISHER, S. & RUBINSTEIN, I. (1955) *The effects of moderate sleep-deprivation on social influence in the autokinetic situation.* Unpublished paper.

FISHER, S., WILLIAMS, H. L., & LUBIN, A. (1957) *Personal predictors of susceptibility to social influence.* Paper read at meetings of American Psychological Association, New York.

FORD, R. W. (1957) *Wind between the worlds.* New York: David Mc-Kay.

FREUD, S. (1922) *Group psychology and the analysis of the ego.* London: Hogarth.

FRIED, M. H. (1959) The Family in China: the People's Republic. In Ruth Anshen (Ed.), *The family: its function and destiny* (Rev. Ed.), New York: Harper & Brothers.

FRIEDRICH, C. J. & BRZEZINSKI, Z. K. (1956) *Totalitarian dictatorship and autocracy.* Cambridge: Harvard University Press.

FROMM, E. (1941) *Escape from freedom.* New York: Farrar and Rinehart.

GARFINKEL, H. (1958) *The rational properties of scientific and common sense activities.* Unpublished paper.

GOFFMAN, E. (1955) On face-work. *Psychiatry, 18,* 213–31.

―――――. (1956) Interpersonal persuasion. In Bertram Schaffner, M. D. (Ed.), *Third conference on group processes.* New York: Josiah Macy, Jr., Foundation.

―――――. (1957a) Alienation from interaction. *Hum. Relat., 10,* 47–60.

―――――. (1957b) On the characteristics of total institutions. *Proceedings of the Symposium on Preventive and Social Psychiatry,* Washington, D.C.: Walter Reed Army Institute of Research.

―――――. (1959) *Presentation of self in everyday life.* Garden City, N.Y.: Doubleday Anchor Books.

GOURLAY, W. E. (1952) *The Chinese Communist cadre: key to political control.* Cambridge: Harvard University Russian Research Center.

GUILLAIN, R. (1957) *600 million Chinese.* New York: Criterion Books.

HELSON, H. (1948) Adaptation-level as a basis for a quantitative theory of frames of reference. *Psychol. Rev.,* 55, 297–313.

HINKLE, L. E. & WOLFF, H. G. (1956) Communist interrogation and indoctrination of "enemies of the state." *A.M.A. Arch. Neurol. Psychiat.,* 76, 115–74.

HOFFER, E. (1951) *The true believer.* New York: Harper & Brothers.

HOFFMAN, M. L. (1953) Some psychodynamic factors in compulsive conformity. *J. abnorm. soc. Psychol.,* 48, 383–93.

—————. (1957) Conformity as a defense mechanism and a form of resistance to genuine group influence. *J. Person.,* 25, 412–24.

HOVLAND, C. I. (Ed.) (1957) *The order of presentation in persuasion.* New Haven: Yale University Press.

HOVLAND, C. I. & JANIS, I. L. (1959) *Personality and persuasibility.* New Haven: Yale University Press.

HOVLAND, C. I., JANIS, I. L., & KELLEY, H. H. (1953) *Communication and persuasion.* New Haven: Yale University Press.

How to be a propagandist (1951) Ed. Dept., Peking: People's Publishing Co.

HUANG, Q. K. Y. (1954) *Now I can tell.* New York: Morehouse-Gorham.

HULME, KATHRYN. (1956) *The nun's story.* Boston: Little, Brown & Co.

HUNT, R. N. C. (1957) *The theory and practice of Communism.* New York: Macmillan.

HUNTER, E. (1951) *Brainwashing in Red China.* New York: Vanguard Press.

—————. (1956) *Brainwashing.* New York: Farrar, Strauss, and Cudahy.

HUXLEY, A. (1958) *Brave new world revisited.* New York: Harper & Brothers.

INKELES, A. (1950) *Public opinion in Soviet Russia.* Cambridge: Harvard University Press.

—————. (1954) The totalitarian mystique. In C. J. Friedrich (Ed.), *Totalitarianism,* Cambridge: Harvard University Press.

JANIS, I. L. & KING, B. T. (1954) The influence of role playing on opinion change. *J. abnorm. soc. Psychol.,* 49, 211–18.

KATKOV, G. (undated) *The political opinions of the Soviet citizens.* Oxford: St. Anthony's College.

KELMAN, H. C. (1958) Compliance, identification, and internalization: three processes of attitude change. *Conflict Resolution,* 2, 51–60.

KING, B. T. & JANIS, I. L. (1956) Comparison of the effectiveness of improvised versus non-improvised role playing in producing opinion changes. *Hum. Relat., 9*, 177–86.

KRACAUER, S. & BERKMAN, P. L. (1955) Attitudes toward various Communist types in Hungary, Poland, and Czechoslovakia. *Social Problems, 3*, 109–14.

KUBIS, J. F. (1957) Instrumental, chemical, and psychological aids in the interrogation of witnesses. *J. soc. Issues, 13* (2), 40–49.

LEA, C. H. (1887) *A history of the Inquisition of the Middle Ages.* New York: Harper & Brothers.

LEITES, N. & BERNAUT, ELSA. (1954) *Ritual of liquidation.* Glencoe, Ill.: The Free Press.

LERMOLO, ELIZABETH. (1955) *Face of a victim.* New York: Harper & Brothers.

LEWIN, K. (1947) Frontiers in group dynamics: concept, method, and reality in social science. *Hum. Relat., I*, 5–42.

LIEBERMAN, S. (1956) The effects of changes in roles on the attitudes of role occupants. *Hum. Relat., 9*, 385–402.

LIFTON, R. J. (1954) Home by ship: reaction patterns of American prisoners of war repatriated from North Korea. *Amer. J. Psychiat., 110*, 732–39.

—————. (1956a) *Chinese Communist "thought reform": the assault upon identity and belief.* Mimeographed paper.

—————. (1956b) "Thought reform" of Western civilians in Chinese Communist prisons. *Psychiatry, 19*, 173–95.

—————. (1957a) The group "re-education" of six Westerners in a Chinese Communist prison. *Proceedings of the Symposium on Preventive and Social Psychiatry,* Washington, D.C.: U.S. Government Printing Office.

—————. (1957b) Thought reform of Chinese intellectuals: a psychiatric evaluation. *J. soc. Issues, 13*, (3), 5–20.

LILLY, J. (1956a) In *Illustrative strategies for research on psychopathology in mental health.* Group for the Advancement of Psychiatry Symposium No. 2, New York: G.A.P. Publications Office.

—————. (1956b) In *Factors used to increase the susceptibility of individuals to forceful indoctrination: observations and experiments.* Group for the Advancement of Psychiatry Symposium No. 3, New York: G.A.P. Publications Office.

—————. (1957) In *Methods of forceful indoctrination: observations and interviews.* Group for the Advancement of Psychiatry Symposium No. 4, New York: G.A.P. Publications Office.

LINDSAY, M. (1950) *Notes on education problems in Communist China.* New York: International Secretariat, Institute of Pacific Relations.

LINTON, HARRIET B. (1955) Dependence on external influence: correlates in perception, attitudes and judgment. *J. abnorm. soc. Psychol., 51,* 502–7.

LIU SHAO-CH'I. (1951) *How to be a good Communist.*

LIU SHAW-TONG. (1953) *Out of Red China.* New York: Duell, Sloan, & Pierce.

MEERLOO, J. A. M. (1951) The crime of menticide. *Amer. J. Psychiat., 107,* 594–98.

————. (1954) Pavlovian strategy as a weapon in menticide. *Amer. J. Psychiat., 110,* 809–13.

————. (1956) *The rape of the mind: the psychology of thought control, menticide, and brainwashing.* Cleveland: World Publishing Company.

MILLER, J. G. (1957) Brainwashing: present and future. *J. soc. Issues, 13,* 48–55.

MILLIN, L. (1955) *Interview with the Reverend Leslie Millin.* DSI Report No. 6/55, Directorate of Scientific Intelligence, Defence Research Board, Canada.

MILOSZ, C. (1955) *The captive mind.* New York: Vintage Books.

MOLONEY, J. C. (1955) Psychic self-abandon and extortion of confession. *Intern. J. of Psycho-An., 36,* 53–60.

MOUTON, J. S., BLAKE, R. R., & OLMSTEAD, J. A. (1956) Personality and yielding. *J. Person., 24,* 339–47.

OHLIN, RUTH. (1954) *The passion for unanimity.* Unpublished paper.

ORNE, M. The potential uses of hypnosis in interrogation, in Biderman, A.D. and Zimmer, H. (Eds.), *The Manipulation of human behavior.* New York, Wiley 1960 (in press).

ORWELL, G. (1949) *Nineteen eighty-four.* New York: Harcourt, Brace & Co.

PACKARD, V. (1957) *The hidden persuaders.* New York: David McKay.

PYE, L. W. (1956) *Guerilla Communism in Malaya.* Princeton: Princeton University Press.

RAPAPORT, D. (1951) The autonomy of the ego. *Bull. Menninger Clinic, 15,* 113–23.

REDL, F. (1942) Group emotion and leadership. *Psychiatry, 5,* 573–96.

REINERS, W. O. (1959) *Soviet indoctrination of German war prisoners.* Cambridge: Center for International Studies, M.I.T., unpublished paper.

Report on Communist China based on the experiences of three Canadian Jesuits in Kiangsu Province. (1955) DSI Report No. 11/55, Directorate of Scientific Intelligence, Defence Research Board, Canada.

RICKETT, A. & RICKETT, ADELE. (1957) *Prisoners of liberation.* New York: Cameron Associates.

RIESMAN, D., GLAZER, N., & DENNEY, R. (1953) *The lonely crowd: a study of the changing American character.* New York: Doubleday.

RIGNEY, H. (1956) *Four years in a Red hell.* Chicago: Henry Regnery.

ROGGE, O. J. (1959) *Why men confess.* New York: Thomas Nelson & Sons.

SANTUCCI, P. S. & WINOKUR, G. (1955) Brainwashing as a factor in psychiatric illness. *A.M.A. Arch. Neurol. Psychiat.,* 74, 11–16.

SARGANT, W. (1957) *Battle for the mind: how evangelists, psychiatrists, politicians, and medicine men can change your beliefs and behavior.* Garden City, N.Y.: Doubleday.

SCHEIN, E. H. (1949) *The effect of group interaction on the judgment of physical stimuli.* Unpublished M. A. thesis, Stanford University.

——————. (1956) The Chinese indoctrination program for prisoners of war. *Psychiatry,* 19, 149–72.

——————.(1957) Epilogue: something new in history? *J. soc. Issues,* 13, 56–60.

——————. (1958) *Social disorganization, belief change, and collaboration with the enemy.* Unpublished manuscript.

——————. (1959) Brainwashing and totalitarianism in modern society. *World Politics,* 11, 430–41.

——————. (1960) Interpersonal communication, group solidarity, and social influence. *Sociometry,* 23, 148–61.

SCHEIN, E. H., HILL, W. F., WILLIAMS, H. L., & LUBIN, A. (1957) Distinguishing characteristics of collaborators and resisters among American prisoners of war. *J. abnorm. soc. Psychol.,* 55, 197–201.

SCHRODER, H. M. & HUNT, D. E. (1958) Dispositional effects upon conformity at different levels of discrepancy. *J. Person.,* 26, 243–58.

SCHWARTZ, B. I. (1951) *Chinese Communism and the rise of Mao.* Cambridge: Harvard University Press.

SCOTT, W. A. (1957) Attitude change through reward of verbal behavior. *J. abnorm. soc. Psychol.,* 55, 72–75.

SEGAL, H. A. (1954) Initial psychiatric findings of recently repatriated prisoners of war. *Amer. J. Psychiat.,* 111, 358–63.

SEGAL, J. (1957) Correlates of collaboration and resistance behavior among U.S. Army POWs in Korea. *J. soc. Issues,* 13, 31–40.

SHERIF, M. (1936) *The psychology of social norms.* New York: Harper & Brothers.

SINGER, MARGARET T. & SCHEIN, E. H. (1958) Projective test responses of prisoners of war following repatriation. *Psychiatry, 21,* 375–85.

SKINNER, B. F. (1938) *The behavior of organisms.* New York: D. Appleton-Century.

SMITH, L. B. (1954) English treason trials and confessions in the sixteenth century. *J. Hist. Ideas, 15,* 471–98.

SMITH, M. B., BRUNER, J. S., & WHITE, R. W. (1956) *Opinions and personality.* New York: Wiley.

STEINER, H. A. (1959) Ideology and politics in Communist China. *The Annals of the Amer. Acad. of Polit. & Soc. Sci., 321,* 29–39.

STEPHENSON, R. (1958) Communist controls and satellite evasions: their political and social consequences. In Society for the Investigation of Human Ecology, *Second Seminar on the Hungarian Revolution of October, 1956,* New York.

STRASSMAN, H. D., THALER, MARGARET B., & SCHEIN, E. H. (1956) A prisoner of war syndrome: apathy as a reaction to severe stress. *Amer. J. Psychiat., 112,* 998–1003.

STRAUSS, A. (1959) *Mirrors and masks.* Glencoe, Illinois: The Free Press.

TALMON, J. L. (1952) *The rise of totalitarian democracy.* Boston: Beacon Press.

TENNIEN, M. (1952) *No secret is safe behind the bamboo curtain.* New York: Farrar, Strauss and Young.

U.S. Department of Defense. (1955) *POW: the fight continues after the battle.*

WALES, N. (1939) *Inside Red China.* New York: Doubleday.

WALKER, R. L. (1955) *China under Communism.* New Haven: Yale University Press.

Wang Tsun-ming, anti-Communist. (1954) Washington, D.C.: George Washington University Human Resources Research Office.

WEI, H. (1955) *Courts and police in Communist China to 1952.* HRRI Research Memorandum No. 43, AFP & TRC, Lackland AFB, Texas.

WHITING, A. S. (1955) The new Chinese Communist. *World Politics, 7,* 592–605.

WHYTE, W. H., Jr. (1952) *Is anybody listening?* New York: Simon and Schuster.

————. (1956) *The organization man.* New York: Simon and Schuster.

WINOKUR, G. (1955) "Brainwashing"—a social phenomenon of our time. *Human Organization, 13,* 16–18.

WRIGHT, MARY C. (1959) Modern China in transition, 1900–1950. *The Annals of the Amer. Acad. of Polit. & Soc. Sci., 321,* 1–8.

YEN, MARIA. (1954) *The umbrella garden.* New York: Macmillan.

YU, T. C. (1955a) *The propaganda machine in Communist China.* HRRI Research Memorandum No. 37, AFP & TRC, Lackland AFB, Texas.

—————.(1955b) *The strategy and tactics of Chinese Communist propaganda as of 1952.* HRRI Research Memorandum No. 39, AFP & TRC, Lackland AFB, Texas.

INDEX

Accusation meetings, 290
Adjustment, social, 259
Adorno, T. W., 105, 252
Agents in coercive persuasion, 299–304
  administrator, 301
  arrestor, 299
  cellmate, 302
  guard, 300
  indoctrinator, 301
  interpreter, 301
  interrogator, 300
  judge, 303
Agrarian reform, see Land reform
Alcoholics Anonymous (AA), 272
Alienation, Marxist, 263
Altered psychological functioning, 159
Antisemitism, 95
Anxiety, 145, 156, 214, 215
  conditioning, 206
Arrestor, 299
Asch, S. E., 133, 197, 203, 224, 250
Attitude change
  and behavioral compliance 160–163
  and commitment, 165
  conclusions, 191
  determinants, 167–193
  experiments, 241–253
  integrated, 164
  and interrogation, 179
  post-prison experiences, 186–191
  vs. "refreezing," 164
  in repatriates, 164
  rewards and punishments, 181
  and role shift, 246
  "significant others," 189
  situational factors, 189
  in "struggle" meetings, 176
  theories, 241–253
  unintegrated, 163

Barker, C. H., 290, 299
Barnett, A. D., 45, 57, 291

Bauer, T. J., 44, 204
Becker, K., 154, 159
Behavioral compliance 160–163
Berkman, P. L., 109
Berkowitz, L., 252
Berle, A. A., 41, 79, 86
Bernaut, Elsa, 79, 100, 221
Bersohn, M., 53
Bexton, W. H., 209, 223
Biderman, A. D., 196, 204, 221, 226, 275
Bonnichon, A., 88, 150, 161
Brainwashing, 60, 151, 184, 195, 205, 211, 239, 246
  defined, 9, 200
  see also Coercive persuasion; Thought reform
Brandt, C., 27, 32, 34
Brinton, C., 92
Brzezinski, Z. K., 70, 77, 84, 98
Buddhism, 40
  see also Zen Buddhism
Bureaucratism, 54, 55, 91

Cadres
  creation of, 54
  and group discussion, 49
  nationwide influence, 295
  training of, 49
Carothers, J. C., 272
Cartwright, D. P., 253
Castro, Fidel, 88
Cellmates, 302
"Changing," 129–136, 255, 277
  big-brother system, 279
  cognition, 129, 239
  cognitive theory, 233
  "company man," 278
  in juvenile gangs, 278
  loyalty shifts, 278
  in mental hospitals, 279
  in non-Communist settings, 277–280

"stool pigeon," 279
vs. "unfreezing," 129
Chen, T. H., 80
Chen, W. H. C., 45
Ch'en Yun, 31
Cheng feng (party reform) movement, 33–39, 75
  intra-Party morale, 35
  Leninist concept, 34
  reasons for, 34
  tendencies, 34
  pre-prison experiences, 112
Chinese Communist Party (CCP), 25–42, 84
  combat state, 84–91
  Constitution (1945), 85
  development, 25
  and local populace, 170
  personnel, 169
  prisoner contact, 169
Chinese People's Volunteers (CPV), 287
Chiu, S. M., 80
Christie, R., 271
Chu Teh, 31
Coercive persuasion, 112–193, 213, 205, 269
  agents involved in, 299–304
  analysis (outline), 112–193
  basic stages, 213
  cognitive process, 196
  conclusions, 283–285
  determinants, 111–193
  effects, 111–193
  and guilt, 140–156
  hypnosis, 197
  identity problems, 196
  initiation rites, 230
  learning theories, 205–211
  mechanisms, 196
  in non-Communist settings, 269–282
  perception of take-over, 112
  post-prison experiences, 115
  pre-prison experiences, 112
  prison experiences, 113
  psychoanalytic formulations, 196, 211–220
  psycho-physiological stress, 196
  situational factors, 112

social psychology, 117–139, 197, 221–256
stress theories, 199–205
structure, 111–193
theories, 195–256
Cognitive theory, 233–241
  and distortion, 238
  formulations, 240
Collectivization, 53
Communications
  breakdown in, 102
  of cellmates, 134
  by interrogator, 135
  mass media, 134
  public vs. private, 76
  studies, 252
  and totalitarianism, 76
Communism
  Chinese vs. Soviet, 37
  logic of, 238
  vs. nationalism, 39
Communist ideology, 64–74
  all-inclusiveness of, 70
  basic goals, 65
  dynamics, 68
  leaders, 74–84
  materialism vs. idealism, 67
  "people's standpoint," 89
  in prison, 80
  unity of theory and action, 69
Compliance, definition of, 247
Confessions, 50, 114, 148, 243
  false, 148, 183
  forces acting on prisoner, 121
  public, 41, 100
  religious, 41
  repudiation of, 243
Confinement, solitary, 177
Cooperatives, agricultural, 47
Counter-revolutionary activity, 50
Cressey, D. L., 273
Crime, 49, 87
Crutchfield, R. S., 252
Cuban revolution, 88
Cultural themes, Chinese *vs* Soviet, 39–42, 108

Davies, S. J., 289
Defectors, 56, 109

Defectors (*continued*)
  motivations, 109
  see also Prisoner of war (POW)
Dejaegher, R. J., 44
Dissonance reduction, 241
"Double-think," 245
Drugs
  sensory deprivation, 201
  truth serums, 204

Ego guilt, 148
Ego identity, 221
Ego neutralization, 211
Erikson, E. H., 65, 131, 221
Escape From Freedom, 105

Fainsod, M., 78
Fairbank, J. K., 27, 32, 34
Fantasy, control over, 262
Farber, I. E., 196, 205, 208
Ferreus, 66
Festinger, L., 98, 197, 241
Fisher, S., 209, 250, 252
Followers, 78, 104–110
  escape from self, 105
  psychological factors, 104–110
  self-sacrifice, 106
  in totalitarian society, 106
  "true believers," 109
Ford, R., 90, 171
Formalism, 36, 54
Freud, S., 218
Fried, M. H., 26
Friedrich, C. J., 70, 77, 84, 98
Fromm, E., 104
Fu Cheng-sheng, 295

Garfinkle, H., 239
Geneva Convention, 286
Goffman, E., 196, 221, 224, 261, 276
Gourlay, W. E., 49
Government, Chinese, coalition, 33
Griffith, W., 91
Group
  cells, 176
  discussions, 40, 290, 296
  indoctrination, 48
  pressures, 250, 252

"struggle" meetings, 176–179, 291,
    296
Guard, 300
Guerrilla warfare, 27, 91
Guillain, R., 49, 56, 70, 108, 263
Guilt, 87, 141
  anxiety-guilt, 145, 156, 213
  by association, 141
  broadening of, 214, 236
  captor's view, 140–144
  channeling, 214
  conditioning, 206
  vs. crime, 235
  ego or identity, 145, 148–152
  failure to act, 142
  generalized, 219
  for harmful action, 142
  for having knowledge, 142
  incorrect attitudes, 141
  loyalty, 145, 154
  "objective," 156
  of "others," 141
  persona (face-to-face), 145, 152
  for personal faults, 142
  political, 67
  prisoner's view, 144–155
  proneness, 147
  recognizing, 147
  situational, 145, 155
  social, 67, 146–148, 220
  special role of, 140–156
  transfer of, 212
  types, 141, 145
  and "unfreezing," 156

Helson, H., 133
Hinkle, L. E., 39, 80, 196, 203, 222,
    299
Hitler, 94
Hoffer, E., 79, 104, 263
Hoffman, M. L., 252,
Hovland, C. I., 197, 252
Huang, Q., 99, 185
Hulme, Kathryn, 261
Hungarian rebellion (1956), 75, 109
Hunt, R. N. C., 67, 252
Hunter, E., 196, 200, 205
Huxley, A., 196
Hypnosis, 197

Idealism, 67
Identification, 247, 255
  with authority, 212
  with cellmates, 131, 151, 230, 238, 249
  defensive mechanism, 213
  and internalization, 249
  with interrogators, 249
Identity
  change, 189, 229, 230
  collapse, 224
  confirmation, 225
  crisis, 131, 164
  denial, 223
  destruction, 224
  diffusion, 227
  guilt, 148
  levels, 225
  problems, 196
  resolution, 165
  shifts, 297
  stresses, 225
  of students, 49
  theory, 221–233
Ideological unanimity, 55
Imprisonment, 58–61
  for espionage, 58
  for propaganda purposes, 58
  and property seizure, 59
  revenge on West, 59
Indoctrination, 184, 301
Influence
  altered psychological functioning, 159
  not discernible, 158
  types and degrees, 158–166, 248
  theory, 257–282
Informers, 45
Initiation, psychology of, 230
Inkeles, A., 77, 93, 103
Internalization of behavior, 247
Interpreter, 301
Interrogation, 179
  father-child relationship, 180
  military, 204, 275
  prison, 51
  Russian, 223
  and "unfreezing," 180
Interrogator, 300

communications, 135
  establishes guilt, 88
  initial contact, 172
  Machiavellian, 144
  sadistic, 174
  superego surrogate, 212
Interviews, purpose of, 10

Jacobinism, 66
Janis, I. L., 246
Juvenile gangs and loyalty shifts, 278

Katkov, G., 264
Kelman, H. C., 197, 247
King, B. T., 246
Korean War, 47, 53, 109, 147, 234, 286
Kracauer, S., 109
Kubis, J. F., 204
Kuhn, Irene, 44
Kuomintang (KMT), 27, 235

Labor reform, 50, 81
Land reform, 44, 47, 168
Language
  Chinese, 171
  ideological, 91
  of masses, 73
  study, 73
  and "unfreezing," 171
Lea, C. H., 87
Leaders, 98, 92–104
  basic traits, 92
  cell, 182
  group, 293
  "the idealist," 93
  psychological factors, 92–104
  role in movement, 92
  sense of omnipotence, 100
  success of, 92
  types, 92
Leites, N., 79, 100, 221
Leniency
  calculated, 183
  in prison, 172
  technique of, 38
  uses of, 38
Lenient policy, 286–289
Lewin, K., 117, 253

Liberation movements, 30, 85
Lieberman, S., 246
Lifton, R. J., 32, 40, 49, 80, 107, 133,
    145, 183, 196, 213, 216, 221, 233,
    299
Lilly, J., 209
Lindsay, M., 28
Linton, Harriet B., 252
Literacy training, 246
Liu Shao-chi, 51, 35
Liu Shaw-tong, 49
Loyalty guilt, 154, 155
Lubin, A., 250
Lundy, R. M., 252

Mao Tse-tung, 25, 35, 47, 68, 75, 85
Marxism, 69
    sinification of, 35
Mass persuasion, 46
Materialism, 67
"Mechanism of escape," 105
Meerloo, J., 79, 104, 156, 196, 205,
    212, 217
"Menticide," 212
Messianism, 64
Methodology, 7, 20
Miller, J. G., 196, 201
Millin, L., 293
Missionary movement, 59
    after take-over, 44
Moloney, J. C., 196, 211, 217, 226
Morale, intra-Party, 35
Mouton, J. S., 252
Mutual surveillance, 103
    pao chia, 45
Mysticism of leaders, 93, 100

Nationalism, Chinese, 39
Neuroses of war, 224
"New man," 79, 103
    creation of, 52
Nineteen Eighty-Four, 78, 98

Ohlin, Ruth, 62
Ongoing relationships with "significant
    others," 189
Opinion change
    in small group, 253
    terminology, 259

Orne, M., 204
Orwell, G., 78, 98, 245

Papal Inquisition, 86, 87
Pavlovian formulations, 205
    in coercive persuasion, 200
    mechanisms, 204
Peer influence, 280
Persona (face-to-face) guilt, 152
Physical "liquidation," 44
Post-prison experiences, 115, 138, 186–
    191
    initial contact, 187
    with "significant others," 189
    situational factors, 189
Post-Yenan period (1945–49), 43
Power struggle of leaders, 74, 79
Pre-prison experiences, 112
Prison
    administration, 301
    cell, 113, 150, 152, 167
    cellmates, 153, 302
    "changing," 134
    debilitation, 174, 204
    diet, 175, 232, 236
    discipline, 114
    experiences, 113, 134, 137, 163,
        172–186
    facilities, 171
    goals of, 114
    groups, 182, 227
    guard, 300
    hygiene, 175
    identity crisis, 133, 164
    indoctrination, 184, 253, 291, 301
    information sources, 234
    interpreter, 301
    interrogations, 179, 300
    interrogator, 51, 303
    isolation, 177, 209, 300
    management, 184
    manuals, 51
    peer-group relationships, 180
    procedures, 51, 80, 88
    propaganda, 233
    psychotic defenses, 122
    punishment, 150, 174, 181
    "refreezing," 137
    regimen, 113, 159, 174

rewards, 181
role-playing, 152
songs, 210
stress, 175
"struggle" meetings, 176–179, 182, 193, 284, 291
Prisoner
age factor, 172
American, 283
British, 286
CCP approach to, 283
vs. cellmates, 235
contact with CCP, 169
as hostage, 59
and local populace, 170
motivational state, 208
not inner-directed, 168
not politically sophisticated, 168
psychological state, 167–172, 226
situational factors, 167
uncommitted, 168
Western, 58, 235
Prisoner of war (POW)
American, 53, 56, 160, 206, 209
British, 286
resistance of, 226
Propaganda
anti-American, 47
materials, 293
in mass media, 46
oral, 47, 49
in prison, 114, 169, 233, 299
Psychotic defenses, 122, 133
Public Security Committees, 45
Punishment, uses of, 181
see also Prison, punishment
Pye, L. W., 33, 85

Race discrimination, 95
Rapaport, D., 225
Rationality, sociological concept of, 239
Reality testing, 259
Recruits, Chinese Communist, 25–27, 31
Red Cross, 286
Redl, F., 218
Re-education
recoding of reality, 216

rewards, 215
steps in, 215
working-through, 215
see also Coercive persuasion; Thought reform
"Refreezing," 136–139, 255
in non-Communist settings, 280
Repatriates, 158
altered psychological functioning, 159
American, 187, 190, 265
attitude changes, 163
internalized beliefs, 249
paranoid, 139
pro-Communist, 191
psychotic, 139
types of, 189
Resistance, 123, 252
to confession, 123
to influence, 161
patterns, 212, 226
in prison, 161
training, 231
Revolutionary colleges in Communist China, 49, 267
Rewards, uses of, 181, 215
Rickett, A., 165
Riesman, D., 168
Ritual of liquidation, 100
Ritualism, 75, 81
Ritualization of belief, 259–268
Role-playing, 152
denial of role, 223
and deception, 227
in prison, 152
Rousseau, J. J., 66

Sadism, 174
Santucci, P., 196, 205, 210
Sargant, W., 196, 200, 205, 224
Schein, E. H., 80, 131, 133, 189, 196, 204, 222, 252
Schneier, Inge, 165
Schroder, H. M., 252
Schwartz, B., 25, 32, 34
Secret police, 45
Sino-Japanese War (1937), 34
Sherif, M., 253
Singer, M. T., 252

Situational guilt, 156
Skinner, B. F., 207, 209
Skinnerian formulations, 209
Sleep deprivation, 208, 209
Smith, M. B., 100, 259, 262
Social guilt, 146
    proneness to, 167
Social influence, 241–253
Social psychology of coercive persua-
    sion, 221–256
Socio-economic change, motivation
    for, 82
Soviet purges, 100
Stalin, 85
Stealing in prison, 155
Strauss, A., 196, 221
Stress, 199–205

Talmon, J. L., 64, 70
Taoism, 40
Tennien, M., 44
Thorndikean formulations, 209
Thought reform, 9, 43–61, 216, 228,
    267
    after take-over, 43–61
    avowed aims, 52
    CCP viewpoint, 53
    conclusions, 60
    evaluating, 283
    in group, 290–298
    implicit aims, 54
    important movements, 48
    leniency phase, 107
    passion for unanimity, 62–110
    visible effects, 55–58
    see also Coercive persuasion
Totalitarianism, 75, 76
Transcendentalism, 86

Unanimity
    coercing of, 102
    forces to consider, 63

functions of, 109
image of, 63
passion for, 62–110
"Unfreezing," 120–129, 233, 254
    Alcoholics Anonymous, 272
    in Army basic training, 271
    aspects of prison, 125–128
    attitudes, 123
    of basic personality, 127
    vs. "changing," 129
    cognitive distortion, 238
    forces acting on prisoner, 121
    and guilt, 156
    identity crisis, 131
    in interrogation, 180
    in mental hospitals, 273
    in non-Communist settings, 270–277
    and physical strength, 125
    and prison confession, 121
    in religious orders, 271
    and resistance, 125
    self-image, 126
    social-emotional support, 126
U.S. foreign policy, 190

Wales, N., 31
Walker, R. L., 49
Wang Tsun-ming, 32
War neuroses, 224
Wei, H., 45, 87
Whiting, A. S., 109
Winokur, G., 196, 205, 210
Witchcraft, 272
Wolff, H. G., 80, 196, 199, 203, 222,
    299
Wright, Mary C., 27

Yen, Maria, 49
Youth movements, 57

Zander, A., 253
Zen Buddhism, 211